Dominic Reeve wrote his acclaimed first book on Romani life, *Smoke in the Lanes*, in 1958. Since then he has written four further books, including *Beneath the Blue Sky*. He lives and works in a semi-nomadic style with his partner Beshlie, an illustrator.

Also by Dominic Reeve

Smoke in the Lanes

To Beshlie –
too many talents, too little rewarded.

'The Romani-*rai*'

Dwellers in cities work for a wage,
Gold could not buy for me such a cage.
Out on the common, beneath the blue sky,
Who is as free as the Romani-*rai*?
Masters I smile at, none call me a slave.
Strolling in the heather, monarch am I –
Who is a king like the Romani-*rai* ...?

Chorus:
I'm a Romani-*rai*, I'm a true *diddikai*,
I build my mansions beneath the blue sky.
I live in a tent and I don't pay no rent –
And that's why they call me the Romani-*rai*.

Up on the Downs

Every year the thoughts of most travellers, especially from the southern half of the country, turn towards Derby Week, held in June at Epsom. Epsom is one of the most famous race-courses in the world and, during Derby Week, the focus of international attention. There is a magic and excitement in the air which no other race meeting seems able to rival, for ordinary punters, the nobility and travellers alike.

Most travellers, as opposed to the licensed fortune-tellers and the fairground operators (who are situated across a road some little distance from the grandstand) tow their trailers onto a sweep of allotted ground, sloping upwards, adjoining the course. For this privilege a hefty charge is made. Once, I have been told, travellers could stop almost anywhere on the Downs without payment but over the years the Stewards of the Course have succeeded in adjusting that situation. At one time it even seemed that travellers would be banned from the Downs entirely. This mean-spirited plan was, thankfully, defeated and replaced by the scheme charging for each trailer-caravan. Alas, however, the charge for admission has risen so dramatically that the attendance figures have dropped accordingly. I fear it is no longer as fashionable.

The majority of travellers would start appearing on the Downs on the Friday and Saturday prior to the Race Week. The early arrival is caused by their desire to attend 'Show-out Sunday'. This is the day when hundreds of *spielers* and stall-holders set up in business for the day, whatever the weather. They stretch in lines, sometimes three or four, of half a mile or so in length, facing the grandstand. There is a curious combination of fairground and Petticoat Lane in the atmosphere, and always a seething mass of people, almost all travellers, walking, talking, and buying. The enthusiasm of the stall-holders is echoed in the vigour with which they mount their sales-pitches. Their stock is aimed almost entirely at travellers, especially in china, glass and even rugs. It is a pleasure to witness.

The first year that Beshlie and I pulled on for Derby Week was 1964. It was Saturday, in the early afternoon, when we approached the town of Epsom, unsure of the way to the right area of the Downs. However, as we entered the town we saw several other lorries and trailers – some of immense length like landliners, others short and cobby, gliding in from various directions and all making for one road: we sensed it would be wise to follow. Hence, after a long but steady gradient we found ourselves approaching the Race Course, and traversing a short entrance-road to the 'Travellers' Park'.

There were already masses of trailers and motor vehicles, spreading haphazardly over several acres from beside the road, down a steep incline, up a hillside, and on to a flat area at the summit, over to a fence marking the boundary. We decided to make for the far side as it seemed a little less crowded, and we knew that our lorry would easily manage our comparatively small trailer up the hill without undue strain. (This could not be said for some lorries of a similar size which were, at that moment, being required to pull great trailers of twenty-three feet and more up the incline, which was proving almost too much for them – to the chagrin of their owners.)

As we drove down the hard track lane beside the field, in order to ascend the hill and enter at the top, I was able to distinguish many people whom I knew, some beside their trailers and others in small groups conversing together. All was activity: men, women, and children all busy in setting-up their homes and contents for the coming week.

Reaching the entrance I drove in, passing several 'rough and ready' turnouts, and on through a collection of small 'tourer' trailers, a dozen or more, and sleek cars. These last belonged to some settled-down Devonshire Romanies who had come up purely for a week's holiday, and to savour a feeling of their past culture! A little further on I reached four or five very 'travellery' lorries and huge shining trailers. Observing the lorries to be 'lined-out' in a very fancy manner, with ornamentally-carved wooden ladder-racks and side 'raves', also picked-out and scalloped, I realised it was the family of Old Mosey and Louie Smith.

Not having met for over a year, but having my eye for a vehicle decorated in the colours and style of those of his own family, Old Mosey had appeared from his trailer and was observing us with interest.

'Oh my blessed loving God!' he cried, on recognising me as we neared. 'I never knowed it was you, my boy – pull in alongside us!'

I was more than pleased to do so, as they were a family for whom, without exception, I had great affection and respect.

'You'll be safe there, along've we,' Old Mosey reassured me. "Cos there's some bad old people pulled up here this year – some proper *beng* tails, by all accounts.'

Old Louie emerged with two Crown Derby mugs of tea, which Beshlie and I gratefully accepted: it was sweet and strong and of a pleasing colour.

Old Louie had a very Romani look: her hair was black and worn in two braids, while her features had about them the beauty of an ancient carving, weathered and gnarled.

Hoop-shaped gold earrings and three or four thick gold chains adorned her, and several of her fingers carried thick gold rings. Her deep-set dark eyes smiled a welcome. Her manner, alas, she seemed unable to turn away from a kind of professional mournfulness: over the many years that we knew her I cannot recollect her ever making an optimistic statement on any subject!

'Miserable old weather, ain't it?' she remarked, despite the sunshine of a warm June afternoon. 'I should like to be pulled-in on a nice little plot somewheres,' she continued. Adding, surprisingly: 'You can get some funny old weather this time of year.'

Despite their comparative wealth (in comparison with my own, anyway), she seemed unable to forget her earlier years, spent in bender tents and then in wagons, mostly around London, when the elements were of such impact on one's life. I too carry those feelings with me.

Old Mosey, spruce in panama hat, fall-front trousers, and red braces, a coloured handkerchief at his throat, inspected my little Bedford with both admiration and pleasure, noting each and every detail of the body's construction, and those of the paint-work and 'lining-out'. Two of his sons had similar vehicles, and he owned a large Bedford TK, of the same age as my own. It was necessary for him to have such a lorry in order to manage his trailer, which was a twenty-three-foot Vickers four-wheeler, of probably three tons in weight.

There was a very large attendance that year, and all around us were other trailers pulling on or setting themselves steady and aright. Shouts, greetings, laughter, and shrieks rent the air, and spasmodic short-lasting dog fights broke out as terriers and lurchers leaped down from the lorries and attempted to assert territorial rights.

'Hullo, Uncle Mosey,' came a constant stream of greetings from those arriving, or passing by.

Old Mosey, then in his seventies, had been on the Downs for Race Week since his boyhood just after the First World War. He could recall times when motor vehicles were a rarity among Romany people, and ninety per cent of them were still living with horses and wagons. An astonishing sight that must have been, so many in one place. It was, of course, during those times that many Romanies were immortalised by the artistic creations of the likes of Sir Alfred Munnings, Dame Laura Knight, and the superb Augustus John, the last being remembered to this day as the greatest Romani Rye of all time.

Old Mosey reminisced to me: 'I can call to mind them times, when I was a little *chavi* up here, an' me dear old father had the bestest wagons an' horses amongst all travellers,' he boasted, with the refreshing lack of modesty that characterised much of his speech.

'Old *bori ryes* would come up to me poor old father an' say: "Well my good man, I never seed such pretty wagons and

horses in all me life. If I fetches me camera could I take a picture of 'em – an' you yourself of course?"' He paused in filial
reverence, continuing: "Course me dear old father'd draw a
few shillings, wouldn't he? An' me poor muvver'd *dukker* a
few of the *rawnies*, so they always came out a bit ahead, don't
you know – an' that's in them days when a pound was worth
something, Lord love me.'

'Those were the days, Uncle Mosey,' I agreed.

'Them was the days,' he exclaimed. 'I remember once, on
these very hills, when me father was talking to an old 'fessor
about this an' that. An' after he finished talkin' the old *rye*
sez to me father: "Mr Smith, you got what no learning from
books could ever teach you – you knows it all!"'

At that moment we were interrupted by the sound of a
piano-accordian being played in a wailing tone, accompanied by a chorus of gloomy-sounding voices. Casting our
eyes in the direction of this lachrymose noise we beheld a
collection of persons, mostly male, with absurdly placid
countenances, pallid and sickly-looking, somewhat dwarfed
by a large banner which the most stalwart held aloft,
proclaiming: *The End of the World is Nigh. Let Jesus Save
You!*

My brain, not always so alert, realised that the unfortunate persons were in the grip of some kind of, possibly
contagious, lunacy. Seeking to ingratiate myself with them,
and possibly to raise their spirits I enquired brightly:

'Did you get the winner, today?' This question appeared to discommode them slightly.

'God was the only winner today!' retorted a particularly unhealthy-looking man of some forty years, anoraked, bespectacled, and grey of face. He showed no spark of humour nor of warmth.

'Ah!' I replied knowingly, 'but I believe He was disqualified for Moving in Mysterious Ways!'

Far from laughing at this jovial witticism the whole party, as one, regarded me with stony distaste.

'You will remember what you have just said, at the Day of Judgement, when you face the Lord Jesus,' announced a middle-aged woman from under a grizzled mess of grey hair which gave every impression of having been fried.

With much whispering, subdued chanting, and occasional cries of 'Praise the Lord' they moved away on their sad and pointless crusade.

Later, I believe it was in the late seventies or early eighties, their place was to be usurped by a huge collection of wealthy-seeming French Romanies, who appeared one Race Week with new trailers, new Mercedes vans, and a vast marquee. The latter, when erected, sported a large flag emblazoned *Gypsies for Christ*. They were to hold meetings each evening, which they did. Unfortunately, however, since their grasp of English was limited, and the travellers' understanding of French all but non-existent, more time was spent admiring their motors and trailers than gaining any insight into their message by the English travellers.

They were my first experience of Born Again Christians, later to prove a rather fanatical band of well-intentioned Bible fundamentalists, whose simple fire-and-brimstone message has presently been embraced by a large number of British Romanies, and throughout Europe too I am led to believe. As a life-long agnostic I am naturally a little depressed by this, and can only hope that it will pass, like other fashions. To me blind faith is as stupid as blind atheism: surely the great adventure of life is *not* to know what, if anything, follows death. It is the one fact to which, up to now, no convincing reply has been given. I can only say that I have never heard of a war being caused by agnosticism. Unfortunately, I must admit, WE DON'T KNOW (even if honest) is not a vastly inspiring message! 'There's a nest of *dinilos* – complete cranks, fuckin' idiots!' said Old Mosey, pulling his hat brim down low over his eyes and squinting after them contemptuously.

My mind returning to Old Mosey's description of people of yesteryear admiring his father's wagons and horses, it once again occurred to me that a brand-new lorry and a decorated trailer are but the equivalents of a fine young cob and a painted wagon of days gone by – and have taken no more, or less, effort to acquire.

Beshlie was still busy in the trailer setting out the china

and vases, picture frames, bird-cages, and other breakables, all of which must be 'packed down' for each journey.

Transporting one's complete home, with all one's worldly possessions, is a far cry from the average Caravan Club member's comparatively spartan lifestyle – with sleeping-bags and plastic cups! (Several non-traveller visitors have expressed astonishment when told that the ornaments did not stay on their shelves or behind the tiny 'fiddle-rails' during each move!)

Once all was completed we sat and devoured a lump of cooked bacon and salad with great pleasure, surveying the scene outside with much interest as trailers still continued to arrive. Our only slight trepidation was caused by the fear that 'bad' people might draw in beside us. To have such people nearby during a fair, or indeed at any time, can utterly destroy one's peace in every sense. For, alas, such people, usually with 'bad' children too, take no heed of their neighbour's feelings, nor of threats or even violence unless extreme; and thus they never, under any circumstances, moderate their voices or behaviour, even in the early hours – sometimes, if drunk, singing at the tops of their voices right through until dawn! Over the course of the years we have ourselves so suffered – finally, after consecutive sleepless nights, have left such meetings as human wrecks! Then needing several days in which to recover. And all in the name of pleasure!

By seven o'clock people were still pulling on. However,

our fear of a quarrelsome neighbour was alleviated by the arrival of an almost new Rolls Royce saloon car, towing a long residential Jubilee: it was Morris Hendry, a successful motor-dealer who, although the owner of a Birmingham car-front, still lived in a trailer from choice. His elegant wife and teenaged son were in the latter's E-type Jaguar. Not, perhaps the *average* traveller family!

Towards eight o'clock everyone retired to their respective trailers in order to don their finery for an evening out. Many of the public houses in the town of Epsom, and its environs, would close their doors for the week, being unnerved by the influx of unaccustomed trade! Other landlords, however, being either courageous or grasping, would open their doors, though with a seeming air of sufferance on the part of many: they liked the money, but not the people who were spending it. The choice of public house would vary according to the tastes of the particular travellers, the 'rough and ready' ones preferring the unadorned, barrack-like 'beer shops', while those of us intent upon a form of social mountaineering would choose a Lounge Bar in an accommodating public house of the hotel variety, more often used to catering for those who feel their natural habitat to be the stockbroker belt!

That evening those of us who affected to prefer the last kind of establishment headed for the Bridge Hotel which lay about two miles from the Downs, next to a golf-course whose members usually frequented it. Apart from, of course, during Race Week.

We had all squeezed into Old Mosey's son David's silver-coloured Mercedes 280 saloon, eight of us, in some discomfort but good spirits.

The car-park was filled to overflowing with expensive limousines, new vans of all sizes, and trucks too – all easily being recognisable as belonging to travellers, at least to the attuned eye.

'I should park over the road, on that green, David,' advised Old Mosey. 'If you gets in that car-park someone'll put a dent in the motor, specially after a few drinks – remember what happened to Bobby's new BMW ...'

We pondered on the fate of Bobby's new car with great sorrow. He was the son of one of Old Mosey's brothers. The unfortunate young man, upon returning to a car-park, discovered his brand-new motor had been reversed into with such force that it was a write-off. Having saved up for a considerable time to buy it, he was naturally shattered at its loss.

'He ain't never been right since, dear blessed boy,' said Old Mosey sadly.

It seemed a sensible suggestion, and within moments we were joined by others who had the same idea.

Amy, Nellie, and Beshlie were all wearing new dresses, in bright block colours, their hair lacquered, teetering on flashy Italian stiletto-heeled shoes. Gold jewellery gleamed about their persons, the fashion then being for lumpy gold bracelets, each link bursting with as many solid-gold charms as it would hold. Old Louie, who was restrained in black, was even more fulsomely laden with gold chains, sovereign earrings, and a variety of gold rings on most of her fingers. It was, to my eyes, a pleasure to see ostentation proudly displayed.

David, Henry, Old Mosey and myself were all attired in lightweight suits of faintly luminous fabrics, Old Mosey still clinging to a form of tailoring that owed much to travellers' suit-stylings of some decades before. He still liked to have his jackets with yoke-backs, and scalloped pocket-flaps, and sometimes even demanded the notorious 'fall-front' design of trousering. We had all abandoned our daytime yellow elastic-sided boots for their kin in shining black. Sheeplike we may have been, but we *enjoyed* being so.

The lounge bar was almost full, but by a stroke of good luck we managed to take possession of a table in one corner at which a bewildered *gaujo* man had been sipping warily on a half-pint of bitter beer.

He was soon dislodged by the simple expedient of Old Mosey remarking to him:

'Excuse me, Sir, but there's a lady outside asking most particularly to speak to you very urgent – she said could you step out straight away, please?'

Gazing at us with a mixture of apprehension and fear the

man, who I supposed to be some form of local white-collar worker, rose and left with a nervous grin. I placed his half-consumed glass of beer in a plant pot nearby, and we all sat down.

'*Kushti*,' said David, approvingly.

'I'll get the drinks in,' offered Henry politely and Old Mosey winked at me.

We gave him our orders in turn which he memorised with some difficulty, eventually becoming so confused that I went up to the bar with him to assist. Utter chaos reigned there, with five men and a girl confronting a wall of would-be drinkers and serving them with all the speed they could muster. It was only nine o'clock – how would they stand the pace until eleven that night? The atmosphere was already ripe and heady, many of the customers loosening their ties and mopping their brows.

'Here's a struggle to get a poxy drink, bruv,' growled a red-faced man next to me. It was Cock-eyed Jim, a London-traveller living in a council house in Staines. He smiled a gap-toothed grin, and his eyes seemed to stare simultaneously at the men on either side of me.

I often think of him amusing me by recounting when by chance he was near Windsor Great Park and the road was temporarily closed to allow the Queen to pass by. With nothing better to do he left his lorry and seated himself in the sunlight beneath a tree. However, suddenly being beset by severe stinging-pains in his groin, he realised that he had inadvertently sat down upon an ants' nest – the occupants of which were wreaking revenge!

'I jumped up like I'd seen the Devil,' he said. 'An' I starts a-runnin', don't I?'

'"Oi," shouted me bruvver, "ain't you gonna wait for the Queen?"'

'"Fuck the Queen!" I sez an' druv off!'

After several rounds of drinks the cordiality of the over-heated room was taking effect and several women had began singing, in sentimental mood, to a rather indifferent reception. Generally speaking, those who chose more lively numbers in such company were more likely to be well-received.

Of the more vigorous type of performer was a once-beautiful, though by now slightly fading, woman of perhaps fifty-five years old, who rose from her seat to sing. She was a legend among travellers in this country and Australia and she was soon in the full throes of her favourite ballad: 'I'm going to Lingerlonger – down in Larawonger!' Charm it may have lacked, but vitality it did not, and the whole room fell into respectful silence during the entire recital, ending in a burst of genuine applause. A lovely person, alas now dead, she will endure in my memory for all time, not least for the glorious abuse that she heaped on her husband. In one quarrel, not long after returning from one of their frequent trips to Australia, I heard her shout at the retreating form of her husband: 'Here you! You with the humpty-back, what you got from fucking all them kangaroos . . . '

The time passed, conversation flowed, and elegance dissolved into perspiration.

'I'm sweating like a *baulo*, Louie,' said a vast blond woman from a nearby table, a small glass in her hand.

'Funny old weather,' Louie agreed affably.

Men and women sat at separate tables, as is the custom on such social outings, thus ensuring no restrictions on their very different subjects of conversation. It has always been so.

Old Mosey had been looking uneasily towards the bar where a number of especially sinister-looking semi-traveller men were crowded together.

'Them's London-hounds, see 'em?' he said, looking over furtively. 'They carries *yoggers* an' all – they'd *mar* a man for three grand, like me dead father they would.'

'What're they doing in here?' I asked.

'I think it's all to do with that Blackie and Andrew – all to do with them *chordi* motors they been trying to ring,' said Old Mosey under his breath.

'See that big one,' he continued softly, pointing to a tall, strongly built man with thick grey hair, wearing a silk and mohair suit. 'He's the one what got throwed out of the Jag in the Dartford Tunnel last Christmas when they had that bit of trouble, don't you remember? Anyway, he got up without a scratch on him by all accounts. Lucky, or what?'

At that moment an altercation broke out between one of the London-hounds, a small, dark, greasy-faced man, and one of the bar staff, who he accused of neglecting them.

'You're treatin' us worse'n fuckin' dogs, mate,' he shouted. 'Let's have some service or I'll jump over that bar an' knock your fuckin' head off.'

Sensing that this could be a real threat the barman called to his colleagues and, as one, they hastily hauled down a steel grille to separate them from the irate customers.

The London-hounds became so incensed by this obviously hostile treatment that they started to hurl tables and chairs at the grille, behind which the bar staff cowered. The grille did not budge, rather did the furniture collapse in pieces upon impact.

Screams and shouts erupted from the travellers, many of whom had not been aware of what had been happening at first. Up till that moment they had been peaceably enjoying themselves. However, knowing that the law would soon arrive in force they began streaming from the exit.

'Let's git off – the *gavvers* will be here directly,' warned Old Mosey. And at that moment they arrived. A dozen or more grim-faced constables descended from a white van, with two patrol cars besides.

Shouts from one or two of the thoughtful travellers

warned the Londoners of the arrival of the police and they managed to filter outside into the throng just before the police entered the building. Witnesses proved non-existent and statements were not forthcoming. But our little party had already slipped away quietly. After a goodnight drink in Old Mosey's trailer we were soon abed, to be woken sporadically through the night by the noisy return of late revellers.

Show-out Sunday dawned bright and sunny, skylarks trilling overhead in the morning light. I was up by half past six, but few others seemed awake. I surveyed the scene with great wonder. Trailers had obviously been coming in until quite late in the evening – there must have been five or six hundred on the Downs, many lodged sideways-on up the steep gradients of the hill before us. In order to sit level the owners of these trailers had scooped out lumps of turf and dug holes for the wheels that were 'up' the hillside, clicking the trailers in like plugs into their tailor-made sockets. With characteristic optimism the owners did not doubt the ability of their vehicles to haul the trailers out on departure.

In those days almost every family owned a watchdog of some sort. These would be chained beside the trailer, some with kennels, some without. They were usually terriers, lurchers or alsatians, the latter being in the minority. It was unfathomable to me, but it always seemed that the rougher the family the more dogs they seemed to possess, often as many as seven or eight.

There was one woman of particular eccentricity, known as Black Mary, who was single and middle-aged, and lived with her elder brother Creddy. Black Mary owned a splendid Westmorland Star trailer which her brother towed with his TK lorry. On the back of the latter he had a canvas-topped wagon-like structure, with a Queenie fire-stove, in which he lived. That in itself made them unusual, but their strangeness was further exaggerated by Black Mary owning a pack of between thirty and forty Yorkshire terriers. These fearless and aggressive little animals would surge out without warning on the unwary who happened to approach their owner's domain.

Black Mary was incredibly skilful at *dukkering* and she supported her brother and herself, and her pack of dogs, from her efforts. Each day when she returned from 'calling' she would, about fifty yards distant from the trailer, shout out and the pack would flood out to greet her, knowing she would have a sack of food for them. A curious sight indeed. Over the years I encountered them far down in Cornwall, and once in Western Scotland. They were rarely in one place for long; they were true travellers in all senses of the word.

Another way you could determine status, within the curious definitions of traveller society, would be the presence of a tent or even a portable shed. The higher classes always possessed at least one, sometimes two, small square-framed tents – to be used as kitchens or bathrooms/lavatories, though one tent was never used for both purposes. The rougher travellers (and for some reason, most Irish) dispense with such amenities and rely on nature to provide cover for natural events. Eventually we ourselves became so equipped, the first being wooden-framed and covered in green canvas. However, fashion-fool that I am, I soon switched to the lighter aluminium-framed, coloured-plastic versions which are now universally used by travellers – with added refinements such as deckle-edged roof pelmets made in almost any colour requested.

The trailers that are specially designed for travellers are never equipped with sinks or indoor lavatories – travellers would be rightly offended by their use. This seems to mystify some *gaujes* to whom I have mentioned it. Yet to me it seems wholly understandable.

I sat down on the trailer steps and rolled a cigarette, releasing Barney who raced around in delight at being free, causing every dog in the vicinity to bark in protest from their tethers.

I had decided to enjoy the week, freeing myself from the drudgery of 'calling'. It was an unusual feeling for me. The possibility of a lucky bet or two on Derby Day floated enticingly in front of me.

By half past eight there was some faint show of human activity, though many would not bestir themselves until far later. Old Mosey and most of his family, however, were soon about and eager to inspect the stalls. Amy, Nellie and Old Louie were a little worse for wear, rather haggard in the sunlight. All three wore headscarves to cover the roll-curlers in their hair. Amy and Nellie were both dark-skinned and, Amy particularly, could only have been Romani. Bird-like and snappy, they chastened their menfolk to hurry themselves.

Beshlie came out of the trailer in a long dress of blue and pink floral pattern, with pink shoes and scarf.

'That's a pretty dress,' Old Louie said agreeably, backed up by the younger women with perhaps a touch less sincerity, for both were of a slightly jealous nature.

Harry and David wore dark suits, straw hats and sunglasses, resembling closely the popular conception of Mafiosi!

We sauntered down the hill, through the trailers, with occasional greetings to or from the occupants, each of us commenting on particular vehicles or trailers which took our fancy.

We suddenly saw one of the most ornate Vickers Morecambes that any of us had ever seen, which proved to be much to Old Mosey's liking.

'That's a *kushti chat*,' he said, pointing with admiration. 'I reckons I'll have meself one like that.' Mosey was not a man to discuss such matters with his wife, rather would he make all the decisions himself. Old Louie, after forty-two years of his company, had long decided not to question his wishes, in order to have a peaceful life.

'That's a nice trailer, Uncle Mosey,' said Henry, tall and blond, a bit Scandinavian-looking. 'How much would it weigh?'

'Trailer like that'd go over three ton, on my life,' replied Old Mosey.

'Not much good for your little Bedford Joey, eh Henry?' David was laughing – he and Henry were the best of friends.

'If he had a four-speed gearbox he'd pull him all right,' Henry assured him.

'Like its grandmother's cunt it would,' added Old Mosey.

'Here! *Dik* at them blinds, Farver!' Amy was pointing at a long Astral trailer with drawn-down pink Venetian blinds at each window, the owners still abed.

'That's what they calls ammunition-blinds – they costs some *lovell*, don't you worry!' Old Mosey was always master of the malapropism. Without the benefit of being able to read or write he was, nevertheless, a conversational adventurer of great style. He could, with pride, trace his ancestry back through respected Romani families for many generations.

As we arrived not far from the first row of stalls he drew our attention and pointed:

'*Dik* here! There's old Bob and Vi from out of Canning Town. They bin here every year since I was a child – must be ninety year old, dear old people.'

I peered in the direction he was indicating and beheld a very sad yet strangely inspiring sight. For there, surrounded by a scattering of spectators, stood the figure of an ancient man. Pouchy and grey of face, under a battered bowler hat, and clad in a shabby overcoat and down-at-heel brown boots he was being slowly and painstakingly bound up in chains, from his head to his toes. This was being executed by a small, frail-looking woman in even greater decay than he was. Wisps of floaty grey hair protruded in a thin hazy veil from all around a green beret. Her old tweed coat was drawn together with a large safety-pin, while her spindly legs were loosely connected to a pair of over-sized ankle-boots trimmed with imitation leopard skin. Her pale face was thin and wan, and she emitted faint high-pitched cries intermittently, which seemed to vanish immediately into the atmosphere. They were possibly to encourage both the old man and the audience, in an effort to build up a feeling of tension and anticipation. At length, the ancient man trussed up like a turkey, she placed a sack over his head, pulled it down and tied it securely at his ankles. Having completed this she gingerly pushed the shapeless bundle over on its side – where it lay without movement on the ground.

The number of spectators had grown somewhat and the

little woman faced the unenthusiastic crowd with some fire, crying out, in a shrill, thin voice, 'Five pounds! Five pounds! Five pounds against ten sez he'll be up an' free in less than two minutes!' But, alas, no one would take the risk of such a large speculation. With feigned disgust she lowered her offer.

'One pound! One pound! One pound against two!'

At this she had a few takers, me among them, out of sheer admiration for their age and dedication.

After a few more shrieks of encouragement she realised that no more money would be forthcoming, so with a kick at a completely inert bundle and a shout of 'Goo-on, Bob!' she affected to scan a stop-watch. Of course, neither of them had been on this planet for so long without perfecting their act; so it was that, after one minute and forty seconds, grunting and gurgling with exertion, still wearing his bowler hat, the disreputable figure of Bob struggled free from the sack, a faint smile of triumph playing about his stubbly features.

The crowd, who had obviously thought, or at least hoped, that he was moribund, dissolved slowly and without enthusiasm.

'Dear old *mush*, I thought he'd *kerred* himself in that sack, didn't you, Uncle Mosey,' said Henry, pleased at his obscene question.

'*Kek! Kekker!*' said Old Mosey in affected disgust. 'You'll have us took in a minute, with talk like that.'

We wandered down the aisle of stalls. Old Louie bought a large cut-glass crystal vase weighing thirty pounds or more.

'Carry that, my Mosey,' she said, thrusting it at her husband.

'Nah! You bought it – you carry it!' he replied ungratiously.

'I shan't cook you any more sheep's paunches for your tea,' she threatened. 'I'd have done better to have the Devil than have a man like that,' Louie concluded, glaring at Old Mosey.

'Now, now, don't say that, Aunt Lou,' pleaded her daughter-in-law, who had just joined us. The latter was of an amiable and placid nature, and was sometimes distressed by the spirited altercations and arguments which were regular occurrences in the family of her husband.

At every step, and all around us, were people that we knew, and we were making slow progress, constantly stopping either to talk to friends or to admire the Crown Derby and Royal Worcester on display for sale. All such stalls were clustered with travellers, both men and women, many attempting to 'have a deal' with the sellers. The last were a hardy breed, often of traveller extraction, used to haggling and the encouraging sight of ready cash. Many buyers would save up all year to buy whatever took their fancy at Show-out Sunday.

The hot sun of June beat down upon us, and by midday

Old Louie began to complain of feeling 'faintified'. So we sat down on a little hillock overlooking the scene. By that time dozens of travellers' vehicles were parked all about the vicinity of the stalls, mainly belonging to those who had driven up there for the day, as opposed to those of us who were actually stopping on the Downs. Most of the day-visitors had brought food and drink with them and were seated on the ground beside their cars, enjoying splendid meals of cooked meats and salads and bottles of beer or wine. When in such surroundings I would invariably reflect on how infrequent it was for Romanies to be predominant in a crowd. I felt it must be rather a similar situation that Jews experience on visiting Israel.

Amy and Nellie had both purchased some Crown Derby plates, while Beshlie, alas, confined herself to buying two miniature stainless-steel water-carriers to match our full-sized ones, which were in daily use. At that time, having expended most of our capital on the new lorry, we were in no position to enjoy carefree spending – as was perhaps to be the case in later years. However, health, youth and wealth are to be appreciated, in that order. At least we had two out of three.

That year, 1964, almost everyone was looking at least a little picturesque and colourful; the strangulating social conventions prevalent until the end of the 1950s seemed, in those heady days, to be gone for ever. The age of romance, visually at any rate, seemed to have entered our lives and we were better for it. Closet dandies paraded quite openly, with hitherto undreamed-of excesses in fashions; while women revealed their new-found freedom and standing. 'Make love, not war' struck me as being an eminently sensible message and surely only those of a mean spirit could fail to applaud it.

We staggered wearily back to the trailers about two o'clock and we all sat down outside in the sunshine, devouring sandwiches which Old Louie had generously provided and which she insisted Beshlie and I should share with them. In truth I have experienced much open-handedness from travellers of all sorts and in all situations – from those living outdoors with only bender tents, those with wagons and trailers, to those living in properties of their own.

'I think there could be one or two fights goin' off this afternoon,' announced David, who had returned from his stroll across the ground. 'They reckons Boxer Tom's son is challenging an Irish boy, one of the Cashes I think, an' a few of the young Stanleys wants a go as well.'

'We'll have a walk up there in a minute,' said Old Mosey. 'I likes to see a good *cor*.'

After a cup of tea apiece we slowly set off, meandering down the hill to the bottom and up the other side, Old Mosey breathing hard with the exertion. Young boys in smart cars or pick-up trucks, often belonging to their fathers, drove at high speed up and down the inclines and steeper slopes, frequently avoiding collision by only a matter of inches. Some of their vehicles bore the searing scars of previous not-so-lucky encounters.

'These young *chavies* don't know what it is to have to struggle for a crust of bread – they've had it all gid to 'em,' grumbled Old Mosey, with some justification.

'Oh *dordi*,' said his son, for he had heard it all before.

At the top of the hill, quite near the entrance from the road, a large, close-packed collection of men and boys had gathered in a circle. It was the Ring, which flourished each year under the management of travellers, for travellers. It was the simplest form of gambling. A man in the centre of the ring would toss two old-fashioned pennies, spinning them high in the air, and those present would bet as to whether they landed 'two heads' or 'two tails', upon which large sums were often wagered. Off fails – one head and one tail – do not count. During the years prior to the 1970s one could bet as little as a few shillings with the official 'banker' who ran the gambling, but in later years the minimum stake became a five pound note. Inflation had found its way everywhere!

The man in charge that year, and for several years after, was a dark-haired, well-dressed, suave-looking man called Swaley. He was shouting hoarsely, his voice harsh and rasping from overuse.

'Ten pounds he heads 'em! Ten pounds he heads 'em – come on boys, let's see your money!'

Men of all ages, flushed with either triumph or disappointment, were plunging their hands into wads of notes, some kept on the ground under the toe of their boots, and betting with abandon. Many were having side-bets with their neighbours, the man next to me betting a hundred pounds a time! Some would leave in delight, much richer; others would do so in deepest gloom, having lost every penny on them.

There was one famous gambling man whose entire year would revolve around the Ring during Derby Week. One year, having a luckless spell, he succeeded in losing all his money and his motor and trailer as well. His family of six would have been homeless had not some of his relatives, with controlled generosity, provided him with an old trailer and an ill-served Escort van. Yet the very next year, this extraordinarily adventurous man was fortunate to win over twelve thousand pounds. That year he left the Downs at the end of the week with an almost-new lorry and the 'Show' trailer which had been brought there as a sample by its maker. Alas, however, until his premature death, he rocketed upwards and downwards in prosperity. Like the true gambler he really owned nothing – it could all disappear on the turn of a card.

His hobbies had been gambling, boxing and hare-coursing, and for his tombstone Beshlie produced a linear design in his memory, which cleverly incorporated all those interests in the one motif. It was received with great approval by his family and was reproduced on the black marble headstone to assist, one hoped, the immortalisation of his fame.

Old Mosey and David declined to try their luck in the Ring, though Henry and I did.

A quick and surreptitious glance at my rather thin wad of notes apprised me that I had some fifty pounds in my pocket. I decided that I would chance ten or twenty pounds of them and, should my luck be bad, trust that I would summon up the strength to withdraw before losing the rest. I could but hope!

'Ten pounds he heads 'em! Ten pounds he heads 'em!' Swaley was still rasping encouragingly.

'Go on then,' I said, parting with a ten-pound note.

Up went the coins, spinning close together, and down – one head one tail.

I tried again, with another ten pounds.

Up, so close together, glistening in the sun, and down, down.

I had won. A good feeling.

A small Irish boy next to me, perhaps eight or ten years old, pulled my sleeve and looked up at me, his face speckled, his eyes not child-like.

'Ah, sure I've only two pounds left, mister. Would you have a side bet wit' me for that?'

I agreed, and won his two pounds. He spat resignedly and

immediately demanded more money from a large paunchy Irishman, sweating profusely, who I presumed was his father and was clutching a wad of five or six hundred pounds.

He handed the boy a fiver. 'No fuckin' more!' he said.

From then on my luck held, and I wisely managed to force myself to retire when I found myself a hundred pounds ahead.

Henry, who was down some fifty pounds, affected to be delighted by my winnings, though I knew him to be feeling sickly.

'Luckiest man in the world, Uncle Mosey,' he declared. 'He've only justy gone an' won hisself a nice little hundred *bars*!'

'How about that Sonny Loveridge?' responded Old Mosey grimly.

'He've lost seven hundred an' fifty pounds in an hour – an' his wife looks like killin' him stone-dead!'

'You've got to feel lucky or it's no good,' I said defensively.

'How about Amigo's boy, then?' continued Old Mosey, warming to his theme of domestic disaster. 'About three years ago it was; he had himself a nice bit of ground just out of Egham, with a lovely prefab on it, with full rights to be there. As well as that, like me dead father, he had a nice tidy trailer an' a new Jeep up there for the week. An', my blessed Lord I'm tellin' you no lie, he got to gamblin' with some up-country travellers an' lost the lot! Every blind thing! He walked off these Downs with nothin', only what he stood up in. His dear wife an' little *chavies* had nowhere to lie, no home, no nothin', an' he ain't back on his feet yet, I heard.'

I felt no useful purpose would be served by disagreement. 'You're quite right,' I said. 'Definitely a silly thing to do.'

At that moment there was a slight surge of people to a point about fifty yards to our right, and we could just make out the flailing fists of two young men stripped to the waist and aiming blows at each other. It was soon over, however, with the slighter of the two participants withdrawing owing to a badly cut cheek, from which blood was streaming.

To his shame, he was led away by a large Irish woman, his mother, who swore vengeance upon almost everyone in sight.

'Only bits of boys, just playin',' pronounced Old Mosey with great contempt.

We hung about impatiently for a while, awaiting the materialisation of the rumoured contest between the two well-known pugilists, but neither appeared. Hence, after watching one or two further uninspiring contests between aspiring champions, we drifted back to the trailers.

I must confess that bare-knuckle fights are not the most edifying of spectacles. One of the most harrowing that I have ever witnessed was held on a Sunday morning in winter, on a council site in a south London borough. News of the contest spread widely by word of mouth among travellers within a good radius of London. Both contestants were well-known and each had their supporters.

The day of the fight dawned dank and cold with a threat of snow in the air. We were stopping near Slough at the time. I wasn't sure of the fight's whereabouts and drove to the site under the guidance of a long-term friend, Billy the Kid. When we arrived, the road outside the trailer-park was dense with closely packed travellers' vehicles of all ages and descriptions. Denizens of the nearby houses were peering from their windows, sensing that something unusual was happening, not knowing what it was.

Inside the council site, as is more or less universal, there were rows of trailers standing next to each other, lined up on individual plots – sometimes two or even three on each. All around the perimeter were high walls. Teenage children and younger ones too were perched up high in order to secure a vantage from which to view the proceedings.

The contest was due to commence at ten o'clock, and one of the participants and his supporters were already there and waiting. He was a tall, thin but muscular young man called Creamy. His hair was crew-cut and his features were gaunt and determined. He was sparring with an imaginary foe, his fist moving with incredible speed while he gazed about him through pale grey eyes.

Before long, his opponent Jimmy arrived, accompanied by his cousins in a new red pick-up truck.

Jimmy was also tall and of unusually powerful build, indeed more so than Creamy. His face was broad and white, scarred by many close encounters of the knuckle kind. His eyes were blue, and he glanced across the crowd trying to assess how many of his own family and relatives were present to support him. They were there in strength.

Two older men, obviously ex-fighting men, thickset and looking knocked about, were the referees.

Without any preamble, other than to strip to the waist, the contestants were soon facing each other.

'I just want to say,' said Jimmy to his opponent in slightly slurred tones, 'if I fall down, let me get up. And if you fall down, I'll let you get up. Alright?'

'Alright,' agreed Creamy.

'Okay then, get to it boys!' urged one of the heavy men.

After a few minutes it became apparent that it was to be a battle of speed and skill against strength and courageous stamina. Creamy, light-footed and agile, danced around his opponent in the fashion of Muhammad Ali in his prime, and was soon delivering sharp and smashing blows to the face of the slightly surprised Jimmy. The latter was even more astonished when, minutes into the fight, one of the blows caused him to fall to the ground for an instant before recovering himself. The main disadvantage for Jimmy was the speed of his opponent, who managed, time after time, to dance backwards before landing a punch.

'My dear blessed Saviour, *dik* his *mui*!' shouted Old Mosey, who had arrived with his son just as Creamy struck the unfortunate Jimmy straight across the mouth, causing him to spit blood and grunt in discomfort.

Being an old-style East End and travellery type of competition, there were no rounds as such and no rests or medical attention. Thus the conflict progressed for fifteen or twenty minutes without Jimmy succeeding in landing more than a few telling punches on his agile foe.

A thin splattering of sleety snow began falling. The spectators shivered in their overcoats but the fighters continued their punishing ritual. Suddenly lunging, Jimmy managed to drive home a thudding blow to the ribs of Creamy, who flinched in pain but skilfully danced himself out of trouble once again, before continuing to concentrate on the head of Jimmy. After well over thirty minutes the pace was not visibly slackening, but both of Jimmy's eyes were half closed, with cuts round them, his mouth was bleeding and both ears had swollen to nearly twice the size. He was indeed a sorry sight. Even the most insensitive among the audience were beginning to be sickened by the sight, yet all were moved by the prodigious courage of a man willing to take such a battering without admitting defeat.

Perhaps another ten minutes of contest went on until, without warning and to our utter astonishment, Jimmy suddenly raised his hands in victory! We were all struck dumb with surprise, until those close to the combatants passed word to us that Creamy had 'given' the contest to Jimmy. Creamy was unable to proceed as he had broken his wrist owing to the force he had used. The injured Creamy, suffering from a broken rib as well as his hand, was ferried to hospital by his family, while the victorious though almost unrecognisable Jimmy proceeded to the nearest public house for a well-earned celebration.

We later learned that he had had to spend two days in bed before his injuries subsided to a bearable level.

As we made our way back to our trailers we halted for a minute or so in order to speak to a pair of very aged travellers of our acquaintance who were resting on the grass.

It was Amos and his cousin Joe, both in their late seventies and looking considerably older. Their faces were deeply furrowed and sunburned to a deep coppery brown. Each wore a coloured handkerchief around the neck and a heavy gold-plated ring. Their eyes were twinkly and humorous. Old Mosey reminisced with them, for they were lifelong associates though not related to him.

A youngish black-haired man passed by, very travellery, accompanied by an attractive Romani girl with dark ringlet hair. Their eyes were only for each other.

'Ain't that your Jasper?' enquired Old Mosey of Amos.

'Sure it is,' Amos replied, grinning widely.

'What's he got – a new woman then?' asked Old Mosey.

'Since he got divorced he has a new woman every week,' laughed Amos, adding, 'He loves 'em and leaves 'em, eh Joe?'

Both the old men became convulsed with laughter at this thought, and were brought almost to the point of hysteria by Joe asserting through his mirth, 'Fucks like a ferret I shouldn't wonder!'

We felt unable to improve on those sentiments and left them, tears rolling down their cheeks.

'That Jasper'll get himself killed one of these days if he goes on like that, messin' with travellin' girls,' forecast Old Mosey. 'He should go down the town an' get himself one or two of them *lubnis*, if he wants to carry on like that.'

'Certainly he should,' we agreed.

On each evening we proceeded optimistically to a variety of public houses as near to the town as we could find. Sometimes the elusive 'good time' was experienced, sometimes not. On Derby night itself all the members of the Stanley family who were stopping on the Downs were in the same hotel as ourselves. We welcomed this because almost all of those present were either accomplished singers or stepdancers, and we were virtually assured of an evening's entertainment. One after another they obliged with both modern and old-fashioned songs. The eldest brother,

Johnnie, was so talented a singer that he really deserved a wider audience than just that of the travellers. He was much esteemed and revered in that society, however, and would hold his listeners spellbound. His cousin Tommy was present too and, outside the pub after closing time, he danced for us on a small square of board. The speed and variety of his steps were the cause of great wonder and admiration in us. As one of his old uncles declared to me, he was 'an artist with his feet'.

By Friday morning, Beshlie and I were quite exhausted after the feverish excitement both before and during Derby day. Like a number of other people, we were ready to leave for quieter pastures and by midday we were packed. We said our farewells to Old Mosey and family, and to other friends.

I hadn't made up my mind in which direction we should head but finally decided to make for Devonshire. I knew that at that time of year there would be no shortage of travellers already stopping there. It should not be difficult to find company, should we desire it.

An ancient Romani woman, who was long settled-down in one place in rural Wiltshire against her inclinations, once observed to me when we stopped for a night in a green lane near her settlement, 'You'm like the birds in the sky, young man. You goes where you likes, but we'm stuck here like *crewts* in a pond, an' cain't go nowheres.'

Down the Country

O ne of the most rewarding aspects of my little bronze and gold lorry was that, to the observant and knowing at least, it cried out that it was a traveller's vehicle – by reasons of its colours and adornments. No journeys could be undertaken in it, in any part of the country in that period of time, without encountering similar lorries. We would always raise our hands in friendly salutation as we passed one another, whether we were acquainted with the drivers or not. So great was the popularity of the Bedford J-type lorry from 1959 until the early 1970s that they became firmly established as the favourite of travellers. Such is the fickleness of fashion, however, that the advent of the Ford Transit and Bedford CF, both in lorry and van form, succeeded in edging them out completely. In *some* ways we are like the rest of society: upper-class travellers came to the decision that the J-type Bedfords had become 'too gypsified' for their grander status.

We ourselves were fortunate in so far as we had obtained ours during their heyday of popularity, and I have never since owned a motor which has afforded me more pleasure. (The reader's contempt for me will know no bounds when I confess that I have actually had recurrent dreams of that vehicle – which has certainly never been the case with any of my succeeding ones!)

After pulling off the Downs at Epsom we headed south and, bypassing Salisbury, decided to spend one night on a lay-by not far from that city, and then to travel straight down to Plymouth the day after. The country near Salisbury seemed a little unfriendly to me but we spent the night on the lay-by without interruption.

Just before we set off in the morning, a grey-painted Bedford lorry, a year older than our own as I could detect from the number-plate, drew up just behind us. I saw that it had a spray-engine and several drums of bituminous paint on the back. The driver jumped down from the cab, clad in a paint-spattered boiler-suit, and I recognised him as Henry Lichen's brother-in-law, Albie. He was a fine-looking man, six feet tall, with weathered features and thick, upstanding, white hair. We shook hands and exchanged gossip; he was likeable and good-humoured.

'It's all right for you, Albie, I can see you've got your bit of bread for today,' I smiled, nodding at his engine and the paint.

'I've got a dear little three-bay barn to paint,' admitted Albie cautiously. 'I might earn meself a crust, but there won't be no butter on it!'

'Huh! Butter on both sides, more likely,' I chided him.

He rolled his eyes and grinned. 'Where are you making for?'

I told him and he enlightened me as to which of his own class of traveller were to be found in Devon just at that time, and where. 'I expect me cousin Tom would get you in where he's pulled,' he suggested generously. 'It's a pretty place, just outside of Barnstaple.'

I thanked him warmly, but did not feel able to tell him that, at that time, I was not looking for a stopping-place where I would have to pay rent. Rather was I hoping to be with the company of travellers taking 'French leave' (as they called it) and stopping here and there, for as long as they were allowed, on roadsides or scraps of wasteland. At that moment my earnings were too stretched, and our savings too scant, for me to enjoy the luxury of such added overheads as rent! Later in life I came to reverse my opinions on such matters, to some extent.

In any event I felt in a reasonably elated frame of mind, optimistic as ever. I trusted that Devon would advance my intention of becoming a member of the small and exclusive

band of successful 'muck-hawkers', in the mould of Henry
Lichen, the Compost King!

After we had been travelling for some time we gradually
found ourselves spinning through the wet, flat, low-lying
side of Somerset towards the hills of South Devon, its red
soil smiling at us from the fields, and my spirits rose still further. We had been in Devon previously, though not for
several years. On our last journey into the county we had
been beset by mechanical troubles which, though not too
serious, were nevertheless sufficient to bring on mild neuroses in Beshlie, and caused even my own stout heart to
quail.

At that time I had been alternating between gravel-path
laying and scrap-iron collecting, and had discovered that
both forms of occupation were being more than fully
exploited by almost the entire population of Devonshire
travellers themselves. It had not been a successful time for
me, but I believed it to be but a temporary set-back. I
instinctively felt that a new assault on the West Country,
with our presently more exalted turnout, would prove to
bring about a change of luck.

Past Honiton, then bypassing Exeter, we climbed the
once-dreaded Telegraph Hill, over the gradient of which we
soared with ease and complete lack of nervous tension. How
unlike our previous ascent when, engine boiling, crawling in
first gear, we barely managed to reach the summit. Upon that

last climb, quite near to the top, and lying with his head no more than two feet from the passing traffic, was a matt and dirt-caked figure of indeterminate age, face blackened by a combination of exhaust fumes, dirt, sunburn, and possibly a layer of charcoal. As we passed slowly by he suddenly sprang to his feet and mouthed obscenities at us, arms flailing and eyes protruding in fury. We remarked on his appearance and the lunacy of his manner in some wonderment to each other and then, having enough worries of our own, he soon disappeared from our thoughts.

We were not a little astonished, therefore, to perceive the same figure, in apparently the same condition, still occupying the *same spot* beside the highway, and still living out what appeared to be his own private game of charades! (As the Broadmoor inmate said to the Jehovah's Witness: 'Lunacy can take up many disguises!')

The sun was shining full in our faces, flashing in opalescent reflection from the metallic paint of the lorry's bonnet, and we smiled at each other.

Just as we picked up speed, along the flat road that ran along the hilltop, we noticed five or six travellers' lorries attached to trailer-caravans on the car-park of a small transport café on the opposite side of the road. As we were passing the travellers happened to be leaving the café. Galvanised by the sight of us, they all waved in happy and curious greeting, which we returned enthusiastically. I felt a little sad that our roads were in opposite directions, especially as I recognised two of the men, Crippled Jesse and Eddie Little, both old friends. When one is moving, especially if alone, it is always heart-lifting to encounter others in the same situation: the sense of being an alien from another world is partially removed.

Beshlie, who has never enjoyed long journeys, was becoming restive and wished that we would go no further. Selfish in my youth, however, and becoming even more so in advancing years, I dismissed such complaints. Plymouth, or very close to it, was my destination.

So on we went, down through the outskirts of Bovey Tracey, on past Ashburton, South Brent, Ivybridge, Plympton. As we passed through the last-named place I kept my eyes glued to the left, as there was a car-park there on which travellers would sometimes be allowed to spend a week or so. Sure enough, three trailers were standing together on the far side, but a quick appraisal showed me that they were Irish people, not personal friends, so I pushed on towards Plymouth.

In those days, a mile or so before the city of Plymouth, the road divided: the left fork led to the city and the right fork led to Saltash Bridge and Cornwall. Between the forks was a large piece of rough wasteland, perhaps an acre in size. For several years running, during the summer months, this ground became the main stopping place for all the long-distance, roadside-dwelling class of travellers who wished to spend a little time in that part of Devon: in fact it was almost the only place where one could stay. (Later a council site was provided and was built where a former cliff fortress had once stood. It was, however, only accessible by means of a narrow, hairpin-bending lane, which was almost impossible to negotiate with a long trailer-caravan and lorry. Was it some kind of fiendish trick? one was forced to wonder.)

Within minutes after we had passed through Plymstock, glimpsing some settled-down travellers in trailers and chalets on our left, there, ahead of us lay . . . Arcadia!

On the wasteland there were perhaps twenty-five luxurious, immaculately maintained Vickers and Westmorland Star trailers, their polished stainless-steel ornamentations shining like mirrors in the sun. Besides those ultimately rococo and opulent homes, there were, rather overshadowed, several Jubilees, two small Carlight Specials (like our own), and a few Eccles Travellers. The latter were just beginning to dwindle as their fashion faded. I would say that it was not until the mid- to late 1970s that Vickers and Westmorland Stars, as well as their poor relations, Aaros and Portmasters, developed to their fullest splendour – to finally climax in such extravagance that they must, I am sure, remain unrivalled in our time. I could deduce at once that the vast majority of the trailers present were owned by the families of Price and Lee and that most of them would be known to me.

We jolted up over the kerb and on to a compressed-mud track which broke off in several directions, leading to various separated family-groupings of trailers. Upon sighting us a pack of mongrel dogs, from terrier-size to greyhound-lurchers, ran around us, growling and sniffing suspiciously; these were followed by a collection of little black-haired children, also curious to find out who was pulling on. The dogs, ascertaining by instinct that we were not enemy intruders, soon lost interest and wandered back to their respective homes, while the small children, some of whom were known to us by sight, smiled or just gazed at us non-committally. A number of men appeared, for in those days very few of that 'breed' of travellers went out 'calling' – preferring to be supported by the skills of their wives and their *dukkering*. Some of the men were sitting in their trailers, others were cleaning their lorries and vans, while yet more standing around a large smouldering stick-fire, talking animatedly. Once we had decided on a place to stay, some of them began walking over, casually, towards us: I recognised them as being Old Boggy, his cousin Nin, and two of his sons, Rudolph and Crimea, each of whom was leading a small boy by the hand. I was much delighted to see them for Old Boggy was one of my favourite members of his family. Deep coppery of complexion, his Indian ancestry very evident, he possessed a ready smile and natural good manners – which characteristics all his sons were fortunate enough to inherit. With five daughters and six sons he had done his best to ensure that there would no noticeable decline in the Romanies for some time to come.

We all shook hands and exchanged greetings, and they pointed to a vacant spot near to their own trailers, slightly horrified by the space we had chosen.

'Don't pull over agen that hedge, old kid,' warned Old Boggy, gesturing behind our trailer. He continued, 'Keep outa that old hedge – it's full of *beng* tails! An' just over the other side is Peg-Leg and then Old Black Mary – an' they must have sixty *jukes* 'tween 'em, God kill me! You wouldn't get two minutes sleep in a *rati*, wi' all of 'em barkin' an' hollerin'.'

'Well, aye,' agreed his son Rudolph. Beshlie did not look overjoyed on hearing this, but we had little choice.

We pulled the trailer round in an arc, backing it in longways against a low bank next to Old Boggy – as far from the hedge as possible. In such surroundings experience teaches one that it is perhaps unwise to station oneself close to any natural cover, under which the grass is indeed frequently greener – fathoming out the reasons for which may present little difficulty!

Scarcely had we unpacked our bits and pieces and set everything to rights when we became aware that three more trailers were pulling on, ending up within about thirty feet of us. Two Eccles Travellers and a small Vickers, drawn by long-bedded lorries, each smartly painted in two colours, two TKs and an old Austin. On the backs of which, like strange archaic birds of prey, perched delicately handled vibrating rollers. It was, I realised, upon catching sight of the snow-white hair of the driver of the leading lorry, Charlie Brasspin and his family. The Brasspins were originally from Northern England, but seemed to spend most of their time in the West Country, the men tarmacadam-laying and the women *dukkering*. They were a close-knit family, some of them blond, others red, and still more black-haired: Charlie himself was completely white-haired, though no more than forty-five years of age. Noisy and aggressive among themselves, like seagulls, they were generally reasonably affable to outsiders. Their main faults were their open envy of those with newer and better possessions balanced by their utter scorn and contempt for those who were worse off. Like most who were stopping on that ground, their womenfolk set out each day with lace and, whenever the opportunity arose, *dukkered* the receptive. The skill and dedication with which all the women fulfilled their arduous task was worthy of the deepest respect.

Two of the Brasspin boys, Rainbow and Joey, both in their late teens, sauntered over, ostensibly to speak to me but really, I knew, to inspect my little lorry. This they did with a mixture of pretended enthusiasm and thinly disguised jealousy.

'A pretty motor, Uncle,' observed Joey. 'How old is it?'

I told him.

'Would you have a *chop* for me brother's TK?' enquired Rainbow, shaking his head of thick red curls.

'Nah!' I replied. 'I've only just got it.'

'He'd give you a nice bit of money to *chop*, on my word he would,' persisted Rainbow – 'ain't that right, Joey?'

'Sure he would,' agreed Joey, loyally.

'Nah! I don't want a TK, too big for me,' I answered sharply and decisively, for it was no time for any hesitation.

After a few more comments on my lorry the two boys wandered off.

The only complaint that I could have possibly voiced about that first new lorry of mine was that it was *too* attractive! Its reserved tones of colour, its varnished-oak body, and all the little additions which gave it a character of its own, were to make it a constant target, a source of biddings from travellers of all kinds who coveted it during its first year of life. Most especially, however, did the offers flow in from the class of travellers with whom we were then stopping. It was flattering, but nonetheless could become tiresome. I retained the little Bedford for just under two years, until someone made me an offer which I felt it would have been financially unwise to refuse.

Beshlie and I consumed an aromatic curried-vegetable stew at about five o'clock, connected our tiny black-and-white portable television to the lorry battery, and relaxed, feeling that life could offer no greater refinements! However, upon viewing the local news programme, soon after six o'clock, we were somewhat disconcerted to see an aerial photograph of our trailers appear on the screen, having been accomplished by means of a helicopter. Listening to the commentary, we were in no way amazed to find that the report was strongly slanted against our presence being allowed to continue on the wasteland. Council officials, their pleasing Devonshire accents somewhat tarnished by the narrowness of their expressed opinions, were calling for our removal, coining what was then a new phrase: we were a 'health hazard'! (The latter phrase was once shown up in its true meaninglessness by a letter-writer to a local New Forest newspaper who objected to the ponies being allowed to wander through the streets of Lyndhurst as they were wont to do. This demented correspondent quoted their presence as constituting 'a definite health hazard'. One dares not speculate upon the numbers of persons who may have expired from the inhalation of gases from pony-droppings – before the arrival of the health-giving emissions of the internal combustion engine!)

We were slightly disheartened by the news item, and realised that our time between those busy highways was to be limited by bureaucrats, as always working in the guise of Public Health or Town and Country Planning; the last, particularly, seeming to be an unaesthetic body with no direct link to tastefulness – as a visit to almost any town or city in recent years will confirm.

Outside, I discussed the television feature with some of the men, many of whom had been stopping there for upwards of a month. All were confident that we would be able to extract at least another two weeks or more before action on the part of the council would commence. 'We've had no papers yet,' said Old Boggy. 'Have you, Fearless?' 'Not one,' confirmed Fearless. 'An' if they do bring any I'll eat 'em, dear Lord Above I will!'

He smiled strangely at us and nodded to himself. Fearless was a short yet incredibly thickset man, almost as broad as he was tall. His red face was scarred from fights and accidents; he was subject to 'fits' of a violent nature which had, over the years, been the cause of his being arrested and placed in protective custody for months on end. He was, with justification, viewed with wary alarm by all those around him. Thankfully, he was stopping on the far side of the ground, away from us. His condition was rumoured to have been activated by his being hit on the head by a house-brick by a *gaujo* with whom he had been having a dispute when he was but ten years old. He had been in a coma for three weeks, and the damage to his personality did not make itself strongly evident until he became an adult, we were told. Both of his parents were first cousins, as were his grandparents, and I have often wondered whether such a combination could result in such catastrophic behaviour.

That evening I spent in a local public house with Boggy, two of his sons and a son-in-law, where we engaged in a quiet and peaceful tournament of dominoes, for a penny a spot! Without imbibing too much beer, we returned happily and without mishap by eleven o'clock.

The next morning, Friday, was hazy with the promise of sunshine to come – a good omen.

In the sixties and seventies it was common practice for the itinerant muck-hawker to load his wares into used chicken-feed paper sacks, this being before the adoption of plastic bags as universal containers for almost all kinds of goods.

Henry Lichen had advised me that owners of battery hen or broiler-house establishments would invariably be happy to sell sacks for any price slightly in excess of waste-paper value. Thus, having spotted a large chicken farm some two miles or so from our stopping-place while on our way there with the trailer, I was soon knocking on their door. Within moments I had secured five bales of a hundred bags each for a pleasingly low outlay. In reply to my query as to the whereabouts of a riding-school in the locality the agreeable bag-seller directed me to one, only a mile distant.

I followed his directions and discovered the stables with no difficulty. I drove into the yard and was confronted by a somewhat stalwart young lady, with freckled face and pale ginger hair worn in one long plait. She showed me the midden, a finely decomposed sawdust and manure composition: it resembled peat and was a cheering sight. It was indeed even more cheering when she requested but a pound a load and assured me that I could take all I wanted.

Not being skilled or practised in the art of bagging up in those early days, I found that the constant unaccustomed stooping and bending took its toll on the shocked muscles in one's back. I would suffer acute pains after completing the forty bags which I had demanded of myself that I should sell each day. Necessity and determination, however, triumphed in the end: within a year I was able to increase my numbers to fifty or sixty bags an hour, while experiencing little or no fatigue whatsoever. Over twenty-five years later I can still perform the same labour, though sometimes, I fancy, an unfamiliar weariness creeps over me. Perhaps I am not immortal, after all!

There was an occasion, at a later date, which was somewhat fearful. I had been bagging up at an equestrian centre where they not long previously burned most of the stable-clearings, which were a wood-chip mixture. However, the remains seemed quite good, black and rich-looking and of an enticing odour, a little of it still smouldering calmly.

Alas, impatience and lack of care caused me to fill two or three of the sacks with overheated manure and ash. As I drove from the stables, unknown to me the contents of the paper bags was fanned by the movement of the lorry. Stopping at a red traffic-light and pedestrian crossing, I was somewhat astonished to be addressed by an infinitely respectable middle-aged lady on the pavement beside me. Tapping on the window rather daintily, she said, without emotion, 'Excuse me, but do you know that your lorry is on fire?'

My horror knew no bounds when I observed smoke and flames pouring from at least six of the bags towards the cab of the lorry. Rushing round and climbing aboard the lorry's rear I managed to cast the semi-incinerated bags and their contents into the gutter and trample the flames. Fortunately for me the rest of the bags were unaffected and tragedy was averted.

Little did I realise, when I first commenced my muck-hawking career, that I was actually starting it at the very worst time of the year – too late for spring-planting and too early for autumn. The gardens of suburbia in midsummer are, in the majority of cases, too lush, crowded and green to accept the addition of manure. However, later experience taught me that not everyone would realise that such was the case, and so sales *could* be achieved if one persevered. So it was that my self-taught apprenticeship was one of great hardship, but matters could only improve with the changing of the season. Had I not been fully experienced in the vagaries and soul-destroying qualities of door-to-door salesmanship over a number of years I might have been tempted to give up. I had set myself at an additional disadvantage by calling at Plymouth: it had, apparently, long been regarded as a very difficult town from which to extract a living – unless a Devonshire native, born and bred.

In succeeding years, when in Devon, I tended to concentrate upon the coastal areas of Torbay and its surroundings, the inhabitants of which, commonly in retirement and often from other parts of Britain, seemed less confirmed in their automatic opposition to persons calling at their doors. However, even in the face of opposition, both human and seasonal, my sales in Plymouth during my first day were not to be entirely despised. The bags disappeared in twos and threes, such that my already high opinion of the 'little apples taste sweet' theory of retailing was in no way diminished. My luck improved still further when, glancing at random down a side road, I saw a crescent containing eight or ten towering Victorian residences, each standing in its own grounds. The first one at which I knocked resulted in an immediate purchase of four bags by an academic-looking elderly man of hesitant manner and slightly stammering speech.

The second house was less well maintained, with once-green paintwork flaking from the door and window-frames, and the garden wild from neglect. Several large old garden vases and urns could be glimpsed through the evergreen shrubs, the paths were overgrown, and the crumbling remnant of a once-charming little ha-ha was just perceptible in the distant wilderness beyond the hassocky lawn. At the windows of the gloomy old house there hung torn, sun-bleached velvet curtains, and uneven, haphazardly lowered Venetian blinds which veered crazily across the dirty panes. At some other windows long tassels of beads, multi-coloured, once exotic, dangled in profusion, some broken and spilled on to the ledges like brilliantly tinted peas. There was about the place an atmosphere of sorrow or grief, or of desolation come of age – it was hard to tell which. Its aspect excited me; my hopes, as ever, were that within that decaying dwelling I might discover a person of not too straitened circumstances who might feel inclined to become a beneficent donor to my own cause of financial self-advancement. Mine was not the quest of a dubious con-man or robber seeking to engage in lies or tricks: more the search for the materialisation of the kind of good fortune which I had always intuitively felt to be my due!

A long verdigris-covered bell-pull hung inside the twilit-seeming porch, beside a heavy front door set with iron studs and enormous moulded iron hinges across its width. As I tugged upon it I could make out what sounded like the tinkling of myriad tiny bells, echoing from within.

After a short pause, as the bells fell silent I could hear the sound of approaching footsteps, slow yet not faltering, and the great door was slowly eased open. A largely built though somewhat wizened housemaid of very advanced years stood regarding me suspiciously from behind thick-lensed, perfectly circular spectacles with gold frames. The uniform she wore, of stiff-looking black and white, strongly accentuated the yellowish pallor of her skin; her eyes fluctuated alarmingly in size behind the great magnification of her lenses, her features devoid of identifiable expression other than suspicion.

I knew that the surest way to leave unrewarded would be to upset her.

I smiled politely, trying not to expose my gold tooth, and said: 'Good morning, I wonder if I could ask you to be kind enough to let me speak to the lady or gentleman of the house?'

'What do you want? What's your name? Where are you from?' demanded the domestic with excessive coldness, expression unchanged. As I was seeking in my mind for a reply, piercing cries echoed from the far end of the nocturnally lit hallway. 'Gertrude! Gertrude! Who is it?'

Eventually I was able to discern in the distant vastnesses a bulky figure coming gradually closer, edging forward in slow, painstaking, lopsided steps. When about thirty feet distant, I distinguished the figure as that of an aged woman, leaning heavily upon a thick walking-stick. Her curiously ungainly movement was evidently occasioned by the fact of there being but one leg visible beneath the hem of her voluminous serge skirt – the missing one had been replaced by a wooden stump of the variety usually associated with pirates or ancient mariners of any sort in days long past. However, despite a dumpiness of form, and the missing limb, it was a person of distinct character who finally proceeded into the rays of sunlight in the doorway. At least eighty years old, her hair was bleached a bright yellow-blond, ringletted, and with a row of sleek kiss-curls swinging across a tall brow. Vivid cornflower-blue eyes were carefully outlined with mascara and pencil, her skin was taut beneath a generous layer of theatrical make-up, her mouth slashed in a neat bow of shining scarlet lipstick.

Although I have never prided myself on being either an artist or an imbecile, I nevertheless share their alleged fascination with the bizarre – a side of my character which, perhaps, I have never sought to nourish in the way that it should have been.

The maid bobbed obsequiously, if rather stiffly, at the approach of her employer and offered her assistance, but was peremptorily gestured away – at which she withdrew into the dark recesses, grumbling inaudibly to herself, leaving us alone.

'Good morning, Madam,' I said, smiling.

'Good morning. How can I help you?' enquired the gentlewoman pleasantly, listing to one side where she stood.

I launched enthusiastically into the reason for my call, stressing the efficacious and beneficial results which must surely be obtained from the application of stable manure to her gardens, stressing that she might well be advised to follow the theory that where there was a supply, then surely would a demand follow.

During what only the cynical could describe as my spiel, the old woman's blue eyes stared fixedly at me, her smiles growing. Convinced that I was making good progress, I smiled back. 'Tell me,' she at length remarked, amiability personified, 'do you know the Lord Jesus?'

So taken aback was I by this unexpected enquiry that I was only just able to stifle the instinctive reply, 'No, but does He want some for His garden?'

Wisdom prevailed and I merely shook my head, feeling my chances of making a sale were slipping away.

'You have a very good face,' she continued. 'What a pity that you do not know the Lord Jesus.'

'Oh dear,' said I, becoming more and more depressed.

'Yes,' mused the ancient woman, 'I am interested in faces. Until my accident, when I lost my leg, I was a plastic surgeon. Yours is a good face – but you should know the Lord Jesus.'

A definite crank, I thought.

'I remember when I was staying with dear Gracie,' she went on, still staring closely at me. 'I lifted her face, and Marlene's too. Beautiful women both, in their own ways. Would you like to see their photographs, which they autographed for me?'

'Yes, I would like that,' I replied, surprised by her offer and suddenly finding the encounter of great interest.

She pivoted and advanced awkwardly for a few paces. 'What do you think of my leg?' she suddenly demanded.

I obligingly, if unwillingly, regarded the foot and ankle protruding from the hem of her skirt.

'No! No!' she shouted irately. 'Not my old leg! My *new* leg, I meant.'

'I'm sorry,' I answered, a trifle unnerved. 'Oh yes, well I call that a very nice leg, from what I can see of it.'

'It is a nice leg – look at it!' snapped the old person in apparent indignation, raising her skirt up to where her knee should have been, and disclosing a socket into which her lower thigh was stuffed.

A momentary wave of nausea swept over me, but I managed to steady myself. It brought back a memory of when I had once been calling in a suburb of Great Yarmouth and had observed an old man gardening in the sunshine. He was wearing only a sleeveless vest, which had left the stump of one missing arm hanging, fully visible, for the seven or eight inches of its length. I was younger then, but for some unfathomable reason the sight had turned my stomach over and I had vomited into a nearby gutter.

We turned through an archway from the hall and entered a large sitting-room, furnished in a kind of decaying opulence, each nook and cranny filled with objects of age and interest. Even I, limited though my knowledge of antiques was then, could readily appreciate the heady scent of monetary value which was clearly present.

I recollected the story of a Brighton 'knocker' who had gained entry to such a house and managed to purchase its entire contents for only a few hundred pounds. His delight may well be imagined, therefore, when he obtained fourteen thousand for just *one* of the pictures therein. Could he, one wonders, have been the sort of businessman who might have been viewed as unscrupulous? How can one judge?

The voice of the ancient surgeon cut across my ponderings.

'There!' she exclaimed, pointing with her stick while hanging on to a little inlaid table to steady herself. 'There's Gracie, and there's Marlene.'

I examined the framed photographs on a shelf opposite. Each was in faded sepia, each strongly autographed. The faces of both women, such great celebrities in their lifetimes, stared flatly back at me, no hint of emotion visible on their rather expressionless and unreal features. To me they looked as remote as Aztecs. But I could see that they were highly thought of by their owner, so for no other reason I was fulsome in their praise.

She seemed delighted by my reaction and announced: 'Since I retired as a surgeon I have taken up portrait painting – and I would like to paint you.'

'Well, thank you,' I replied, utterly astonished. 'But I'm afraid I haven't much time at the moment. I have to sell my bags of compost—'

'Never mind that,' she interrupted. 'I expect I could buy them. Would you like to see some of my pictures?' I assented readily.

She shuffled to a cupboard and began to extract large numbers of canvases from it, mostly about two or three feet square in size. She thrust half a dozen or so in my direction. Alas, though no authority on the techniques of oil-painting, I was sufficiently aesthetically attuned to realise that they boasted no quality of either colour or line. I could have done as well myself.

Having them displayed for my admiration was enough to make me all but tongue-tied for any kind of comment. Floundering desperately, I eventually enquired, 'How could you describe the mode in which you paint?'

The pictures, without exception, appeared to me to be somewhere between the kindergarten and Grandma Moses on a bad day. So I was slightly taken aback by her reply.

'I paint,' she said confidently, 'in the style of the Old Masters.'

This engaging modesty appealed to me. She then suggested that I might sit for her on an afternoon in the following week. Over two hours had passed; as always to me, time was money.

'Um, yes,' I faltered slightly. 'About the bags of compost, I have twenty left, and I will offer them to you at a remarkably reasonable price.'

'How much will that be?' she asked. I apprised her of the figure. She extracted the amount from a finely embossed leather handbag and gave it to me.

'You will find Mr Yurin, the gardener, in the greenhouse. He will tell you where he wants it to be stored,' she informed me.

At that moment we heard a sound of crashing and splintering from somewhere in the rear of the house, followed by faint cries. The surgeon betrayed neither surprise nor alarm. 'The house is collapsing, you know,' she remarked, adding: 'It was Christmas Day when cook fell through the kitchen floor – and we knew then that it must be the dry rot.'

I looked sharply at her, but she showed none of the

feelings one might have felt appropriate in such trying circumstances, with a house falling down about if not one's own ears, then at least about those of one's unfortunate cook.

'A very bad thing, dry rot,' I sympathised. 'Would you like me to try to get something done about it? I have a friend who specialises in the tr—'

'No, thank you,' she interjected. 'It has already been treated by a proper firm, and it cost me seven hundred pounds. I had hoped it had been cured.'

After fixing upon an afternoon during the following week for me to suffer a portrait-sitting – a date which I felt a little dubious that I would keep – I took my leave and went to consult with an ill-tempered Mr Yurin, whose accent led me to conclude that he and his forebears were from Staines rather than the Russian Steppes. He grumbled incessantly at the thought of his being expected to dispose of the fertiliser around the wilderness-like gardens in his charge.

I finally left, and my spirits were lifted when, upon inspecting the little wodge of notes with which I had been presented, the amount proved to be well in advance of what I had requested. I was so elated by my day's takings that I returned to the equestrian centre and bagged up a further forty, the energy fathered by success, ready for the next morning's assault on suburbia.

When I reached the trailers all was placid and quiet in the

afternoon sun. Traffic streamed by on either side of us, the drivers of both cars and commercial vehicles and their passengers casting looks of wonderment, malice, envy, or even goodwill in our direction as they sped by. The children played at their secret games, and dogs and men lolled in the shade.

For the most part, the women had still not returned from their long day of hawking. Some would be picked up at an appointed time and place by their menfolk in lorries or vans, others would trudge wearily back on foot, while those who had experienced a reasonably successful day might arrive home by taxi – not a very common occurrence I might add . . .

The lives of women of that branch of traveller society is one of some hardship, and would be daunting indeed to those who had not experienced it from girlhood. Luckily, however, this was the case with most of the women there, almost every one of whom had accompanied their own mothers on such daily expeditions when they were children, and they were usually well versed in the art before entering their teens. Sheer force of character combined with staying-power would enable them to keep trying, despite the denigration from many an uncivil householder, until perseverence brought a little reward their way. The pedestrian journey of the itinerant 'caller', whether buying or selling, is sometimes a desolate trek, difficult and arduous indeed. It is a method of earning a livelihood upon which unlimited abuse is heaped and for which no credit is given. Yet surely those who strike out for themselves, from the humble 'knocker' to those in big business, *gaujo* or traveller, should be accorded more respect than those whose only ability is to visit the job centre each week or merely sit at home safe in the knowledge that the God of Giro will prevent them from having to endure any *real* privations of the kind suffered by unfortunates in bygone years, and still suffered by those who are without state aid, even if through choice.

Beshlie and I sat in the shade of the trailer and munched on some cheese and cold cooked vegetables. Barney crouched nearby, watchful for any scraps we might fling in his direction, which he would skilfully apprehend in mid-air.

The Prices and the Lees were all of an old-fashioned 'breed' of traveller, with a great reverence for old traditions of Romani behaviour. They would never visit when another family was eating a meal, be it outside round the fire or in the trailer, nor would they enter another person's trailer except by invitation, unless it should be that of a close relative. And they taught their children to respect other people's belongings, and their elders. All such habits could only prove advantageous to themselves and add to the chances of harmonious living with their neighbours.

The Brasspins, however, were not finding the area very

rewarding on that occasion; the men were unlucky in their searches for tarmacadam-laying contracts. They returned home later that afternoon very out of temper, quarrelling vigourously among themselves. Apparently, they had agreed to re-surface the driveway of a large suburban house near Exeter, only to have the owners of the property renege on the agreement at the eleventh hour when they had actually arrived with hot tarmac and were about to commence laying. Charlie himself was in a fine state of wrath at such disgraceful behaviour, and with some right on his side in my opinion.

'My dear God Almighty, I never seen such a man,' he grumbled, lying on the ground surrounded by his sons, all sweating profusely in the sunshine.

'We only fetched the tarmac to the house an' was just goin' to start a-layin' it when the man, a real *bori rai*, comes out like a bulldog. He said we told his dear wife lies, an' he was goin' to phone the *muskeros*! I thought he'd have a heart attack there an' then. He was the colour of a pickled cabbage! I tried everything with him – 'ticin' him, beggin' him, threatenin' him even – but he wouldn't have none of it. So what could you do? We had to *jal*. We ended up doin' a couple of poverty little jobs, just to get back the money laid out. Unluckiest day I've had for years, my old kid.'

I commiserated with him, knowing that his spirits would

not be restored until he had found a 'lemon' to help him recoup his losses, both to his pocket and to his ego. I had too often found myself in the same situation.

The boys soon wandered off to their own trailers, only Charlie remaining. We offered him a cup of tea, which he gratefully accepted, and joined us in the shade. His snow-white hair and sideburns, and black eyebrows and moustache, coupled with piercing eyes, gave him an arresting appearance, not easily forgotten. Of course, of this he was not unaware and indeed was fond of relating the following anecdote, as something of a highlight in his later life: apparently he had been accosted by the owner of a biscuit factory in the Midlands who was about to launch a new range. Upon seeing Charlie, he immediately envisioned him suitably attired in the full costume of a Spanish hidalgo of a former century, and desired to use the image for reproduction on the proposed brand's tins. Although much flattered by this offer of immortality, Charlie had felt it necessary to decline it on the grounds of modesty. 'It'd be no good if some old *rai* or *rawnie* was just sittin' down for their bit of tea, would it, if they was to *dik* me photy on the biscuit-tin and say: "Here, that's the feller who done me drive!"' he said drily, ''Specially if they was a bit narked with the job!'

We had to agree that a quiet genteel tea-party might well have been disturbed!

*

An added complication had been brought into all our lives by reason of the fact that a nearby factory, where we had been collecting our water from an outside tap at the side of the premises, had rather unreasonably turned off the supply. This forced us to try a variety of alternative sources, mostly without success. The nearest garage took the ungenerous step of demanding a high payment for each can or churn that was filled at their premises, despite the fact that we had all been buying our diesel and petrol from their pumps.

As always, the numbers of trailers grew almost daily, and so did the local reaction. Demands for our removal increased in volume, through aural, pictorial and written means. It was obvious that the end was near, and the ground had become overcrowded to a degree that was almost unbearable. In all Beshlie and I had spent a fortnight there, quite long enough for me in those days. There were threats from the council that we would be evicted on Monday so I decided to pull off on the Sunday, rather than be involved in the confusion and chaos which I knew would ensue.

As we were so far 'down country' we decided to venture further; to aim, eventually, for Land's End in Cornwall, which was utterly unknown country to me then. None of the others wished to proceed in that direction, almost all choosing to head back towards Bristol, London, or in some cases to the east coast in time for the holiday season and *dukkering* on the beaches. At one point it seemed that the Brasspins might accompany us, but at the last moment they changed their minds and decided on North Devon instead. Overpowering as a family, constantly squabbling and sometimes actually coming to blows, I felt no great sorrow over their change of plans.

On Sunday morning, quite early, the skies heavy with the threat of thunder, we were off again, this time into the unknown.

Stow Fair, 1959

My first visit to Stow Fair, which is held twice annually in the little Cotswold town, was to the spring fair of 1959. It was before we became mechanised and we were stopping, with our two horses and a living wagon, some twenty miles from Stow, on a smallholding which was owned by a settled-down Romani who found it useful for his horse-dealing business. His heart was still on the roads, and he was forever 'going away' for varying lengths of time in an ornate Vickers traveller-style trailer which he kept for the purpose. Named Jack Smallbones, he was a fine-looking man, tall and erect, of about seventy years of age. Despite his years he had not a grey hair among his dense black locks; his eyes were of the deepest 'Gypsy black' and his almost olive skin stretched tightly across his thin features, especially over his aquiline nose. He would usually wear a black velour hat and a knotted, coloured neckerchief tied crosswise: he was of the outlook that to look 'gypsified' was a matter of pride.

'You can't hide what you are,' he would say. 'And you shouldn't try.' Not for him the lounge suits and collars-and-ties of many of his latter day counterparts.

Black Jack was a widower, his wife having been a Welsh *gauji*, but his three sons and one daughter had all married back into traveller families and were moving about the country. One or other of them, or sometimes two at a time, would come and stay in one of his fields, until they were evicted by the local council and planning authorities. 'Twenty-eight days in any one year' was all that they were officially allowed. It is very depressing to see the enforcement of those petty regulations in a so-called free society. (Eventually, I suspect, after all the miscarriages of justice, uneven convictions, racial antagonisms – particularly towards travellers, even from Home Secretaries – combined with a thorough examination of our history, including slavery and transportation for trivial crimes, and also – until recently – our official attitudes to illegitimacy and homosexuality, we will at last not fail to appreciate that we are part of the most hypocritical nation in the world. However, I digress!)

Jack was intending to take two good-sized cobs, both coloured, to the fair with the aim of either selling them outright or engaging in a remunerative *chop* should the opportunity be presented. To my delight he invited me to accompany him in his aged horse-box. Converted from a smallish pantechnicon, it was of 1939 but still 'tidy' in its own way. It was a 'bull-nosed' Bedford, originally a lorry, and had been hand-painted a rich dark blue. As far as Black Jack was concerned its only handicap was that it was made before the refinement of synchro-mesh gears. Instead it possessed the more archaic 'crash' gearbox, necessitating double de-clutching at every change, either up or down. Once learned (as I later discovered with my own first lorry) it was a rea-sonably easy feat – even if a somewhat acrobatic one! Jack, however, had never fully mastered the technique, hence every gear-change was accompanied by rasping grumbles from every sprocket and ratchet in the mechanism – enough to cause horror and nausea to all but the stoutest-hearted mechanic who happened to hear the engine's protestations!

We set off at eight-thirty in the morning on the main day of the spring fair which was, and still is, a Thursday. I climbed up into the cab beside Jack and his eleven-year-old Bedlington-cross whippet bitch who went everywhere with him. 'Come on, old gal,' murmured Jack as he managed to coax the engine into spluttering life, amid clouds of blue smoke. 'Could do with new rings, I reckons,' said Jack casu-ally, adding for good measure: 'Keep her topped-up with oil and water – she'll soon tell you when she'm out of petrol!'

He grinned at his truism and his eyes glittered, darker still, and his long mouth curved in the semblance of a smile, a matchstick-like hand-rolled cigarette hanging from one corner. He was smoking the old travellers' favourite tobacco, 'Black Beauty', which smelled acrid yet strangely sweet: its odour was unforgettable. I remember, in those days, aged travellers would smoke it in clay pipes, sitting round the wood-fires and judiciously priming their *swiglers* with either tea-leaves or hot ashes to supplement the baccy. (I am by no means sure that Black Beauty, with its wrapper featuring the head and shoulders of a dusky young maiden with an enticing smile, is still available. Possibly it *is* still obtainable, though in these days of political correctness I suspect it could only be presented as 'Beauty'!)

It was a beautiful May morning, my favourite time of the year, with the undoubted promise of a glorious day. I was intensely excited at the prospect ahead: it was as thrilling to me as the thought of a visit to Disneyland is for the average ten-year-old boy in other circumstances. The age of innocence was, and to some extent still is, upon me.

Shuddering and creaking, the gearbox protesting even louder than usual as Jack forcibly manhandled it against its will, we proceeded, with occasional surprising turns of speed, across the open, sweeping Cotswold country, turning eventually on to a road marked: *Stow on the Wold 10 miles*.

Jack was lively and enthusiastic company with a lifetime of ducking and diving behind him. His tales of horse-dealing were legion – in some he came out clearly ahead, in others he lost. The modern phrase: 'win some, lose some' could never be more aptly applied than to the profession of horse-dealing. Everyone is out for themselves and though they are the best of friends, when in the throes of a deal each adheres to the adage: There's no love in dealing.

Not, of course, that there are no principles at all. For example, no decent man would sell a thoroughly unreliable horse, maybe a *bouncer* (kicker), to a man to use on his wagon and thus to transport his family and worldly goods. The same, in its own way, may be applied to the motor-trader of today. Though, alas, I have found fewer scruples shown by many motor-dealers than were shown by their horse-dealing forebears.

'You'd have to get up early in the morning to catch Black Jack,' said another dealer, a man called Pincher Moore, later that day, having failed dismally in a good-natured attempt to deceive Jack over the fitness, age *and* character of a seemingly impeccable chestnut pony which he was attempting to *chop* for one of Jack's cobs – and trying to draw some money as well!

It was well nigh impossible to judge Jack's financial state by his appearance, which although cultivated was always rather shabby and broken-down-looking: his tall lace-up brown boots were cracked and worn, his old-fashioned tailor-made fall-front trousers, pipestem-legged, were ragged and stained and his heavy Derby-tweed jacket, with yoked back and half-moon pockets, hung uneasily on his tall frame. Only his bright neckerchief and well-brushed velour hat showed any sign of attention. He was of a dying breed of old-style dealers, once to be found spread all over the land and now almost disappeared – their places having been taken by smarter, slicker, maybe even cleverer men, who lack the charm of their forebears. He was rumoured to be a million-aire, though this was never either discounted or confirmed at his death: Jack was too wise to let the world into his secrets. Brought up in bender tents and wagons, forever on the move, with no education other than that concerning horses and buying and selling them, taught to him by his father, his was a story of success in the face of disadvantage and preju-dice, and admirable indeed.

As we turned down from the main Oxford road into the little town of Burford we passed several easily recognisable travellers' lorries which had parked alongside of the shops, probably for refreshment after their journeys.

'There's Sonner an' his boy,' observed Jack, pointing to a smart little Bedford lorry, painted dark maroon and lined out in straw colour; a large belt was painted on each door, with a horse-shoe buckle, and the owner's initials in gold leaf within its circle. The latter was a favourite decoration on the vehicles of Romanies in those times – sadly to die out as the need for anonymity, by reason of prejudice, became more pronounced.

'A nice little lorry,' remarked Jack. 'Just the right age – I likes a motor about two years old what's nicely used to the roads.'

We both laughed at his witticism and he inhaled deeply on his wizened cigarette. His roll-ups were so thin and small that they often attracted attention.

'Here, Uncle Jack,' said one youngish traveller to him one day in my presence, 'you'll be had-up for starvin' they fags!'

On my first viewing, Burford seemed a picturesque and architecturally agreeable place, though the number of antique shops and tea-and-cakes establishments led me to suspect that the grip of commercialism was not entirely lacking in the spirit of its denizens.

We reached the end of the downward gradient towards the limit of the town, went over a small bridge and took the left fork, travelling upwards and across open country for almost ten miles until we joined the main road to our right, leading still upwards into Stow. As we approached the town, which was no more than half a mile distant, we beheld lines of travellers' motors of all sorts, ages, and conditions, drawn up along the grass verge which was just wide enough to accommodate them.

In the late fifties, before the magically affluent years of the sixties and seventies, the majority of travellers, and particularly the old-fashioned ones, had only recently surrendered their horses and wagons in favour of the imagined luxury of the much-praised motor and trailer. As an experiment in a new way of living they tended, either through choice or necessity, to purchase elderly commercial vehicles, already clapped-out by the time they acquired them: hence breakdowns and other disasters were none too infrequent. (It was a tribute to the young men of that era that, despite having only just become motorised, they nonetheless seemed to absorb the intricacies of the ancient engines which they faced with incredible ease and confidence.) Mostly favoured was the twenty-five- to thirty-hundredweight lorry; and much in front of the others in the way of choice was the old thirty-hundredweight Bedford lorry. This single-rear-wheeled truck, sturdy, reliable, and almost indestructible, was always in great demand and remained so, in its different guises (the 'bull-nosed', the 'frog-fronted' and the 'mouth-organ-fronted', to give them their travellers' nicknames) until the 1970s when Ford Transits superseded them like a swarm of locusts.

Besides the Bedford, in those days, there was the Austin Lonestar lorry and the long-defunct little twenty-five-hundredweight Commer lorry or van. The latter were quite popular but did not possess the power of either Bedfords or Austins. This did not, however, always dissuade optimistic owners from forcing these game little motors into almost impossible feats of towing, getting heavy living-trailers stuck on hills and, in the last resort, causing the engine to blow up. Disaster indeed.

As most of the vehicles were distinctly shabby when pur-chased, in the way of old commercials, they were invariably hand-painted by their new owners. The latter fact in itself was responsible for the colourful and imaginative shades which were combined, though these adventures in colour were mainly practised by those who had come accustomed to the cheerful sight of brightly painted wagons and saw no reason to give up old habits.

Those who pined to give the impression of a more rarefied and genteel background tended to be drawn to shades of mushroom, beige or grey – often in two-tone. In fact the last of the Bedford lorries to be produced were almost *all* two-toned grey or mushroom – sprayed of course, no longer hand-painted. Everyone was going up!

Though many readers might sneer at the attention paid to motor vehicles, they should stop and think: those lorries had become the new equivalent of wagon-horses for their owners – they therefore looked for the best that they could afford. That travellers' vehicles became recognisable from those of *gaujes* was a tribute to their ingenuity.

Even today, in these more uniform times, it is easy for the initiated to pick out a traveller's motor, be it lorry, van, or limousine.

Nowadays manufacturers supply towbars direct from their factories, designed to fit any specific model, but this was not so until the mid-seventies for lorries and vans. Nobody except travellers used such commercial vehicles for the towing of trailer-caravans. So local blacksmiths and general metal-workers were called upon to fashion and make towbars; many a 'mauken' was produced, often in so heavy a guage that a ten-ton armoured tank could have been pulled; or alternatively so light and flimsy that they were liable to stretch or bend when a trailer was attached. The earliest towbars were almost invariably of an elongated vee-shape, jutting out a foot or so from the rear of the chassis in order to provide clearance for the corners of the lorry body so as not to come into damaging contact with the trailer when nego-tiating very sharp turns. (I remember once, at Appleby Fair, when a traveller had just arrived with a splendid brand-new Westmorland Star trailer which he was pulling with a long-bedded lorry with an undershot towbar. While reversing too sharply he succeeded in severely crunching both one corner and the complete front window of the opulent home. Though somewhat staggered by the event, he managed a brave face and announced his intention of returning to the maker, fortunately not too far distant from Appleby, for repairs. One could not help but feel, however, that his enjoy-ment of the week must have been slightly curtailed. Mine would have been.)

However, travellers always seem to emerge as natural improvers, and there gradually evolved the square-shaped step-bar. The latter was universally adopted; it was more pleasing visually as well as being of practical use for assisting one's progress up into the back of a van or on to the bed of a lorry. In later years, they fell out of fashion, being dubbed 'too travellery'. Fashions, of course, dominate almost everything in the travellers' lifestyle – from clothes to motors and, especially so, trailers. Of the latter, the fashions are marked and distinct, those at the top financially setting the pace and style. As there are, at the time of writing, only about four manufacturers of traveller-style trailers, the choice is not very wide. It is, however, a natural progression from the time of the wagons, when there were only a small and select number of makers – each clearly recognisable from each other.

'Here's some people here already, kid,' observed Jack, eyeing the line of vehicles appraisingly. 'This good bit of weather's don it an' fetched 'em all up here. We should've *awved* in a bit earlier.'

As we had the two cobs aboard, the grass verge would not have been near enough to the horse-sales area, so we decided to carry on in the hope of finding a space among the other horse-boxes. And so we passed along the grass verge and some rows of cottages until we were opposite the main road into Stow itself. Here, on the left hand side, was the entrance to a small road, little more than a lane. Several constables paced around the edge, and a sergeant too.

As we turned in, I was astonished by the scene before us. On each side of the lane, though mostly on the left, were both wagons and trailers, and intermingled with them were stalls, all seemingly owned by travellers and all displaying the kinds of goods which would appeal to their discerning clientele. Some stalls were piled high with Crown Derby and Royal Worcester china, with heavy crystal cut-glass vases in a variety of shapes and colours as an added attraction. Others showed plates and tea-sets decorated with hand-painted scenes from old-style Romani life – wagons and horses and groups seated round wood-fires predominating. Still more carried huge displays of stainless-steel water-cans, bowls and buckets, wash-stands and jugs, all of which are part of every traveller's possessions.

Amazingly embroidered cushions of unimaginable vulgarity and delicately stitched pillows and bed-covers glittered in the sunlight. Carpets and rugs of all descriptions, and of all qualities, were hung out for inspection. Money was changing hands, after vigorous haggling, almost everywhere one looked. A group of Irish travelling-women, hair peroxided, with huge gold hooped earrings and thick gold chains around their necks, were struggling with a roll of carpet, their strong accents strange amid those of the English travellers. Their several little children were all reddish blonds, with heavy freckles.

Other stalls were filled with bird cages, piled up upon each other and side by side, in which, singing loudly and sweetly, were 'mules' – mostly canaries crossed with goldfinches, and a few crossbred with bullfinches or linnets. On the ground a variety of bantams and gamecocks were seated rather mournfully in wire-fronted boxes: the last I knew would surely sell. At others were dogs, puppies too, all either terriers or running-dogs. The lane was packed with humanity, almost exclusively Romani people – for this was before the advent of the New Age traveller or even the Weekend Gypsy!

Some were modern, the men in slick drape suits, which were still in fashion then; the women in smart frocks with no little excess of gold jewellery. However, in by far the greatest numbers were the old-fashioned (a term of praise among travellers), and these latter were more pleasing to the eye. The women were in plaid skirts of ankle length, their hair braided and watered-down; many carried wicker *kipsies* – these baskets were filled with lace or trinkets to hawk around the town or on the environs of the fair itself. Here were men, both young and old, in large-brimmed hats or snappy trilbies with coloured scarves at their necks – *diklos*, as they were called. They were almost universally wearing the once-popular elastic-sided jodhpur boots, in vivid shades of yellow or red-tan. The majority were attired in the tailor-made style of the period: many-pocketed, with scalloped flaps, the jackets were either yoke-backed or with pleats at each shoulder; while the trousers were often fall-fronted and always had

raised seams down the outside of each leg. Some of their features were derived from the films of American Smart Society,
while others had hung on from the Edwardian era. They
were generally preferred in black, navy blue, or dark brown;
and, combined with the boots, hats and neckerchiefs, they
presented to the world, for a few years, the characteristic
Romani style. Perhaps not up to the sartorial standards set by
the *Tailor and Cutter* but nonetheless pleasing for all that.

Indeed there was a firm situated in Rugely in Staffordshire
whose enthusiasm for the style was so great that they would,
upon request, send a self-measuring chart to anyone interested. Fully conversant with Romani requirements, they
would make and despatch the garments for a mere few
pounds: sent, of course, COD! The variety of their cloths
was truly amazing, perhaps the most alluring of which were
moleskin or the legendary 'Owd Dog'. I obtained a suit from
them in black moleskin, and it afforded me immense pleasure and lasted for several years, being worn in all weathers
and under conditions guaranteed to ruin the average fabric
within months, if not weeks!

Our progress down the lane was of necessity slow owing
to the throng of people, of all ages, across its width. Until
then I had not fully realised the extent of Black Jack's popularity. At every yard or so someone would jokily shout:
'Hello, Mr Smallbones,' or 'Hello, my Jack, how are you?'
or some other pleasantry. The younger greeters always

respectfully addressed him as 'Uncle Jack', which is the Romani way. Many a gnarled hand, decorated with a heavy gold buckle-ring or a mounted sovereign, was thrust in through the cab window to shake his hand.

'You know some people here, Jack,' I said, in awe.

'Well I ought to,' he replied. 'I bin here every year, bar one, since I was a dee-little baby on the titty-bottle!' At that moment a small dark man in a straw hat poked his head into the cab, grinning broadly, to display broken stumps and missing teeth, huskily remarked, 'Hello Jack, my old cousin. Got that bit of money you owes me?'

He said it as though joking, but there was an underlying malice beneath the false smile. Jack was not over-pleased, I could tell. He grunted and drove on. 'Fuck that Fincher,' he growled, his mouth a thin straight line. 'He ain't a monkey-man, is he? His father was just as bad. Huh! Both on 'em poxy monkey-men – ringtails the two of 'em.'

However, a few yards of movement and more proffered handshakes and Black Jim was restored to his amiable self.

After about a quarter of an hour we reached the bottom of the lane past the end of the stalls. The last one consisted of a shameless array of virtual rubbish which none but the most optimistic could have considered saleable. It was run by a north-country man of dubious origin, with only a touch of traveller in his pedigree, one would have assumed. He was of middle age, with a bulldog-like wife, and had a complexion of such pallor that his sojourn in this world seemed very temporary – though those who had known him for many years explained that he had always looked near to death, even when young. His diet consisted entirely of white bread and bacon, fried monotonously by his unfortunate woman, which must have greatly added to his condition. His other handicap was that he was known as Prick: this could not have helped!

At that time – though it was to be discontinued after a few more years – an auction sale of horses and harness and occasional carts and trolleys was held at both the spring and autumn fairs in a small field at the lane's termination. It was there that the dealers would gather, running their horses up and down to demonstrate their movement before they went under the hammer. In 1959 there was little demand for middle- or heavy-weight horses to pull wagons as just then travellers were turning in droves to the greater glory of 'motors and trailers'. Heartbreaking though it was, hundreds of fine wagon-horses were sold for slaughter as nobody wanted them; only riding ponies and hunters could be readily disposed of. Heavy harness was in the same state: beautiful sets in red or yellow morocco, often with silver 'white metal' buckles, would fetch a fraction of their value. And these were frequently sold and then cut up, by unscrupulous vendors, to be used as wall-decorations in many a bijou suburban residence. (Who, in those days, could have foretold that wagons and their coloured cobs and harness would make such a reappearance in the eighties and nineties, largely used by 'weekend Gypsies' in country shows, or even by the New Age travellers?)

We drew in among the horse-boxes, all owned by either travellers or 'London-men' (the last a fairly elastic term enveloping much of the Home Counties!). As luck would have it, there was a space just large enough for Jack to squeeze his lorry into. This accomplished, we lowered the tailboard and led down the two cobs, both of which, being of a quiet and docile disposition, had taken the journey with an air of complete calm. Giving them some hay, we tethered them to the box.

A few small groups of traveller men watched us, some shouting or waving a greeting to Jack, but evinced no open interest in the horses: it was too early for that.

It was not too early, however, for a little weasel-like man whom I recognised as Spider Webb. He was busy showing off a small pony in a black and yellow tub-cart, which he was offering with great enthusiasm to a group of only mildly interested spectators. The pony trotted, fast and slowly, around the space in front of the auction area, lifting his feet high and well. Spider drove straight at us, pulling up sharply to halt in front of our faces. 'Quietest pony what anyone ever seed,' he shouted in an ecstasy of salesmanship, carrying himself along on a wave of his own enthusiasm. He leaped from the tub-cart and skipped over the shafts, placing himself dangerously between the pony's rear and the cart's front. He lay back against the pony's tail – the pony did not move. Spider jumped out again.

'This pony's so quiet he'll follow me about like a dog,' he asserted. 'Look now! *Dik* this!' And he walked a few paces in front of the animal which obligingly followed him. We all breathed a sigh of appreciation. Spider ran under the pony's stomach and crouched there.

'Why a dear little *chavi* could drive un!' he cried, rushing out and lifting one of his granddaughters into the tub-cart and handing the reins to her.

'Goo on, gal! Drive un round!' he urged, assuring the little girl's mother, his daughter, that all would be well. The child, not above four years old and pleased to be the centre of attention, demurely picked up the reins, shook them up and down on the pony's back and expertly trotted the animal round before us.

'Well, like me dead farver, that *is* a quiet pony, my old Spider,' exclaimed a London-man in a velvet-collared camel overcoat standing nearby, his lined and scarred face breaking into his version of a smile.

It was an opening which Spider seized, though events soon proved that this was not the first time that the London-man had seen the pony. 'Is you gonna have a deal wi' me, Sam?' he urged. 'You can see for yourself I ain't offering you no rubbich.' The London-man gazed back non-committally, lighting a cigarette and inhaling deeply.

'That's a pony as I can sell anywheres – an' that's a nice little tub-cart, an' the harness an' all what goes wi' it. Yer eyes is your guide, man!'

'Try an' have a deal wi' him, Sam,' several bystanders coaxed him traditionally. But the London-man was not entirely happy, he rightly knew that Spider would catch him if he could. 'I promised you as I'd give you the fust chance when we was in the pub, ain't that right?' The London-man still remained unresponsive.

Black Jack and I stood watching in silence, leaning against the horse-box. 'Come on now, Sam. Give me what I axed in the pub an' you can take un on now – car an' all.' Spider's little weaselly bronzed face set harder.

'Quick! Hold out yer hand! Or, iffen you ain't got the bit of poke I'll trust you till I sees you next time – ain't that fair?'

'That's fair,' murmured several of his audience. 'Goo on, Sam – have a deal!'

The London-man, however, who was rather worse for drink than he had at first appeared, chose to become rather bellicose at the implied slur on his financial resources. 'I got the readies all right, my old Spider,' he rejoined aggressively. 'Fax the matter is I could show you more *vongar* as ever you could show me, brother – an' I could make you fuck yer mother as well!'

He inhaled hard on his cigarette, his puffy face flushed with anger. This did not meet with the appreciation of those around him, who rapidly became utterly out of sympathy with him in his handling of the matter. 'Gooooooooooooaaaaaannnnnnnnnnn!' they shouted in disgusted unison.

Spider's features set harder still, and he pulled the peak of his cap down over his eyes, drawing in his hollow cheeks with barely suppressed wrath. He stared at the London-man for a moment. 'Go on, you fuckin' hedge-mumper!' he spat. 'Why, I can show you two hundred pounds now, this very minute – an' I'll bet that's fifty more'n you can, fuck-pig!'

'I've got more *vongar* than you ever seen in all your life, an' that's the God's truth,' declared the London-man, slightly stupefied by the atmosphere and his earlier drinking.

At that point I suddenly recollected where I had seen him before. It was at a rather smart roadhouse public house near Croydon a few years previously when I had attended a large coming-out-of-prison party held by fond parents for their son who had just served six years. I remembered Sam, younger and slimmer then. He had been up at the microphone entertaining us, for he had a musical and powerful voice. He sang 'Secret Love', later to be immortalised by a famous and glamorous young lady called Kathy Kirby. He had received tumultuous applause. It had been an unforgettable evening, marred by no mishaps or quarrels: an experience to savour and treasure in one's memory.

'What! I can show you two hundred pounds now – an' if you can top that your're more'n of a man than I took you for!' Spider jeered.

'Go away – please. You're like a fuckin' *dinilo*,' shouted Sam. 'I got more money than you – an' I'll knock yer head clean off to prove it!'

So saying, he tore off his overcoat, flung it on the ground and threw his jacket on top of it. Then he leaped out a few yards to his left into a clear space, automatically striking an old-fashioned boxer's stance straight from the time of the great Romani fighter Jem Mace. Thus, with forearms held vertically and fists clenched, he challenged Spider to defend himself and the honour of his exchequer. Spider, not to be outdone, and despite the pleas of both his daughter and his granddaughter, also removed his outer garments and, leaving his cap on, took up a similar pose. The two circled each other warily, aiming occasional wild blows at one another's faces or bodies. Neither of them were what is called fighting men and the effect of so much circling around caused the semi-intoxicated London-man to reel slightly, and Spider, quick to avail himself of the chance, whipped off the silk scarf he was still wearing and, in one swift movement, wound it round the throat of his unfortunate opponent, who desperately tried to loosen the grip with no success. Spider began to shake him bodily, up and down and sideways, like a terrier with a rat.

He was just about to administer more telling punishment with fist and boot when two constables suddenly appeared, drawn to the scene by the increasing uproar from the crowd which had by then gathered to witness the excitement.

'He's a-killin' my man, policeman!' shrieked a large blonde woman of ferocious aspect beneath her thick layer of make-up. She was unknown to us: she was not a traveller. 'Fuck off, *lubni*,' shouted Spider's daughter. 'My dad wouldn't kill no-one – he'd sooner give 'em a cup of tea, ain't that right?' she appealed to the crowd, many of whom were her relatives, either close or distant.

A buzz of agreement greeted her comment, and the two constables looked at each other in some puzzlement, unsure where their duty lay. Spider joined in, 'What? A-killing him? We was just havin' a talk, policemans, an' just *choppin'* coats, ain't that right, Sam?' The London-man gazed blearily about him, gradually comprehending what was happening.

'Nah. I ain't a-bin killed – we were just havin' a bit of a deal, mate, nothin' to worry about,' agreed Sam, looking around muzzily and sobering slightly at the sight of the constables. At that minute, a bell sounded for the commencement of the auctions, so all was forgotten for the time being – though human nature being what it is, one could be sure that the incident would be re-enacted when an opportunity presented itself: it is the usual way of things.

Black Jack had been gradually joined by several other old dealers, his contemporaries to judge by their appearances, and they ambled slowly into the sale, reminiscing meanwhile on past fairs and on the deals in which they had participated or witnessed.

As the lots of harness, and especially one ornate set in which I was very interested, were not to be sold until after the horses, I decided to walk back up through the stalls and survey the people – some of whom I was bound to be acquainted with.

As it was by then going towards noon, the crowds were even denser than before and the characteristically pitched voices were thick in the air, liberally interspersed with the Romani talk of Borrow's time, or the *poggerdi chib* (broken speech) of today.

That year the spring fair was enriched by the presence, in larger numbers than usual apparently, of both the Prices and the Lees. The latter have managed to achieve, with their adoption of brand new lorries and gleaming trailers while still adhering to the best facets of the old-style Gypsy life, a place of their own. Still cooking their food in black pots over wood-fires and clinging to strangely archaic social traditions and habits, they are always instantly recognisable both in aspect and voice. To me, almost without exception, they have never failed to be very good friends – showing generosity and no meanness of spirit. Even to this day their Christian names are frequently carried on from another age, with an attendant nostalgic charm. What other families have retained such names as Crimea, Righteous, Hope, Bullerman, Romeo, Caradoc or Rudolph? Or among the women: Pemberline, Cinderella, Esmeralda, Rosina, Elvin, Princess or Mima?

Most of the Prices and Lees were there, of course, with their lorries and trailers, though a handful were with wagons and horses. Even those who had become mechanised were still inclined to buy and sell occasional horses, out of interest and for old times' sake.

Many of the other people there were settled-down, driving in for the day from the environs of Swindon, Wootton Bassett, Gloucester or Oxford. Others had come from London itself or its surrounding counties, while some had journeyed from much further afield. However, by far the greater percentage were still on the roads then, either with wagons and horses or motors and trailers.

The change to mechanical transport was to gather momentum to an astonishing degree within the next year or so as travellers sacrificed their horses in breathtaking numbers: within just a few years a whole way of life virtually disappeared. The younger men, particularly, tiring of the slow pace of the old equestrian lifestyle, were anxious, indeed desperate, for the excitement of internal combustion, pining to become part of the modern world. Sad, perhaps, but by no means to be utterly condemned: the rest of society had done it!

However, if any real unhappiness was experienced it was that of the many fathers, often no more than forty-five or fifty years of age, who, either unwilling or unable to learn to drive and bullied by their families to give up their horses, were at the mercy of their sons and had to rely on them whenever they desired, or were forced, to shift from one place to another. This would often have a bad effect on them, sometimes even causing them to relapse into a state approaching premature senility.

So it was that, in southern England and the Midlands anyway, by the early 1960s wagons and horses had almost disappeared. The old stopping-places, still used, were by then dotted with a mixture of trailers and lorries – which created a less aesthetic scenery.

Quite often dismissed as dealers or ex-house-dwellers by both local people of limited intelligence and occasional parochial newspaper reporters of similar brainpower, there were cries of 'Where have all the Gypsies gone?' The grey squirrels had taken over!

As I meandered up the lane I was entranced by the effort that everyone had made. From the children – the little girls in flounced party-frocks, their hair plaited and be-ribboned, the small boys in suits and boots like their fathers – to the adults both young and old: all were attired for the occasion. Alas, it was towards the end of the dressing-up era, 'old-fashioned', that is.

At that moment, I heard my name being called and glancing sideways beheld a shining new Vauxhall saloon car, in the then-fashionable two-toned pink, with flashings of chromium plate about its bodywork. Inside I could see several women of varying ages: there was a very pretty girl of about eighteen, her mother – still attractive despite a gaunt and harassed air – and two old women, obviously sisters. These two looked extraordinarily out of place in the gleaming car; their still-dark hair was braided over their deeply ravaged, sun-blackened countenances. Each wore heavy large gold earrings and exotically embroidered black 'pinnas' over their gaudy plaid skirts.

'How're you getting' on, my son?' enquired the most ancient, who I knew was old Atheliah, the widow of Crippled Jesse. Her face creased in a thousand wrinkles of welcome, her small glittering eyes almost vanishing. 'I ain't a-sid yous in our country lately – too poverty for you, I 'spects!' she grinned toothlessly and introduced me to her sister, her daughter and her granddaughter.

Then in her eighties, she resided on her own property, not far from Malmesbury in Wiltshire, on a piece of land, a long strip of maybe half an acre, secluded up a narrow track. Her husband had purchased the land some time before World War II, before the coming into power of the town planning authorities. Having what is called 'existing rights' as the ground had been used for the stationing of caravans or huts thereon since the mid-1930s, she was able to live there without interference. Some of the time she spent in a little verandah-fronted cabin, or, when she felt restless, she would move into a small trailer-caravan, which one of her sons had bought for her, at the further end of the strip.

'I can't a-bear to bide too long in one place – I ain't a-bin used to it,' she would explain. To alleviate loneliness, her eldest daughter, unmarried and in her forties, and severe and remarkably old-fashioned in appearance, had remained at home – living without any apparent resentment under the domination of her mother. The daughter, Violet, had her own hut-like bungalow (made for her by one of her brothers in a fit of generosity, from the remains of a much larger hut which he had demolished for a nearby farmer). Little bigger than a fair-sized garden shed, it was pin-neat inside, filled with china ornaments and brassware, cosy drapings and a Victorian wood-burning stove, which had originally been in a wagon, on which she could cook: altogether a pleasant home. (Today, of course, it would have been viewed as substandard and uninhabitable by the health or planning authorities; but in those far-gone days one could inhabit whatever one fancied with a grand disregard for the absence of such trivia as running water, bathroom, electricity or sanitation. In that respect, if perhaps in few others, life was as it *should* be. Indeed, if one muses on it seriously, it is really incredible that one cannot live in whatever one chooses, on one's own land, on so small a scale.)

I exchanged a few more memories with old Atheliah and her sister Lovey (short for the more elegant Lavinia), enquired after members of her vast spread-about family, and with a warm glow inside me, I proceeded onwards.

After a while, chatting and joking with acquaintances or friends, into whom I kept bumping unexpectedly – some of whom I had met but recently and others I had not encountered for several years – gossiping exclusively about the insular travellers' world, I stopped at a stall which took my eye. There were crates of puppies piled upon each other and several adult dogs were tied here and there wherever space allowed. Two men were in charge: one was a definite London-traveller, his black hair slicked back at the sides and with a jaunty quiff over his forehead; his sharp pale gabardine suit was long-jacketed and draped, while his feet were encased in black patent leather winkle-picker shoes. His companion was of a more down-country appearance, yellow booted and in a well-worn traveller-style suit from which he seemed to bulge; he was known as Skittles and usually travelled in Hampshire or Wiltshire.

His greatest claim to fame was, perhaps, that he was first-cousin, on his mother's side, to Do-Shit and Don't-Shit – legendary twin-brothers, both of whom were to meet untimely ends within weeks of each other.

Skittles was blond and blue-eyed, aged between twenty-five and thirty. Both his hair and his eyes were faded-looking. He had a faint cast in one eye so that, as he spoke, one eye would stare fixedly at the object of his conversation while the other would gaze to one side, apparently consulting the infinite.

'Cor! Dear blessed Lord!' he exclaimed. 'Been a while since I last sid you, my old kid!'

'Yip,' I agreed. 'It was at poor old Bronco's funeral, isn't that right?'

'Sure enough, that's it, 'course it was,' he answered, shaking my hand in greeting. 'Want to buy yourself a nice *juke?*' he asked, glancing over their stock.

There was, I noticed, a Yorkshire terrier bitch in one crate, with about five puppies not more than about six weeks old, I judged. One was *very* small, the runt of the litter, and I fancied buying it for Beshlie.

I wandered around the stall surveying the running-dogs and the variety of crossbred terriers, including the very ferocious little Patterdale crossed with a Jack Russell. (This last breeding generally producing, in my experience, a fearless little hunting-dog ready to tackle anything in its path regardless of size or pugnacity!) During that time I managed to surreptitiously gain a thorough look at the bitch and her puppies.

Saying that there was nothing there to interest me, I casually paused by the Yorkshire terrier puppies. 'Oh, mate!' rasped the London-man, in a Canning Town accent, sensing my feelings. 'There's some good puppies – I can get the papers an' all for 'em, mate – *kushti* little *jukes*, all on 'em. There's four bitches an' one dog. The dog's the prettiest 'cos he ain't gonna make no size – a puppy like that'd make fifty notes up in London, so help me, Bob!'

'This isn't London,' I rejoined acidly, trying to get back to Skittles. 'Oi, Skittles,' I said. 'If you were to ask me sensibly I'd try to buy that dog-puppy, but the old London-boy's gone sky-high.'

'Don't take no notice of him,' Skittles replied, glancing furtively at his business partner who was by then showing off a pretty blue lurcher bitch to a young Irish-looking traveller and his little son.

'I'll tell you what I'll do,' said Skittles, his faded left eye staring intently into my face. 'We've known each other a good few years an' I wouldn't tell you a lie – what's the good of tellin' lies?' He paused for dramatic effect before continuing: 'All of them puppies an' the bitch come off a dear old *rawnie* woman who's been took bad an' she ain't got no one to look after 'em. I prunes a few trees for her every year an' the dear old woman thinks the worlds of me. "Mr Smith," she sez to me, "could you take 'em on an' find good homes for 'em an' just gimme half the money you gets!" So there you go, *mush*, now you knows.'

'Yes, all right then,' I answered. 'So what are you going to ask me – and don't ask me silly money.'

'Twenty-five pounds,' he said without hesitation.

'It's a nice puppy,' I assented, 'but too much money. I'll give you a tenner and chance it.'

'Oh *dordi!*' cried Skittles, feigning annoyance. 'I'd sooner take him home an' give un to the baby. You'll have to do better than that, my old kid! Hark here! We're getting nowheres!'

He turned and walked along the length of the stall, wheeled round, and, holding out his hand, he exclaimed, both eyes seeming miraculously to focus on me simultaneously, 'I tell you what I'll do, seein' as it's you. I'll take one price, an' one price only – on my baby's life I wouldn't take no less – that's fifteen pounds!'

My hand met his: the deal was done. After his oath I knew that he would make no better offer to me. Thus, in a few minutes more, I had the tiny body of the puppy, who we were to call Moocher, buttoned inside one of the poacher's pockets of my coat.

He proved to be a calm and pleasant little dog, never making any size yet possessed of keen intelligence. Beshlie was delighted with him and he lived on with us for twelve years, siring several litters, or various breedings, in his lifetime.

Although we left Stow Fair in the mid-afternoon, maybe only spending six or seven hours there, it seemed longer with so many sights and meetings to treasure. Besides which, I had bought the puppy and also the set of harness which I had coveted for our wagon-horse. With flashes of red morocco, white-metal horse-shoe buckles and a scarcely used collar, it was a bargain indeed for twenty pounds. As soon as the official auction had finished, the travellers began running their horses up and down, preferring not to put the best of them under the hammer. Some were led at a restrained trot, others at breakneck gallop – encouraged by a man running behind them and cracking a whip. Luckily Jack's younger son, Lias, had arrived and he was more than happy to display his father's cobs for approval and inspection. This task was almost immediately rewarding as both were sold to the same buyer, both destined for use in wagons owned by weekend Gypsies, not for the meat market. The money changed hands and, throwing my harness up onto the box, we set off for home. My mind buzzed and whirled. The combination of 'Smoke in the Lanes' and 'the Wind on the Heath' was almost too much for me.

Stow Fair, 1999

We were stopping on a large traveller-owned trailer-park some thirty miles distant from Stow at the time of the May fair of 1999. The trailer-park was owned by a settled-down Romani man and run partly as a business and partly as a philanthropic enterprise. Nowhere is the old adage 'birds of a feather flock together' better illustrated than by travellers' trailer-parks. Whether council sites or privately established, it is no time at all before they attain their own level. Generally speaking, the private parks are frequented by a zealously clean and tidy kind of resident. Here, both the trailers and their environs were without exception utterly immaculate, beneath even the closest scrutiny.

The council sites, however, are more variable – often through no fault of their occupants – there is frequently little impetus or pride, and a run-down aspect is presented. There are, of course, exceptions, when the 'birds of a feather' syndrome takes over. I believe that in many instances the inhabitants of council sites become justifiably depressed and disheartened by the locations and surroundings in which they are placed. Their common proximity to sewerage-plants, railway overpasses, factories, industrial waste-tips, or complete isolation, engender in the inhabitants feelings akin to those which must have been experienced by the unfortunates confined to leper-colonies in bygone years. The sense of exclusion from the rest of society is very strongly felt. Without the pleasure of green grass or any living plants, behind high wire-fencing or walls, divided up into plots like poultry-runs, these are no places for a once-free people to live or bring up their children. The impression of such 'mini-reservations' is that they were designed by those without the slightest knowledge of Gypsy lifestyle or history.

In 1999, we had the good fortune to possess a nearly new large-windowed, traveller-style trailer, with a square-framed tent in which to cook and wash, and a new silver-coloured truck – a compost carrier de luxe!

It was a far cry indeed from our first mechanised turnout; honesty and hard work had brought their own rewards. Equipped with the necessary up-to-date accoutrements of life, we were stopping among the cream of traveller society. We were up with the Joneses! It was a pleasant experience for one of my easily impressed disposition. But at least I *knew* how difficult it was, and how much hard work it entailed, to obtain, and to forever replace, those very transient objects which comprise so important a slice of the contemporary traveller's existence – and indeed I have always known it.

As had happened forty years previously, we set off for the fair at about eight-thirty in the morning, this time just Beshlie and myself. Having cleaned and polished the truck, and with few anxieties, we felt optimistic that we would have an enjoyable day.

Approaching this time from the London direction, it was not until we plunged down into Burford itself that any nostalgia hit me. As we passed slowly through the little town, seemingly unchanged, the silver paint of our vehicle shining in the sunlight, I could not help but recall my journey, all those years before, in the ramshackle horse-box with Black Jack.

He had, alas, been dead for over twenty years, but my sense of adventure had remained. I realised with some gratitude to fate that, even though white-haired and perilously near to the dreaded and derogatory term 'pensioner', I was still experiencing the same pleasure and anticipation regarding the day before us as I had done all those years earlier.

As we neared Stow on the Wold itself, I noticed that the grass verges, which had once been covered in travellers' motor vehicles, were now bare except for No Parking bollards dotted along their length – and an occasional constable to enforce the message.

Having reached the town, we turned right through the main street. Numerous travellery motors, most almost new and consisting of vans, four-wheel-drive pick-ups, cars and lorries, were crammed in every available parking-space, with a seemingly unlimited number of traffic wardens checking them, sometimes triumphantly, affixing their penalty labels on the windscreens. The latter action was greatly applauded by the majority of the town's populace, whose opposition to the one-day fair just twice a year has grown to epic proportions as they vainly strive to have them abolished.

Indeed, their steely glares towards anyone they suspect of being a traveller, and the disobliging manner in many of the shops, is not to be commended: rather it would seem indicative of a smallness of mind and limitation of outlook.

We found that it was necessary to drive through the town as the fair was now held in the opposite direction from its erstwhile location, when I had visited with Jack. Luckily we had been told of that fact, so were not too put out. It was still held in a lane, as previously. The main difference, however, was that an astute traveller had been able to purchase a large field adjoining the lane, and had fully utilised its resources. Rather hilly, with a pronounced dip down and up again, it was filled with a double line of stalls, stretching from the entrance, down the hill and up the other side, in addition to the stalls in the lane. The stalls lay mostly to the left of the entrance, while on the right there were large numbers of trailer-caravans, perhaps forty or so, a few wagons with the horses scattered around, tethered on plug-chains. A dozen or more horse-boxes were grouped together, having brought their cargoes on the chance of a deal. Several traps and ornate spinner carts were beside them, and were light and graceful sulkies for the trotting-horses greatly favoured by travellers. It was a good sight.

We had been lucky in finding a parking-space within half a mile of the entrance to the fair. It was a quiet residential cul-de-sac, and several other travellers had found it too – it was all but full.

I was somewhat surprised, and rather offended, when, on parking outside one of the bijou residences, I was accosted by its dweller, who complained that the presence of my pick-up would 'keep the light from my front room!' As his front garden was some thirty feet in depth from the road, and my truck was no more than five feet tall at its cab, I could only surmise that his protest was the direct result of either prejudice or senility. Ignoring him, we locked the vehicle and trudged onwards. I did not even allow his promise, for him perhaps the ultimate threat, to call the police to register in anything more than my subconscious. I would not let him spoil the day.

After a few minutes we were there. To enter the lane was to be borne into another world: the stalls were heaped with the usual arrays of finery associated with such events. Both the land and the field, we were soon to discover, were jammed with people, though it was not even eleven o'clock, and more were arriving all the time. Besides the pedestrians there were numbers of riders, mostly young Romani men or girls, all riding bareback with an easy assurance. Seemingly every few minutes, with loud shouts of warning, a trotting-horse and sulky (its driver in crouched position, with legs apart to steady him) would plunge down the lane at break-neck speed – the crowd parting like the sea before it – the pony well lathered but used to the experience. The driver was a young Irish traveller, a well-known winner in trav-ellers' trotting-races all over the country.

Every so often more placid drivers would come through the lane, with coloured horses pulling traps or four-wheeled trolleys: the desire to recapture memories of times gone by was strong and, in many ways, heartwarming.

My first impression of the differences to be seen between that year, 1999, and forty years before was that everyone was infinitely smarter, newer-looking, and that the numbers of the old-fashioned had dwindled considerably. Though underneath those exteriors, the actual individuals remained the same: separate, and proud of being so for the most part, but deeply sensitive of being looked down upon by *gaujes*.

Looking rather out of place among the dressed-up Romanies, there wandered little bands of New Age so-called travellers, their self-consciously cultivated dirty and unkempt appearances jarring strongly with the neatness and flashiness of everyone else. I also became aware of the presence of several of whom I was later to describe as Armchair Gypsies. The latter, almost exclusively made up of those of liberal middle-class origins, often teachers or social workers, could easily be picked out in the throngs of genuine travellers, either by their clothes or their benevolent expressions. They were, and have remained, something of a mystery to me. Usually uninformed as to the true nature of travellers or of the realities of the Gypsy life, but attracted to its romantic superficialities, theirs must surely be a journey likely to end in disillusionment except for the very hardy.

One could imagine my disgust on discovering later, among the stalls in the field, a small marquee housing five or six of the extreme variety of the breed! Around the interior were trestle-tables at which were seated three scrubbed-looking young women of pallid and unexciting aspect, one smoking a noxious Gauloise cigarette. They were offering a variety of pamphlets, soft-cover books, tapes and videos, most of which purported to instruct us on the fate of the 'Roms' in Europe and far across the world. They were too esoteric to appeal to English travellers, too 'far away'.

Indeed, they were unlikely to be snapped up by anyone other than the Armchair Gypsies themselves. At their centre a portly, middle-aged man, with glasses and cairn-terrier-like grey hair, was attempting to sell what proved to be his own literature. He was the author of numerous learned tracts and booklets with titles approximating to: *The Origins of Roms in Southern Bulgaria; The Gypsy's Place in Industrial Britain's Society; Politicising Roms in Britain for the Millennium* etc. It was very trying to survey. Even I was forced to view with a certain ironic amusement that all this painstaking literary outpouring had earned him a university doctorate.

Upon catching sight of me and apparently recognising me, though I had no recollection of him, he found it necessary to address me in Romani, which I felt to be the height of pretension. Affronted, I replied: 'I'm afraid I only speak Romani to Romanies,' and walked away from him.

At the other side of the marquee was a woman with long curly hair and round spectacles, seated on the ground. She was apparently endeavouring to administer running-repairs to her greyish-coloured Arran pullover. Beside her, at a small table, was a tall elderly man with bushy white sideburns. He wore a hand-knitted jumper, truly an alarming exercise in uncoordinated colours of vivid hues, old blue jeans and knee-boots. Upon his table were stacks of video-tapes which, their labels proclaimed, contained the 'Spirit of the Gypsies'. I then realised that the vendor was a once-famous writer who had, in his prime, produced several remarkably fine television programmes, on the East End, the social problems of a single mother, and another on the life of an aged dipsomaniac woman-tramp. All excellent, mostly broadcast to great acclaim, in an era when such subjects had not been regularly trawled.

It now appeared that he had turned to 'the Gypsies'. Coming from the higher echelons of society, an Old Etonian, privileged in every way, I have no doubt that his subjects were fresher to him than they would have been to one from a lower social order. A few minutes of conversation gave me no reason to challenge the verdict given to me by a traveller on 'the video man' later the same day. 'What a prat,' he astutely observed, proving once and for all that the Gypsy's alleged gift of second sight *can* sometimes be in evidence!

Later that day I was shown the video in the trailer of some Welsh travellers. As the cover of the video extolled the virtues of the Gypsy singers therein we were all naturally surprised to discover that several of the singers were not Romanies at all. Their songs and their style contrasted peculiarly and tellingly with those of the genuine Romanies and made rather a mockery of the video's claims. To my amazement, the video even included a long and dirge-like offering from an obvious New Age (hippy) woman of advanced years, mournful expression and limited vocal range. What aspect, one might have reasonably enquired, of the 'spirit of the

Gypsies' did *she* contribute? It was, I fear, yet another example of someone quite unacquainted with the intricacies of the traveller's life relapsing into dreams.

I emerged into the sunshine feeling dampened in spirit, somewhat depressed. Outside I found Beshlie, who had sensibly refused to enter the marquee at all, with an agreeable and old-fashioned Welsh woman called Cinderella. She was stopping on the field with her husband and several married sons and daughters: they were a family, very close-knit, who were at their happiest when travelling in a little band of six or seven trailers – all belonging to their own breed if possible. They had apparently been discussing, in a rather unlikely conversation, a visit by royalty to a town where they had recently been staying. We were surprised when Cinderella, who had the luxury of only a black and white television set which she ran from their lorry's battery, announced: 'I seen the Queen when she was in town, on the telly, in a lovely blue dress – aye, blue's me favourite colour.'

'Isn't yours a black and white set?' I asked innocently. 'My dear blessed Lord!' she exclaimed, somewhat pityingly – and demonstrating herself to be a devoted monarchist – 'it was the Queen, my dear man – they put her through special in colour!' So much for those who doubt the power of our gracious ruler!

Back in reality, and after talking to Cinderella, I began to feel rather better. Indeed so much so that, after a little haggling, I bought two Crown Derby mugs from the stalls, and two dinner-plates as well!

'We'll eat from these – not keep them in the display cupboard,' I declared, thereby raising our domestic standard by several notches.

We wandered to the top of the hill, constantly bumping into friends and acquaintances from all levels of the traveller society. As always, the more old-fashioned bore the more fascinating names or nicknames: Old Bill's Bill, Crimea, Righteous, Sonner, Abraham, Kruger and Elias were there, as well as Peg-Leg, Popeye, Nigger-Boy, Chrome-Legs and Goldfinger – to name but a few – and we greeted each.

I almost ran into Jesus Jake, but just managed to avoid him. Although a nice man, he had nonetheless placed himself at a social disadvantage in recent years as he had developed into a Born Again Christian of the most evangelical and brain-washed kind and felt impelled to press his superstitions upon all who were too polite to rebuff him. Experience had taught me that this could be very wearing, and was to be avoided whenever possible.

There was a public house at the beginning of the lane of stalls, set back on a little green. It was always patronised on fair days by hordes of travellers, overflowing from its doors, the takings during the two fairs probably being substantially greater than the rest of the year put together. That

May, however, the landlord had, in a perverse attack on the very principles of good business, apparently decided not to open his establishment for the duration of the fair. All present were much puzzled and affronted by the strange decision.

After several hours, Beshlie and I decided to wend our way back across the field, aiming for where the trailers were dotted in pleasing disarray, unlike the regimented line of those in official trailer-parks and looking the better for it.

Bill's Bill, the middle-aged son of Old Bill, and his handsome Romani-featured wife Movita (named, she proudly assured us, after the movie star) had invited us to visit them before we left.

'We're up in the corner, by where there's an old Jack donkey tied on,' Bill's Bill had explained earlier, adding: 'You'll see our bits of things round us – my dear man, you can't miss us!'

As, that year, almost all the trailers were Romas, which were enjoying great popularity in the way that fashions go, the task of identification would have been by no means easy, even to the initiated. However, with the directions, and the presence of the Jack-donkey established, we succeeded in finding them with no difficulty, which saved asking. Standing in the corner, as we had been told, the Roma was of the latest model, some twenty feet in length, shining with newness.

Several lurchers and a three-legged terrier lay stretched out in the sun, while numerous bantams of varying size and some ruffled-looking gamecocks pecked optimistically in the muddied grass or attempted dust-baths near the hedgerow.

The remains of a wood-fire smouldered some two or three yards from the trailer and an iron *chitty* stood over the embers, from which hung a large black kettle: it was nostalgia itself for me.

It was the fascinating intermingling of the old-style Romani life with the new which characterised almost all the members of their family.

Bill's Bill, dark-complexioned with a long black Mexican-looking moustache, was sitting inside their trailer and he waved majestically to us, indicating that we should enter. (To be so waved into a traveller's trailer is a gesture of friendship; to be left outside and spoken to from the door is the reverse!)

Movita was standing in a corner of the trailer kitchen, leaning back against the gas cooker, inhaling deeply on a roll-up. The interior of the trailer was almost clinical: the walls and ceiling were of off-white formica, with bands of stainless-steel generously applied to both. Two wardrobe doors, one on each side of the fireplace, were enlivened by ornate full-length mirrors which were widely decorated with the then-popular motif, etched in the glass, known as 'ribbons and bows'. As they were only stopping there for three days they had not bothered to display any china or glass in the cupboards, leaving it all packed away until they were stopping anywhere for a longer sojourn. The floor was covered by high-quality fitted carpet of a lively, mostly red design which would not have looked out of place in the foyer of any suburban Odeon Cinema – and was nonetheless pleasing to the eye.

We exchanged news of our comings and goings since we had last met, which was almost three years before, in Suffolk. A certain amount of gossip and scandalisation added zest to our talk, peppered with malice, and we enjoyed sweet tea in Royal Worcester cups.

Both Bill's Bill and Movita, it transpired, were among the many people at that time who were in fear and trepidation of the advent of the twenty-first century. (That it later proved to be something of a damp squib was largely undreamed-of then.)

'Well, aye, man,' said Old Bill, rolling his eyes dramatically, 'when that old Dillennium comes round there'll be some funny goings-on, you can take an oath on that. 'Specially in them little black towns in the Midlands – we shan't go near 'em. In times like that you'm better off wi' your own company, God kill me, you is!'

The millennium had no great interest for me personally: indeed its only real effect was to remind me of my own mortality and how little of the two thousands I could possibly experience. 'You an' me *pal*, we're old *mushes* – over the hill!' continued Bill's Bill, his message carrying little cheer. 'That's miserable talk! Have some more tea,' suggested Movita amiably. And we did.

After a while the trailer gradually, almost imperceptibly, began to fill with quietly entering visitors, sons and daughters, and small boys and girls who were grandchildren. All were dark, both of hair and skin, and were unmistakeably Romanies, with the natural good manners of their race. More and more kept arriving, young and older, until the trailer was almost bursting at the seams, with nowhere left to sit, leaving many, like urban railway strap-hangers, standing uncomfortably in the middle. Beshlie, being claustrophobic, began to fidget and look slightly hunted. So, knowing the reason, I made our farewells, and we struggled through the throng to the door.

The feeling of upliftment was strong within me: it was the culmination of a day of brief and rewarding encounters, of memories, of shared experiences, of pleasures and tribulations, and of various lightning-etched pictures in the mind.

Weary but happy, we eventually reached the motor, still surrounded by other travellery vehicles, oddly out of place in the infinitely respectable little close.

Noting our imminent departure from outside his house, the aged resident crawled from his front door, and called triumphantly: 'I called the police and you'll all be summonsed. So don't you dare park here again!'

'Fuck off!' I replied in a remarkably restrained tone.

We drove homewards, a fairly quiet Beshlie while I chattered ecstatically about all that the day had brought us: grateful, as always, for the privileges that life had granted me.

Sites to Behold

It was autumn when we pulled on to an old car-park in Surrey, within easy reach of both Guildford and Dorking and the suburbs of Leatherhead. It had originally been intended for the convenience of anglers for it was near the riverside. Over the years, however, it had become a favourite stopping-place for travellers. We had ourselves spent three months there during the previous winter. It was in those years, the 1970s and early 1980s, that councils throughout the land were being encouraged to fulfil their obligations under the Caravan Sites Act, and were supposed to construct sites for travelling people. Alas, however, their actions were slow and, for a variety of lame excuses, far too few sites were even contemplated, let alone actually built. Even to this day, whenever it is proposed that a Gypsy site should be provided one can be assured that protests will pour into the local council offices and newspapers, and consequent delays, or even complete postponements or abandonments of the idea, will occur. It is as though a leper-colony was to be introduced, so strong and invariable is the opposition. Yet, when they *are* occasionally established, their presence rarely evokes any form of disturbance or rise in crime-rates, nor any other kind of social upheaval. One of the most appalling results when they are provided is that, having done their 'duty' in that respect, the council will not too infrequently apply for a Designation Order to affect the area, or even the whole county. The thoroughly deplorable Designation Order entitles the police to move on and harass any travellers who happen to wish to stay within its boundaries – despite the fact that the local council site may be full-up and no provision whatsoever has been made for those leading an itinerant mode of life. It would appear to be a sort of backdoor method of trying to stamp out mobile travellers altogether. It is such persecution that has forced travellers, with no alternative, to pull in on private land – upon which they may at least snatch a few days until the owner has obtained an eviction order.

Ironically, during those years when council sites were being talked about by the authorities, promised but only being built in the smallest of numbers, travellers enjoyed a brief respite from harassment in some counties. By placing their names on lists for the allocation of a plot on the proposed sites they were often allowed to wait in hitherto forbidden locations, sometimes it proved to be for years, until the sites were completed.

For some time, there had been rumours that the riverside car-park was itself to be converted into a council site. This news reached the ever-sensitive ears of the nearest residents, even though none lived less than a mile away, and they immediately began bombarding the regional newspapers with horrific and totally untrue forecasts of what might result from what they obviously regarded as a major disaster in their lives. Indeed, their general opinion appeared to conclude that such a site would constitute something between a sewerage-works and a municipal rubbish-tip in its environmental hazards! Such was their contempt for those whose style of living in no way sought to match or emulate their own. Their letters to the press, as always, made sorry reading and I will not dignify them by quoting from their content. Sufficient to say that, rather surprisingly, their carpings and protests came to nought, and a year later the council completed the site, its situation probably being one of the pleasantest in England.

That autumn, however, the rains came early, and the old car-park, deeply rutted by the wheels of lorries and trailers, quickly became muddy and depressing. When we first arrived it contained but one family in three trailers – the parents, who were of middle-age, were of singularly pleasing personalities and a slight eccentricity which endeared them to me. Their eldest son followed his parents in this way; he was, however, fortunately or not, afflicted by a severe religious mania. The latter condition he was able to further by becoming a pastor in a peculiarly fundamentalist sect, which he achieved by dint of studying, at his own expense, at a 'Bible college' in the vicinity. In later years, he was to travel far and wide across several continents in company with others of his simplistic persuasion, with the aim of inculcating their brand of rather uncharitable Christianity into the minds of the easily led. His actual nature, however, when he was not in the throes of his fire-and-brimstone preaching, was so gentle and calm that my affection for him as a friend was great indeed. Despite his feeling sorry for me because of my lack of religious convictions, and my feeling sorry for him for the reverse reason, we were quite close in spirit – a state which, I felt, mystified us equally!

We had been there for almost a week when our peace was utterly shattered. It was early afternoon and, having returned from 'calling', I was standing talking to Young Tom when the dogs began to bark. Looking towards the entrance, we saw, to our horror, a line of some thirty to forty lorries and trailers making their way on to the car-park.

Without doubt we could both see that they were Irish people: travellers of the roughest kind. Their trailers were old wrecks, dented, many with smashed-out windows and doors hanging loosely from their hinges, while their lorries and battered vans were in no better condition, bald of tyres and without the benefit of road-tax on all but a few of them. There were so many that the car-park could barely contain them, and they pulled so close to each other that they could have effortlessly shaken hands with their neighbours from the windows. Children and dogs abounded, probably about eighty of each! We had suddenly been plunged into hell.

From the size of their lorries, and their equipment, I could see that they were tarmacadam layers. This cheered me slightly for I knew that the whole area had been thoroughly canvassed recently by English travellers, so I hoped that they would not discover enough work to keep them in the area for long. This may appear uncharitable of me, but I had experienced such massed company before, and its accompanying miseries. The vehicles and trailers were, of necessity, so densely packed that it would be almost impossible to find a way through them to go out. I managed to speak a few words to Tom and Young Tom and we each expressed distress at the state we found ourselves in. So few of us, so many of them: civility was our only recourse!

All around us, pandemonium reigned, for they were noisy people and all seemed to prefer short, shouted conversations in peculiarly aggressive tones. The children, from toddlers up, had ascended all the trees, even the bushes, like a flock of starlings, and were hanging from their branches – from fifteen-year-old boys and girls down to tiny barefoot tots. Many of the women were barefoot too, despite the icy cold, their complexions red or strongly freckled, their thick frizzy reddish hair drawn back in ribbons or plaits. One young mother, however, was an exception and both Beshlie and I were astonished by her abundance of curling locks, red-gold, which streamed down her back, to miss the ground by no more than four inches: she was a Titian painting come to life.

All around us their thick Southern Irish accents filled the air. 'Ah! Be Jaysus, Mily,' shouted one large woman from a broken-hinged trailer door. 'Would you tell dem childers to come out've me trailer. Mary, Mother of God! De childers is all heathens!'

Screams and shrieks rent the air, and several radios were turned up, full blast, from different trailers. Dogs whined and barked, and children, down from the trees, fought and squabbled.

After a little cajoling, and difficult manouvering, I managed to leave the ground, luckily selling-out all my bags of compost in only two hits, so I returned by lunch-time.

Utter chaos met my eyes! After only sixteen hours on the car-park the rough and ready Irish travellers had reduced it to a litter-strewn tip: papers, bottles, packages, plastic containers, rubbish of every description was scattered everywhere. Earlier, and later, experience taught me that there are two sorts of Irish traveller, as there are two sorts of English traveller, those who leave rubbish wherever they stop, and those who do not. Unhappily, we were surrounded by the former.

Towards tea-time the police arrived in force, several van-loads, and expressed some concern at the number of arrivals and demanded their removal. Privately they informed Tom's family and ourselves that we would have to leave with the Irishmen if they succeeded in their aim of evicting them. But they agreed that we could creep back afterwards if we so wished without incurring their disapproval: a rather singular suggestion so far as I was concerned.

Luckily I had pulled our trailer on to the very edge of one side of the ground, nearest the river, with a sloping bank to our right, thus allowing for only one side of us to be bordered by a trailer. Our neighbour proved to be a lone old man, with a rusted-out Ford van and a smallish old touring trailer-caravan, hand-painted and severely dented at intervals over its sides. He was grey-haired, shabby-suited and alcoholic-looking, a widower on his own, though with his children and grandchildren scattered about the ground in trailers of their own – while others, he told me, were still in Ireland and were coming over soon.

Late that night, long after we had retired to bed, sometime after midnight, there was an almighty explosion and a flash of fire, combined with the breaking of glass, from his trailer;

and as I jumped from bed and hurried to the door I saw him staggering from his trailer, from which much smoke was issuing.

'Ah! Jaysus!' he exclaimed on sighting me. 'I t'ought it was de end of de world. Oh God, I did that!'

'What happened?' I asked.

'Ah, de fuckin' gas exploded – I forgot to turn it off. An' when I lit me old fag – hup she goes!'

I walked around and inspected the wall of our trailer in some agitation lest pieces of glass or other materials had damaged its surface. Luckily, it appeared to have remained unharmed, which was surprising, for the old Irishman's home was sorely affected.

'I've nothin' to worry about,' he declared, shrugging. 'Sure, I've only old rubbish around me. I'm not a fancy kind of feller since I lost me poor wife, Lord love her.'

Early the next day, alarmed perhaps by such concerted police attention, or for secret reasons of their own, the Irish travellers left as quickly as they had appeared – their ramshackle procession only to be rivalled in dishevelment, in later years, by the New Age traveller convoys.

Relieved that we would ourselves no longer be required to leave by the police as the Irish people had left, we surveyed the ground with disbelief. The legacy of human, animal and other waste they had left was hardly a cause for rejoicing. We all spent half a day in trying to clear it up;

the labour was scarcely a pleasure, and certainly not of love!

At length, it was decided by the council that the car-park would, after all, be made into an official council site, and those who wished to book up as future tenants should apply. There were to be ten pitches, or plots, allotted, and after some thought I decided to put my name forward and it was accepted. The building of the site would take a few months to complete, and in the meantime we moved to another part of Surrey, keeping in contact with the council so that we could be apprised of how the work was progressing.

It was not until March of the following year that we were given the opening date, and thus arrived on the appointed day to witness what could have been, had we so desired, our permanent future home.

As we drove down the lane to the site entrance we were astonished by the transformation of the car-park. Freshly tarmacked, with ten pitches of perhaps seventy feet by thirty, each enclosed by its own wire-mesh fence, every plot contained its own little brick-built wash-house, bathroom and lavatory, immaculate and new. Hot and cold water, bath, flush-toilet, and electricity: such things could, momentarily, turn one's head!

We managed to secure an end plot which was an

advantage in so far as it meant that one was afforded a little more privacy, with a trailer on one side only.

A rather well-meaning collection of people connected with social services, the Gypsy Liaison Officer, a health visitor, and the actual architect of such mini-reservations, were all present, beaming with goodwill and anxious for approval.

At first, to be honest, even I, proud of the hardships and the freedoms of the open road and old-fashioned travellers' way of life, in which I had spent so many decades, was fascinated and seduced for a month or two. Gradually, however, the regular arrival of a man to stamp our rent book, the demeaning feeling of being beholden to authority, and the unfamiliar experience of having unchanging neighbours – no longer coming and going as the fit took them – began to pall. Upon enquiring, I discovered that the denizens of such sites are, or were then anyway, allowed up to six weeks' absence from their plots in any one year, should they desire to take time away travelling – as had been their previous way of life.

Old Tom, Young Tom, a married brother, a married sister, Beshlie and I occupied five of the pitches on one side, while the others were taken by travellers, all known to us, whose lives had usually been spent within a not too distant radius of the spot.

Tom the younger was, just then, still greatly involved in his Bible studies, seeking instruction in the ways of becoming a fully fledged pastor of his chosen church. He even became a supporter of that strange little crew of oddments who produce religious graffiti and supposedly uplifting slogans. Having assisted in the production of the legend JESUS SAVES, white-painted on the side of a local railway bridge over a main road, he failed to share my delighted mirth when a wit had added: WITH THE WOOLWICH!

To add insult to injury, Young Tom's fairly magnetic personality, fervour and lively preachings at local Gospel Halls would occasionally cause religious *gaujes* to repay his sermons by visits to the trailers where, laden with tracts, they would attempt to subvert us. They all appeared to share the mythical conviction that they were in direct touch with the Almighty.

We had, by 1980, moved far beyond the joys of the once-fashionable Bedford J-type lorries and into the realms of Japanese pick-up trucks, which proved both comfortable to drive and admirable in their weight-carrying abilities. On the first that I obtained I boosted its rather characterless appearance by the addition of extended sides made of varnished 'penny-farthing' wood by a skilled wagon-maker. These, to the initiated, looked very travellery, while to the common or garden observer they looked merely practical!

We then, through the auspices of a trailer-caravan-dealer known as Banbury Bob, bought one of the newly produced so-called 'Baby' Portmasters – a smaller edition of its twenty-three-foot namesake. Being about sixteen feet in length, though eight feet wide, the 'Baby' was stainless steel-encrusted, with a coal-fire and twin-wheeled; it was a home of pleasing aspect and was not too heavy for the pick-up to pull. As always, I was in the fashion of the time among travellers!

Our only concession to being site-dwellers was that we felt it might be rather opulent to have two trailers, one for us to go travelling in, and another for Beshlie as a studio in which she could work without having to put away all her artist's materials each day, as she had always hitherto been forced to do in our living-trailers.

I bought a 23-foot-long Aaro 'Travella', which rather resembled a larger version of our Portmaster in shape and design: this I bought from a traveller who was about to settle down on a site and wished to purchase a mobile home. It was only two years old, and I bought it for a reasonable price, which I felt sure I could more than recoup if I sold it within a year or two. With red leather bunks, an end bed-room, coal-fire, formica lining and cut-glass mirrors, it would have made a comfortable spacious home for anyone. Both it and our smaller one were wired up for electricity, so we plugged each of them into the coin-box-operated supply in the bath-house and basked within them, illuminated for all to see.

Although the surrounding countryside on all sides of the

stopping-place was charming and could scarce be equalled in its natural attractiveness, nevertheless I began to feel penned in, no longer proud.

Hence when, in a public house one evening talking to two older travellers, one of them asked me if I had ever thought of giving up my plot, I was tempted. He himself pined to be in that locality, having grown up and spent much of his life thereabouts. He was then in his early sixties and looked at least ten years older. He was complaining of gout, which he told us was troubling him sorely.

'I'll tell you what I'll do,' said he, whose name was Ambrose. 'We'll go down an' *dik* the council *mush*, an' if he's agreeable to me havin' the plot I'll pay you over the odds for that Aaro trailer you've got – I knows the trailer, it come off Alfie's brother – so you'll have a nice bit of money, an' I'll git the plot.'

This seemed quite a reasonable agreement to me, but when I mentioned it to Young Tom and his wife and married sister they all seemed scandalised. They vowed that the old man was a stranger to them, despite his being a native in those parts, and complained that he might have relatives who could cause trouble. Indeed, they accused me of being a Judas, in spite of the fact that Ambrose was of advanced years, semi-crippled, and that his wife was dying of heart disease. In truth he needed the plot far more than I did: so much for Christian charity!

I explained their resentment to Ambrose, but he brushed it aside. 'I ain't worried by them,' he declared. 'They're only old road-siders, I ain't bothered what they does.'

And so, fixing upon a price for my trailer, it was all arranged and they pulled on to the site, amid great hostility from Young Tom and his immediate family, apart from his father who claimed indifference.

'I'll see how you get on,' I said to Ambrose, leaving him there as we pulled out with our Baby Portmaster, to head for a privately owned trailer-park near Staines to which I had telephoned ahead in order to make sure that there was room for us.

After a week had passed I learned that there had been continued friction at the car-park site, and it was rumoured that Old Ambrose had bribed me with the sum of six thousand pounds to let him have my pitch there! This was so utterly untrue as to be ludicrous, but it had apparently reached the ears of the council and the Gypsy Liaison Officer, who were supposed to be taking the matter very seriously.

Not being at all happy at this turn of events, I drove over the next morning, quite early, where I found a morose Ambrose and his invalid wife Florence in low spirits, bordering on tears.

'I never knowed *folki* like it in all me life – you'd think we was fuckin' dossers!' exploded Ambrose, coughing bronchially and gulping for breath. 'They none of 'em won't speak one word to me nor Flo 'ceptin' young George, Bronco's son-in-law, over there – not one poxy word! An' them others – they calls 'emselves Reborn Christians! Reborn Devils I calls 'em!' He spat out through the top half of the trailer door in disgust.

I felt very disheartened by these twists and turns in what was, after all, a completely reasonable transaction. In fact, the whole incident depressed me so much that I suggested it might be best all round if I gave him back his money, took back the trailer and resumed tenancy of the plot, if he fancied the idea. I felt that the aggravation that both he and his wife were suffering could in no way improve their failing health.

'Thank you, young man,' he said. 'But I tell you what, we'll go down an' see the council man an' tell him what's happened. Let's see what the man sez, an' get it all cleared-up about this six grand what I'm supposed to have gid you. Six grand! Lyin' bastards – toe-rags the lot of 'em.'

We arrived at the council offices, alighted from Ambrose's Range Rover, and were fortunate enough to obtain an immediate audience with the Gypsy Liaison Officer of that time. A retired army officer of imposing rank, he was of a politeness and appearance which seemed slightly at odds with his official position – but which, in fact, was greatly appreciated by the travellers. He was not a disliked man.

At first, however, he was somewhat distant and suspicious, for his confidence in the truthfulness of his informants was, at that moment, still very strong.

'No sir! No!' suddenly declared Ambrose, fixing him with a steady gaze. 'I never gid this man no six thousand pounds, nor nothin' like it. All I done was buy his trailer for me an' me dear wife to lie up into. An' surely that ain't no crime, is it sir?'

'Well, no . . .' admitted the officer cautiously.

'Now I tell you what I'm gonna do,' continued Ambrose steadily. 'I'm gonna ask you to fetch in as many Bibles as you like, an' me an' my friend is gonna swear as all I done was to buy his trailer, which I gid him the proper price for. I never gid him no six grand, and nothin' nowhere near it, an' we'll both swear to that on any Bibles you wants to put in front of us, an' in any court in the land, may I go home an' find my dear wife lyin' stiff an' dead on the bed . . .'

'Now, now, Mr Smith,' interrupted the Liaison Officer, rearranging the flaps of his expensive check hacking-jacket as he spoke. 'I'm sure there's no need for that. I'll take your word for it – now could you tell me, Mr Smith, are you stay-ing on at the site after this bit of fuss, or do you want it to revert to the previous tenant?'

He looked questioningly at us, and I agreed to take up the tenancy, for the time being. We shook hands and left. 'Well at least he's all squared-up,' remarked Ambrose calmly. 'You never knows when you might need him – an' he don't seem a bad sort of feller, proper *rai*, you can see that.'

'What shall we do then, Uncle Ambrose?' I asked.

'Well, young man, you been fair about all this,' said Ambrose. 'So if you could just give me two days I'll buy meself another little trailer what I can pull about. In fact I knows of a nice little Buccaneer what 'longs to me cousin Jimmy's boy, so I'll go an' git that tomorrow from Southampton. Then I'll put me bits of things in it an' you can have the Aaro back – an' I'll give you a few *bars* for all what you've done. But I tell you what: I shouldn't leave it empty for long on that old place – 'cos them *dinilos* as like as not'd git someone over to *chor* it.'

And so indeed, within two days, I was the owner of the Aaro trailer again, and the tenant of the plot. However, both Beshlie and myself were greatly disgruntled by the way in which matters had developed and despite a mixture of semi-apologies and half-withdrawals from Young Tom's family it took several years for the wounds to heal, although they did at last.

I put the word out that the Aaro was for sale among various travellers. Luckily, among those I told was a widow named Rosie Wall who had a roadside strawberry-stall near to Winchester.

'What year is it?' she enquired. I told her that, and the price I wanted for it. 'My sister's boy has just got married,' she said. 'An' I know they wants a trailer, 'cos they've only got a little tourer – ain't much of a home, 'specially as she's a big old gal he've got! Would you *chop* it an' a bit money?'

'No, I couldn't *chop*, 'cos I've only got myself as driver, and I don't want to have to pull two trailers about, do I?' I explained.

'Quite right, I can see how you're fixed,' she agreed. 'Anyway I'll tell me sister tonight, they're stopping over agen Watford an' I'm driving over to see 'em. If they're interested will you be in on Saturday or Sunday?'

'Saturday afternoon I'll be home,' I told her. 'Or all day on Sunday. Tell them I'll try to have a deal if they come over. It's a lovely clean trailer that's hardly been lived in.'

'OK, I'll tell 'em. See you,' she said in farewell.

I reached home and told Beshlie, who was pleased though not over-hopeful of a sale.

I went out on Saturday morning, sold all the compost bags, and was back by half past one. Scarcely had I devoured a sandwich and a cup of tea when we noticed a Transit lorry, newly sprayed white, drive slowly down into the site to halt eventually by the entrance to our plot. It was driven by a man in his forties, dark and very foreign-looking, very Romani, accompanied by a younger man, obviously his son, and a pinched-faced red-haired woman with large hooped earrings; she carried a black velvet bag.

All three dismounted from the lorry and walked towards

our Portmaster, in which we were seated watching television. As they approached I opened the door and we regarded each other, a little blankly.

'Is that the trailer what you've got for sale?' demanded the woman, her voice strong and aggressive with a London-region accent, possibly Essex. She looked old-fashioned and I could see that she was the dominant personality of the trio. Unfortunately she was not very likeable.

'That's it,' I agreed. 'Do you want to have a look inside? It's a nice clean trailer – only had one single-woman owner before I had it, so it's never had any bad use, never been ramped around the country.' They all three remained blank-faced and unresponsive at this: unwilling to commit themselves in any way for my benefit.

I showed them all around the exterior, which was almost entirely free from dents of any kind, then ushered them inside. Their eyes darted here and there. 'Have a look – do what you like!' I cried. 'Pull back the bunks, look in the corners, there's not a bit of damp anywhere!'

Mistrustful, as I had known she would be, the thin woman immediately started peering and prying, opening cupboards, drawers, wardrobes, and carefully examining under the bunks for the faintest signs of mould. In fact, there was only one place in the entire trailer that was not perfect: that was just inside the door where condensation had dripped down from the door frame and slightly rotted the floor, just inside the opening. Like a hawk the woman spotted this little patch and made much play of it.

'Here! Come here, Freddie!' she commanded the man, who motioned to the boy also. All three fixed their eyes on to the minute area of rot. 'Oh *dordi*! The floor's going – look here!' she pointed a gnarled, ring-filled hand towards the small patch, continuing dolefully: 'Me cousin had a Aaro trailer, just like this'n – an' they ain't big people, not like the gal my boy's got – an' strike me dead, they went straight through the floor, an' it cost 'em five hundred pounds for a new one to be put in.' She stopped for effect, and I stared back at her.

'You're askin' too much money, my dear man: this ain't a *new* trailer, he's comin' three years old I shouldn't wonder.'

'Just two years old, look on the plate,' I replied.

'Well, I ain't givin' you no twenty-five hundred for it, that's certain sure,' she retorted, very firmly.

'Well, that's what I'm asking,' I answered, before suggesting: 'If you want it, I'll take twenty-four hundred, and that's a cheap trailer. I tell you, it's had no use.'

They huddled together. 'Go outside and talk about it,' I suggested. This they did, walking almost silently about, inspected the exterior minutely, before re-entering it, their faces strained.

'I'll give you two grand for it, an' not a penny more,' said the woman, her thin face taut with determination. I had thought she might offer that amount so it was little surprise to me. 'No, I couldn't do it,' I persuaded myself to reply. 'I don't think we're going to meet – but thank you for your offer ... I tell you what I will do, seeing that you've come over to try to have a deal. I'll take twenty-three hundred pounds and give you twenty-five back for luck!'

'No! I'll give you two grand, the money's here!' she persisted, while her husband and son stood glumly by.

'You think about it,' I advised. 'Have a talk – you won't find a cleaner trailer for the money anywhere in this country.'

Rather miserably they walked away, getting into their lorry and driving away at no great pace. 'They'll be back,' I said, semi-confidently.

'Maybe,' answered Beshlie, as usual no optimist.

Half an hour or so passed when we suddenly became aware of the Transit's presence again: it had slipped quietly on to the ground. All three dismounted and yet again advanced towards us.

'We've had a talk,' announced the woman grimly, 'an' I'm gonna make you one more bid and the one only – an' on my child's life I won't give you no more! I'll give you twenty-one hundred pounds – an' not one penny more, God strike me stone dead!'

'Hold out your hand,' I replied, knowing that the deal was made, and I slapped the thin palm offered. It was strange to conduct a deal of such magnitude with a woman in the presence of her man, one unique to me.

They entered the trailer and the woman carefully withdrew a wad of twenty-pound notes from the old velvet bag and we arranged them in little heaps of one hundred pounds each until the requisite sum was reached. Feeling in my pocket I withdrew a ten pound note and handed it to the woman as 'luck money', which she appreciatively accepted, smiling faintly for the first time in the whole transaction.

They lost little time in hitching on the trailer, and were gone – to disappear from my life for ever. It was not a very dramatic deal, but it was a satisfactory one: my profit was in the category of 'a day's work'. But, best of all, we were free of encumbrances: we could leave the cloying atmosphere of a council site for ever.

We Saw You on the Telly

After many years of toil for little or no return, Beshlie was fortunate enough to dispose of some of her pictures to a greetings-card producer in London, at the upper end of the market. This was only negotiated after a concentrated effort on her part, entailing her wandering around in the, to her unknown, city and knocking on the doors of various card publishers. After a succession of attempts, and some requests for her to return with further work, she at last stumbled upon a firm at which all the directors happened to be present. She was thus able to obtain a full audience who, recognising the worth of her intricate, natural-history-based drawings, commissioned her there and then to produce a series of six.

Slightly distraught at the prospect of having to create a series of six within a short time limit, she was nonetheless elated at the idea of her work being reproduced.

We were stopping on a roadside between Amersham and Beaconsfield just then. It was at that time a favourite stopping-place in the years before the council site was built in the area – after which one was lucky to catch even one night there without being moved on. However, before the site, one could stop without harassment of any description – only 'bad company' might cause a move.

It was conveniently near to London, only about twenty-five miles, and it was arranged that one of the firm's directors would call and collect the work when it was completed. This was done, and we waited trepidatiously for a day or so after the pictures had been collected, but our worries were needless – the paintings were rapturously received, and became an instant success soon after their appearance in card form. In fact, after a few years, Beshlie was to be the recipient of the highest artistic accolade: people of lesser talent began to copy her work, and numerous sub-standard 'Beshlie' cards were in evidence in many a down-market emporium. However, we were slightly disgusted when one of the copyists, who was clever enough to invent a kind of brand-style overall title for her pictures of Beshlie-like little animals and birds, achieved some fame and considerable riches – bursting out with cards, books, china and statuettes! Luckily, both being fairly cynical by nature, we did not allow such things to sweeten our outlook! There was a certain irony in it.

Within two years, Beshlie's cards were becoming quite well known. Some traveller friends were very impressed, and apprised us in awe that Harrods had devoted a whole window to the display of her work: an honour indeed, and one of which, up till then, we had been completely unaware.

In the spring of 1973, the BBC approached the card publishers suggesting that they should make a film programme about Beshlie's work and, what was for an artist, her unusual lifestyle. It was to be filmed for inclusion in the series *Look Stranger* for BBC2.

We pondered for a day or so on what might be the result of such an exercise, and decided that so long as we were given some control over the programme's format, especially in dealing with the Gypsy side of our life, then there was a chance that no harm would be done.

An appointment was made and an affable young woman came to see us in Sussex, where we had gone for the spring, and she seemed assured in her mind that interest would be aroused by the programme and that it should be made. So, quite soon afterwards, we were given a suggested date for the filming: three days in mid-June. With it came an enquiry as to where we would be – they liked the idea of somewhere in Sussex, especially as it was no great journey for them from London.

Somewhat distraught and wondering where a good

situation would be, I suddenly thought of a place where we had once before stayed for a week, with permission from a kindly old lady and gentleman, members of that rare breed: pleasant, convivial landowners!

They owned a large estate, and within its confines, hidden from view and reached by a narrow trackway leading from a private drive, there lay the foundations of what once had been the manor house. The patch of land, although grass covered, was solid-based and level; only its surroundings of grown-in, formal gardens and rockery suggested the house that had once stood there. With its variety of flowers and exotic shrubs and the shade from enormous oak and beech trees on its borders, it comprised a truly delightful, if slightly isolated, stopping-place. There was even a tap for water.

After a journey of about an hour, I reached the dwelling of the major and his wife, again a house in its own grounds. A knock on their front door disclosed that they were at home, and a brief discourse with them was enough to secure their permission to pull in for the filming.

'Television, eh?' said the major, jovially. 'BBC, I hope,' smiled his wife, a severely tailored lady of impressive proportions, whose stature somewhat dwarfed that of the dapper check-suited major. Having reassured them of the respectability of all concerned, I took my leave, saying that we would arrive within a day or so.

That June the weather was especially good, the wondrous midsummer being truly upon us, sunshine every day, and the spell of weather showed no inclination to change.

The appointed day arrived, as bright and sunlit as had been the case for a week or so. The impending arrival of the television crew, producer and director filled us with something akin to fear: a fear that was to prove quite groundless, for a collection of more agreeable persons connected to the media I have never encountered.

They were fulsome in their appreciation of the location itself, realising at once its beauty and romance, and as they were filming in colour they were able to take full advantage of the surrounding flowers and woodlands.

The first day was almost entirely spent on the filming of Beshlie, of her walking through the surrounding under-growth, explaining with love the intricacies of a flower's construction, as seen through the eyes of an artist, or musing on the magical qualities of an insect's armour or a butterfly's wing.

They then showed her drawing inside the trailer and filmed her completed works. They filmed, and were intrigued by, her several finches and singing-mules whose clear-sounding songs enhanced the atmosphere, almost without ceasing. The same attention was given to our tiny terrier, and our elderly lurcher Barney. It was all most picturesque in such a setting.

When the light began to fade in the evening I built up a good-sized stick-fire, and we cooked some food on it and drank numerous cups of tea in its glow, the cameraman still tirelessly filming. It was quite dark by the time that they departed, promising to return by ten o'clock the next morning.

We slept well, in the unaccustomed quietude of the woodland, after the stress of the day – a stress not entirely absent even from the gentle handling of the BBC!

The next morning they arrived promptly, with the somewhat alarming suggestion that they should accompany me on a day's 'calling' with my bags of compost! The suggestion did not meet with unalloyed enthusiasm from me, but I felt it *might* be possible under the right conditions. As luck would have it, I was acquainted with a lady who lived near Brighton, who had been, earlier in her life, an actress of great promise but had sacrificed her career on the boards in favour of becoming a devoted wife and mother to several children. She possessed great vivacity and a lively attractiveness, and I hoped that she might welcome a little break in her domestic routine.

Thus we decided to take a chance, arriving unannounced at her front door. With little or no persuasion, this lovely person immediately agreed to take part in the programme in the guise of a normal housewife, opening the door to me and being offered bags of manure!

To her credit, without any necessity for second takes, without any fuss, she looked out from her front door when I knocked, quite naturally, and even haggled with me when I quoted a price. I am sure, indeed, that few viewers would have guessed that she was a 'plant'. In fact, it was the only false occurrence within the programme, and was apparently no great flaw, as the film has to date been shown no less that eight times over the years, and has yielded many scores of appreciative letters to Beshlie in praise of her work.

Even to this day, years after the programme was first shown, it is not unusual for Beshlie to be accosted in the streets by people from all walks of life, of all ages. 'We saw you on the telly,' they cry, in tones of rapture or delight.

How strange that an appearance on the silver screen can gain more recognition, more adulation, than almost any other form of human activity.

After filming from early morning until twilight for two days, the producer decided that they had enough footage for the programme, and all that was left was to show us packing down our belongings, both inside and outside the trailer, and finally moving off. This we did with the minimum of delay and soon, hitched-on and seated in the Landrover, we were slowly leaving the little haven of peace and tranquility which had proved to be the base for our immortality!

We never stopped there again, in part due to sentimentality. In later years, after the death of the major and his wife, the estate was divided up and sold. Where we had once been filmed there stood a little bijou timber bungalow, as we discovered on a chance visit while passing by a year or so ago. We felt quite sad, and deeply shocked by the rapidity with which the intervening years had flown: life is indeed so short.

A desire for company afflicted me upon leaving the major's estate, and I decided to make for a village near Eastbourne. There, in chalky Sussex countryside, in an area of some refinement, lived a farmer whose amiability towards travellers had become renowned during the previous few years, and was to remain so for some time to come. This most agreeable and unperturbable of men, and his wife, who appeared to be slightly his social superior, could always be relied upon to welcome travellers on their land. They had one particular field, behind the farm and outbuildings and out of view from the roads, which they set aside for travellers throughout the summer months. Indeed, one or two remained there over the winters, but the ground was of heavy clay and, once water-logged by winter rains, the whole field became virtually impassable to motor traffic. Anyone who chose to stay on after early October would surely find themselves marooned there until the following spring. We ourselves stopped there over the course of about ten years; at its peak of popularity I have known there to be thirty or forty families installed there – their electric lead cables snaking into the house and farm-buildings in sufficient numbers as to ensure flutterings of alarm in all but the bravest of electrician's hearts!

A small rent was charged, which was willingly paid, and the 'birds of a feather' syndrome persisted, as ever. Only the more respectable kind of traveller pulled in there, poorer, rough-and-ready families preferring to take their chances of 'catching a day or two' on roadsides, lay-bys and occasional pieces of negotiable wasteland throughout the area. In truth, we had ourselves been only too pleased to avail ourselves of such free stopping-places in earlier years, before age and experience had elevated us to a higher plane.

The day that we pulled in to the farm there were already about fifteen trailers dotted around the edges of the field, and in the centre, too, in little clusters. All were bright and shining, clean and new, in the strong June sunshine, with women and children hovering around them. Several of the women were polishing the trailer windows, while others were shaking rugs and mats from the doors. All was activity.

Sets of garden-chairs and tables, even occasional sun-umbrellas, were an essential part of such travellers' equipment and were much in evidence – giving the impression of a rather splendid holiday camp. To the initiated, however, the

size and makes of trailer, the sight of so much stainless
steel – in the form of water-carriers, dustbins and ornamen-
tation applied to some of the trailers – combined with the
numbers of multi-coloured square-framed tents for kitchens
would all have immediately jumped forward to point them
out as being travellers of a spick and span variety.

No litter of any sort despoiled the field or its environs. As
the saying has it: 'You could eat your dinner off the ground!'
The men were all out 'calling', so there were few motor vehicles apart from one or two cars.

I remember a rather old-fashioned, semi-rough traveller
of my acquaintance who had been to visit such a stopping-
place with a view to possibly pulling in with his family.
'Well, aye, man, too tidy!' he had declared to me. 'The
cleanness of it near enough frit me to death! I wouldn't pull
there.'

I suppose everyone is entitled to his own viewpoint and,
although places maintained in such a manner are in many
ways to be approved, they are a long way from the raggle-
taggle Gypsies – which is indeed their aim, and the direct
result of sensible thinking.

It is indisputable, I fear, that those travellers who retain a
modern equivalent of the raggle-taggle ways are unfortunately their own worst enemies, and bring down upon
themselves the wrath of both householders and officialdom
alike. Between the travellers' varying lifestyles there are few

winners: one mode of life brings about harassment and persecution; while the other seems to encourage envy and malice, jealousy and anger.

As Black Ash Farm was so well-liked and had become widely known, travellers from all over the country were apt to descend upon it. This, of course, made for a greater interest and variety for those who were wont to stop there regularly. It was, nevertheless, a slight cause of anxiety with regard to the character of visitors unknown: better the devil you know than the one you don't!

However, as by and large only sensible and well behaved people chose to stop there the incidents of unrest were few, and those that happened rarely, if ever, went beyond the bounds of spirited vocal exchanges.

As we entered the field through a rather unaccommodating narrow gateway, I noticed a space along the fence on the far side of the meadow and we made our way towards it, slowly and carefully over little mounds and hillocks and deep tyre-tracks.

As we neared the space I recognised that trailers on each side of the gap belonged to travellers well liked by us, old friends of many years, so that made us feel easy in mind.

It was soon after one o'clock, and most of the men were still out about their business. On one side of us was a long Jubilee trailer, and a blue and white-striped tent, belonging to a Devonshire man called Joe Tarr. On the other side of us was the trailer of a man from Hampshire, Mike Smith.

The former, and his wife and children, the eldest daughter among whom was married and stopping on the far side from us, were originally from North Devon. They still spoke with the accent of that county, soft and strong, even though they rarely journeyed down-country themselves, unless for family weddings or funerals.

Joe himself was of sturdy build and faintly bovine in appearance, though perhaps rather more fortunate than one member of his family who had the disheartening experience of being nicknamed Billy the Pig which, apt though it was, must have been somewhat hurtful to him. Despite his slightly unprepossessing looks, Joe himself was a generous and well-meaning man of immense humour and shrewdness. Although unable to read or write, he would conduct his business-dealings with a panache that would have been the envy of many a university graduate. To listen to him when in his cups, favouring us with a rendering of the old folk-song 'Buttercup-Joe', was one of life's noteworthy pleasures. His wife, Mary Jane, his first cousin, was a large blonde woman of an unextinguishable merry disposition, whose laughter was of such remarkable volume that it was audible three fields away.

Their eldest son, Young Joe, had inherited his mother's nature, and her extraordinary vocal strengths. He had recently returned from Australia where, legend had it, he was the only man ever to have been barred from a Queensland public house for the reason of his laughter being too loud! Other travellers who had been in his company at the time spoke in some awe of the event.

Unfortunately these good-humoured characteristics did not run through the entire family. Mary Jane had a sister, Lily, a cheerless woman of about fifty years of age, widowed and embittered, who had purchased a small bungalow and settled down there upon the death of her husband, who had been an astute carpet-hawker.

Mary Jane and Joe, and other relatives, would visit her at first in the suburb of Taunton where she lived, if they were not stopping too far distant. However, their visits became less regular as time went by, and she became more morose. 'She took to being a *gauji*,' complained Mary Jane, winking. 'And when we went round to see her she put newspapers on the seats 'fore she'd let us sit down – well, it made you feel discomfortable, didn't it? I'd never do such a thing in me life – why iffen a beggar was to come in me trailer I'd sit 'em down and give them a nice cup of tea. Wouldn't you?'

However, this mood of low spirits did not last and she went on: 'When our Lily was a young woman, you know, she was very smart, if you can understand me, an' she an' me used to go out muck-hawking by ourselves in me dad's little lorry. Anyways, we used to bag up at an old pig-farm, where the dear man gid us the muck to take it away. It was in a big heap about fifty-foot long an' the *kushti kinder* was over the back, so we had to wheel a barrow over some planks to get to it, then wheel it back full to bag it up on the ground. Well, Lily was a big old gal in them days, she went about eighteen stone or more! An' one day when she was wheeling the barrow across the plank she tripped an' took a step on to the soft muck on the side an' – God strike me down dead – she sunk straight in up to her shoulders, an' it took the old farmer on a tractor to pull her out!'

Upon completion of this tale of human misfortune and its ensuing horrors – the stench apparently, despite constant bathing, having taken a week or more to finally wear off the unhappy Lily – Mary Jane became convulsed by laughter so loud that windows in a nearby housing estate were flung open, the occupants craning out in alarmed curiosity.

As the afternoon wore on, the men began returning in lorries and vans; the majority had been tarmacadam-laying, while others were selling carpets and rugs. Only one other person on the ground, I was informed, was engaged in muck-hawking – that being a young man called Sammy Summers, originating from the north of England.

I knew him slightly through conversations round a midden, when we had both been bagging up at the same place near Leicester, a couple of years previously. There would be a certain kinship, if not competition, between us, which I hoped would be mildly invigorating.

By five o'clock, almost all of the men had returned, and the sound of sizzling frying meat was to be heard, and smelled, from the kitchen-tents. It was good to feel at home, with people of a like mind. We did not necessarily love our neighbours, but at least we *knew* and *liked* them.

At about six o'clock, Sammy walked over to see me. Aged, then, about twenty-six or so, he was already beginning to turn into the overweight figure of a man of middle-age. His hair was blond with a reddish tinge, his blue eyes squinted slightly under the brim of a check hat. His brown smock-coat, once the habitual attire of cattle-dealers and farmers, was tightly buttoned over his protruding stomach, and his once-tan elastic-sided brown boots were ingrained with manure: he looked every inch the young farmer just home from the cattle market. He shook hands and appeared pleased to see me; his soft Yorkshire accent was musical to the ear, and he smiled quizzically at me. He was one of four brothers, all of whom pursued the same occupation, all still moving about in trailers, and all astute and likeable men in their ways.

With the open generosity of many travellers, he told me of a source of supplies of compost – a riding school – in the area. In the cool of the evening I drove over to the riding school, the owners of which were more than delighted to lessen the huge amount of rotting manure which was over-flowing from its bay. It was of a wood-chipping rather than straw base, thus of debatable benefit to the gardener; how-ever, it was given to me for nothing – so everything would be a profit! I bagged-up fifty plastic sacks, all the while being bitten unmercifully by evening midges which hovered in their millions over the dung-heap.

The next morning, I got up early and headed for the outskirts of Eastbourne and, upon encountering a promis-ing estate of privately owned bungalows, commenced my arduous task. Bagging up may be viewed as being hard labour, but selling is the real test of stamina and per-severance.

I began at nine o'clock, and by soon after eleven had sold over half the load, mainly in twos and fours, with an odd half-dozen when my luck was good. The bungalows at which I was calling were of a spaciously appointed variety; each one had a large garden and some had a detached garage some little distance from the dwelling, some being built of asbestos or even corrugated iron.

I was just emerging from the drive-way gates of one such property, there having been no reply at the door, when a small saloon car turned in from the road and entered the driveway. It stopped and the driver, a middle-aged bespec-tacled lady, looked enquiringly at me.

'Good morning,' I greeted her. 'I have just been selling

bags of composted stable-manure along this road, and I wondered if you might be interested in some for your garden – it is very beneficial—'

'How much is it? How many have you got left?' she interrupted. I apprised her on both counts and she said: 'Well, I'll just take two. Will you put them behind the garage? There's a compost-bin there, so lean them against it.'

I hastened out to my lorry and lifted off two bags which I carried, one in each hand, up the drive. She was apparently having some slight difficulty in re-starting her car, its engine coughing dismally. Then, as I rounded the garage, I heard the engine fire. My astonishment may well be imagined, however, when, having placed the two bags beside the compost-bin, some twenty feet to the rear of the garage, I heard the little saloon, engine racing, being driven up the drive and into the garage with no lessening of the revs nor any apparent slackening of speed. And so it was that, in almost complete disbelief, I beheld the little car suddenly burst through the asbestos wall at the end of the garage, causing the entire roof to drop down upon it, and come to a standstill within four feet of where I was standing, engine at last switched off.

It was perhaps indictive of British phlegm that neither the lady driver nor myself admitted, even by the least flicker of surprise, that anything unusual had taken place!

'It was just two bags that you wanted, wasn't it?' I remarked.

'Yes, that's right,' she replied, calm and unruffled. 'Here's the correct money, thank you.'

Endeavouring not to allow the eccentricity of the occurrence to detract from the purposefulness of my continued door-knocking, I was able to dispose of the remainder of the cargo within another hour.

The bungalows were of the utmost respectability and of a style that can be found all over the south of England and indeed elsewhere. Perceiving this one with a very low rockery-style wall along its frontage, in which plants were growing, made me smile to myself.

A year or so previously I had been working in Kent in partnership with a traveller known as White Bob, owing to his pale skin and blond hair. We were engaged in tree-pruning, hedge-trimming, or indeed any other form of garden task. Calling one day on the outskirts of Dover, on just such a bungalow estate, we found a lady who asked if we could remove a low hedge of box, no more than eighteen inches high, which ran along the full length of her low garden wall of rockery in which it had been planted; it was some twenty-five feet in all, I judged.

I quoted a price, which she accepted provided that we undertook to take the hedge away and dispose of it. I consulted with White Bob, who had been knocking further along the road, and we agreed that the easiest and best method would be to run our chain-saw along, at ground level, and cut the hedge from its roots in one long sweep, if possible, and then just dig out the roots.

'I'll git the saw goin', *mush*,' said Bob. 'It needs a bit've oil an' that. You go on round the corner, where I left off, an' see if we can *ker* another little job,' he suggested.

Some two or three houses round the corner, I thought my eyes had deceived me. For there stood an identical bungalow to the one from which we were removing the box-hedge, even down to the rockery wall. I knocked on the door in case they had any pruning that they wished us to undertake, perhaps in the back garden, but there was no reply. At that moment, however, I was struck with the germ of an arresting idea! To avoid filling our truck with the immense length of box-hedge might it not be inventive, and certainly amusing, to transfer it bodily and place it on the existing rockery wall of the unsuspecting neighbour!

White Bob, a person of similarly jokey disposition to myself, immediately saw the funny side of this proposition. Thus having been paid for taking away the box-hedge from the home of the first lady, we stealthily transferred it to the second unknown bungalow-dweller so little distance away. Having completed our devilish operation without mishap we drove from the locality, laughing to ourselves.

In subsequent years I have many times speculated on what must have been the reaction of the outraged householder upon finding the presence of instant hedge along their garden frontage.

After two weeks at Black Ash Farm, we decided to make for the midsummer fair at Cambridge for another week of work and pleasure in equal parts. I hoped.

Our very first visit to Cambridge Fair had taken place in the early 1960s. In those days the travelling people were allowed to stop on the same ground as the fair itself; right down in the town, on a level piece of ground beside the river. At last, however, as the numbers of travellers grew each year, the council – anxious as ever to prevent people from actually *enjoying* themselves except under 'regulation' – banned all but licensed showmen from the riverside green. After some pressure they then allotted the dealers, as the travellers were referred to, a space a mile or two outside Cambridge on the Newmarket road. For this privilege of being placed far out of the town like undesirables we were charged a considerable rent for the week. To add insult to injury, a permanent police presence was stationed at the entrance to the allotted field and all vehicles were checked and noted, both on entry and exit. This did not elevate one's spirits, and there seemed little point in such an expensive exercise.

*

That year there was an almost record attendance for the midsummer fair, and the field on the Newmarket road was crammed to capacity, with an interesting assortment of people from all over England and Wales.

We found ourselves, soon after arriving, surrounded by the families of both Prices and Lees, for whom Cambridge was a regular annual meeting-ground.

Crimea, Caradoc, Rudolph and Elvis, all first cousins, pulled up by our trailer in a new Mercedes limousine and we exchanged greetings with great cordiality. I was pleased that we were there.

Each day I struggled out, bagging up in the early morning at a stable I had discovered nearby, before the heat of the day set in. I attacked Cambridge and its suburbs with grim determination, to return to the ground, quite exhausted, in the early afternoons. I ticked over during the week, and I asked no more than that at that time of year and during a heatwave.

On Thursday evening the annual Showman's Ball was held, in the Cambridge Corn Exchange that year. The latter proved to be a large and depressing building; it was without any interior luxuries, and was furnished with nothing but a vast number of wooden fold-up chairs and a bar, while at one end was a low stage, with a microphone. Without the mass of lively humanity it would have had the atmosphere of a morgue. But, as ever, the energies of the Romanies, who were present in their hundreds, brought everything to life. It was fascinating to see a huge hall filled with nobody but Gypsy people, and to see how handsome and colourful they were as a race. Ravaged though many of them were by the age of thirty, by the never-ending stress of trying to preserve the standards of their lives which they had set for themselves, it somehow seemed to give them a sense of purpose and resolution. Some were dark, almost like Indians, others fair-skinned and blond or redheaded – yet all displayed some special, almost indescribable, quality of aspect or manner which marked them out from *gaujes*. To my mind only Jewish people can be compared to Gypsies in that way. There are great similarities in so many ways. But, alas, I am not able to do more than surmise a connection.

The Showman's Ball was a great success: ending up, as do most travellers' parties or gatherings, with individual men and women, sometimes children too, taking to the stage and entertaining with a song or two – some old-fashioned, others modern. As usual, some of the entertainers were so accomplished that they were almost of professional standard, while others, less musically endowed, would perform with more energy and vitality than actual talent – sometimes, alas, thereby gaining greater adulation than their more gifted brothers or sisters.

In between singers, a random selection of music was provided from the stage by a young man with an explosive stereophonic record-player, to which the more athletic of us danced with great abandon, the livelier the tune the greater the numbers of people taking to the floor. A buffet had been provided earlier, from trestle-tables, upon which all had descended like a flock of starving seagulls. There were still remnants of food, crushed plastic cups, indeed debris of all kinds scattered about the floor. The resulting slippery surface caused several rather corpulent and unsteady ladies to lose their footing and fall to the floor, to find their dresses in no way improved by contact with ice-cream or the squashed remains of hot-dogs!

As it was a major social event everyone had dressed for the occasion in new outfits: the girls and women wore amazingly dramatic garments, as though from some American soap opera; and the men sported a mixture of apparel, all new, from the expensively casual to the formality of tailored silk and mohair suits, gleaming sleekly in the glare of the lighting. (As a faintly dandified person myself I, of course, favoured the latter suiting!)

It was a pleasure to see success shown off so proudly, for those days, in the decade of the 1970s, seemed easy times for all within these shores – and I am sure we will never see their like again, certainly not within the foreseeable future.

Beshlie and I, having danced for some hours, conversation being difficult with anyone owing to the volume of the music, finally left for home just before midnight, leaving only the most dedicated revellers behind.

It had been an evening of no great dramatic incident but rather one of pleasure. And I was, as so often before, filled with gratitude to fate for having sent me, a happy exile, into the world of the travelling-people, to achieve an acceptance and rewards which would never have come my way had I chosen another way of life. The traveller's lifestyle has fulfilled my social, theatrical and material needs. I have learned buoyancy and self-reliance, confidence and adventurousness. I have known admiration, not *envy*, for many in the life, over many years. Perhaps this is no rarity in other walks of life – but I have not heard such sentiments voiced with any regularity myself.

Moving Up

I t had not been very long since we parted from our last horse and wagon in favour of a motor and trailer-caravan: the latter turnout comprising a rather shabby tourer and a rather elderly Bedford 30cwt van which had given its best years in the service of a fireworks factory. The trailer leaked, and the engine of the Bedford coughed ominously: life was filled with strain.

On the brighter side, that spring I had found a small piece of ground upon which the remnants of wartime army occupation were still evident in the shape of overgrown air-raid shelters and crumbling gun-emplacements. It was on the edge of the New Forest, part of a considerable acreage which was rented by an ancient 'Forester' named Mr Pennet. The latter, gnarled and bent-backed and of penny-pinching disposition, was eventually persuaded to allow us to pull in there for 'a month', in return for a small rent, to be paid in advance. It was rather a lonely spot, without water, but was prettily scattered with early daffodils. Indeed, after a winter which we had spent around Birmingham, snowed-up on some lay-bys and moved on from others, in the company of a variety of other travellers, it was not disagreeable to be on our own for a change. With a few bantams pecking about near to the trailer, and our lurcher dog Barney on a chain from the drawbar, it was a fairly idyllic picture: one spoiled only by the chronic ailments which were besetting the old Bedford's engine, and by our own decreasing store of pound notes.

I had been given the whereabouts of a settled-down traveller near Salisbury who was rumoured to have 'several tidy lorries to sell – at sensible prices'. Getting up the next morning quite early, I decided to go over and inspect what was on offer.

After bypassing Salisbury and passing through the village that had been named, I came upon a small settlement consisting of a little square asbestos bungalow, two trailer homes, a hut, and a large old-fashioned-looking tent, through the roof of which a chimney projected some three feet or more, and from which the smell of wood-smoke issued. A yard was at one side of the property, with a tall fence in front, and I could just detect the roofs of several lorries and vans. Two or three crossbred lurchers sneaked about suspiciously, barking intermittently.

The flap of the tent was drawn aside and an old Romani man appeared. I had not seen his like in twenty years: he wore a black hat, a spotted handkerchief about his neck, a thick black suit tailored in old-fashioned Romani style and rather delicate elastic-sided boots.

'Good morning, Uncle,' I said politely, giving him the title as a mark of respect.

'Morning, young man,' he smiled, disclosing two gold teeth.

'I've come about a motor, I've been told you are a good man to have a deal with,' I remarked.

'You wouldn't find a better man in this country,' he assured me, smiling more. 'Fact of the matter is, though,' he continued, ''tis my son's business now – since I lost my dear wife I ain't a-had no heart for it.'

I expressed my sympathy.

'Never mind,' he continued. 'Anyways, my son'll be back sharply, he've only gone to fetch some baccy, so bide here in the tent and have a warm and a cup of tea.'

I was plunged back in time, remembering with pleasure how many of such traveller-tents I had been invited into in previous years. I complimented him on it and expressed my pleasure at its being so 'old-fashioned', which pleased him greatly.

'That's quite right, young man. You can't beat old-fashioneds. An' I can see that you're in the same mind as meself there.'

At that moment we heard a vehicle drive into the yard and a door slammed.

'That's my boy,' said the old man and called out: 'Sam, we'm in the tent – there's a young feller here who wants a bit of trade!'

The flap was pulled back and a tubby, moon-faced but very Romani-looking young man entered, his eyes raking over me, trying to assess me.

'What are you after?' he enquired, nothing if not direct.

'Well, that's my 30cwt van outside. But for what I'm doing I could use a lorry – another 30cwt Bedford if I can find one. Have you got anything? If you have I'll try and have a *chop* with you, and you can be in the drawing-room!' (By which he would know that I would give my van *and* money in a deal.)

'See what you can find to suit this young feller,' encouraged the old man. 'You can see he's here to try and have a deal.' He broke off coughing as a cloud of smoke blew back down the chimney and into the tent.

'God's cuss that *yog*!' he exclaimed. 'The devil's into it!'

With that, we walked across the yard and opened the gates to reveal what he had of interest to me.

'You only wants a Bedford, right?' confirmed the old man's son. 'Well, I've got two – both tidy motors, both come off proper firms, not travellers.'

Both were old bull-nose models, petrol-engined. One was

ten years old, the other was seven. The older was dark green in colour, the other was dark blue. His asking-price for each was high but not outrageous, mere pennies in comparison with those of a decade or so later. The older of the two lorries started up at the first try, while the newer one took much coaxing, and swearing, to fire.

'Needs new plugs, that's all,' Sam reassured me confidently. I nodded, on the fifty-fifty chance that he could be right.

The old man watched everything with great enthusiasm, encouraging us both to try to settle a transaction.

'I likes to see a bit of trade,' he asserted. 'Come on now, try and have a deal, you two – s'help me God, I never seen two slower fellers!'

Eventually, however, having dismissed the newer lorry for various reasons, I managed to have a *chop* for my old van and twenty-five pounds.

Sam gave me one pound back for luck money, and we each gave the old man ten shillings for helping to 'make the deal'.

'Me dear old father loves anything like that,' said Sam, smiling fondly at the old man seated in the tent smoking before the fire.

Before leaving them my eye was caught by an old step-drawbar, which had been made for a Bedford, and I managed to buy it for five pounds. A mechanic acquaintance of Sam's in the next village fitted it while I waited. It always feels wrong to me if I drive a vehicle without a towbar; very incomplete.

Taking a different route homewards and passing the outskirts of Salisbury, I noticed a sprawling car-park, along one edge of which were three or four trailers and lorries, obviously belonging to Romanies. As I neared them I could see that they had not freshly arrived. Lines of clean washing fluttered from a rope attached between two telephone poles behind the trailers; dogs and children were playing nearby, and three men were standing together watching my approach.

There was a tall and muscular man, with flaxen blond hair and a red face; and another, much thinner, who turned out to be his brother. Both were in their late twenties, wearing tailor-made dark suits, ties, and they were noticeably clean and smart. With them stood an older man of very Eastern appearance, his Romani features of an almost red-black tone, his complexion pitted with a thousand tiny craters. His dark eyes gleamed from under the pulled-down brim of a country-gentleman's check hat which sat rather uneasily upon his still-black thick hair; and a red-patterned rich paisley silk handkerchief was knotted crosswise, old-fashioned, at his throat.

We exchanged greetings rather guardedly as we were, at that point, seemingly unknown to each other.

'Hi, *pal*,' said the larger young man. 'Where's you stopping, kid?'

'We're out on the Forest,' I replied. 'On a bit of a farm.'

'Pulled-in, kid?' asked the old man, and I assented.

'You can't beat it, my old kid,' he replied, squinting from the smoke of a thin cigarette, and coughing bronchially. 'Old roadsides is finished,' he continued mournfully. 'All you gets is shift, shift, shift! A *juke's* life it is. I should sooner be settled-down with me bits of things up round me – 'specially in my condition.' He paused and coughed some more. 'I been underneath three doctors, and they can't do nothing for me.'

His sons, for that is who they proved to be, gazed without a great deal of sympathy upon him.

'He won't take no medicines,' complained one of them. 'The last prescription he give to the dog!'

As always among travellers, our conversation veered towards families and origins. As I had suspected, or virtually known, they were members of the Welsh-originated family of Price, a vast and closely related branch of whom travel the length and breadth of the country. I have encountered them in Cornwall and far up in Scotland. To me, they symbolise all that is best that is left of the actual roaming life: they are people who rarely seek the safety of organised official sites, but continue to wander at will, spending but a few days in any one place. And, despite harassment and difficulty in finding even temporary stopping-places, they cling to their habitual ways, still cooking outside on stick-fires, frequently very successful. Many of them own splendid new trailers and motor vehicles, despite their erratic lifestyle, and are the most likeable company for anyone to whom they take a fancy who is not of their own close-knit breed.

'Are you any relation of Boggy or Rudolph?' I enquired, naming two well-known members of the Prices.

'Well, aye! Certainly, *owli* – Boggy's me younger brother, and Rudi's me nephew. Dear blessed Lord above! Never thought that you'd have known them!'

'You must know all the boys, then,' presumed the blond man, who introduced himself as Crimea, his brother as Chasey, and his father as Jack.

'God kill me!' cried Chasey suddenly. 'I knows you – you was stopping in them old lanes round Bury St Edmund's about five to six years ago. You was with a London-traveller, with horses and wagons! Don't you remember, when me and me cousin Fearless come to try to buy that roan mare you had – bid you well we did, too.'

'Yes, I do,' I replied, and my memory recalled him, though his cousin Fearless more strongly. 'Some of old Rudi's boys were stopping with you, and Old Bill's Bill, and Frisco.'

My remembrance brought them great delight.

'God kill me! He knows everyone of 'em – an' I've heared Old Boggy speak of him well, Lord paralyse me, I have!' shouted Jack, warming to me by the second, and me to him.

I admired their shining new Bedford lorries, each painted in bright colours, and their trailers. The last comprised a small Carlight 'Special' (the Rolls Royce of trailer-caravans) and two Eccles Travellers, the latter being one of the most fashionable models in vogue during the 1960s, made especially for travellers.

In later years it has been interesting to note the differing trailers that have been specially made for the traveller market. In the same way that, during the horse-drawn days, there were specialist wagon-makers who traded almost exclusively with Romanies.

They could gauge from the age and condition of my 'new' lorry that I was not too prosperous just then, but they showed me no disrespect because of it.

They were ready and willing to discuss their own livelihoods.

'The women's gone out with a bit of lace, an' trying to do a bit of *dukkerin*',' said Crimea, adding: 'an' we're takin' out a few loads of gravel for the drives.'

'Any good?' I asked.

'Not too bad, old kid,' answered Jack dolefully. 'You can get yourself a crust of bread out of it sometimes, if you comes across the right people.'

'There's some funny people round here, *pal*,' warned Crimea. 'Why, I called on a house the other day an' they was two lisbons! My dear Lord! I only gave the door a couple of knocks, not very hard, an' they runned out, stone-mad, 'cusing me of breaking the door down! They was callin' me everything from a pig to a dog! Never even asked what I wanted, near enough *trashed* me to death.'

We sympathised together about our own encounters at the doors, finding it slightly therapeutic.

After this encounter, I decided to try my hand at gravel-laying, heading homeward with optimism at the thought of a New Horizon!

There were several gravel-pit workings within a radius of only a few miles of our stopping-place. Thus, early the next morning, tense at the thought of the day ahead, impatient yet a little apprehensive, I was early at the gravel works. I weighed the empty lorry on a gigantic weighbridge near to the entrance, and within a few moments I had loaded my lorry from one of the hoppers which contained the washed shingle. Thereupon, armed with a shovel discarded by roadworkers which I had discovered in a ditch, I was in business.

I will not bore the reader with the nervous tension, not to say horrors, involved in the hawking of loose loads of shingle door to door in unwelcoming suburbs. Suffice to say, perhaps, that on my first day in that occupation, on a small estate of privately owned bungalows, I emerged with the grand sum of eight pounds – the equivalent in today's values of at least eighty pounds. It was, to be sure, 'a nice little day'.

In fact, I pursued the occupation for some years. As is said, however, nothing lasts for ever, and by the mid-sixties it seemed as though almost every traveller in the country was doing the same thing, and thus the search for jobs became ever more arduous. It was time for a change.

Years passed and we moved hither and thither throughout the West Country, all of southern England and the Midlands, with occasional northern forays; sometimes on our own and sometimes with other travellers, as has always been our habit.

I had, during that period, managed to *chop* my old lorry for a newer model, a Bedford frog-fronted lorry of only six years of age.

I remember an elderly traveller once saying to me, in regard to the age of vehicles, 'I likes a motor about five years old, one what's nicely used to the roads!'

In any event this seemingly indestructible lorry towed us, and our increasing-sized trailers, with miraculous reliability. It only failed us once, in South Wales, with acute clutch-slip, which was something of a nightmare as we were pulling the trailer at the time. Luckily, however, we were with company so we were towed safely to the stopping-place before nightfall.

Despite forever promising myself the luxury of abandoning the garden-path improvement business, I was still engaged thereon. And indeed, having saved up quite an impressive amount, I decided to invest in our first ever brand-new lorry – an achievement beyond our wildest dreams but a few years before. January 1 1964 would see us with a B-registered motor.

The Bedford 30cwt J-type lorry was the favourite traveller-owned commercial vehicle. They were always supplied in grey primer and, in those days not being frightened of being 'too Gypsy', the owners would show great ingenuity and invention in their choice of colours. Generally two-coloured, with the front bumpers, radiator-grilles and driving mirrors invariably chromium-plated, these gracefully designed, somewhat American-influenced motors were the pride of their owners. Their powerful six-cylinder engines were fast and long-lasting, capable of hauling the largest of travellers' trailers over any hills with which they were presented.

At the time of my decision we were stopping on a car-park near to the docks at Southampton, which was quite fortunate as there was a 'good man' with whom to deal at a Bedford agent in the town. With high hopes I went to see him, and after some haggling and considerable distressed in-takes of breath from him upon inspecting our ancient vehicle, we eventually came to an agreement.

I decided to plunge fully into extras, for was it not our very first brand-new motor vehicle? Psychologically, it would not have been good to hold back, I felt.

It was agreed that the cab would be painted in a pleasing shade of metallic bronze, with gold wings and chassis. The body would be made locally in oak, with a varnished finish; a new and elaborate step-towbar would be made up by a local blacksmith who was familiar with the requirement. As an added refinement I ordered chromium-plating, and, as a finishing-touch, decided to have the doors and the bonnet lined-out in fine red coach-lines. Much shaking of hands and the down-payment of one hundred pounds sealed the bargain: and it was promised for collection within two weeks.

At that time, such a vehicle could have been purchased in primer for about £700 with no extras of any sort, but ours was to be £975 owing to its multifarious additions.

The next two weeks passed slowly, and a slight melancholy overtook me at the thought of our soon-to-be-depleted funds. (The old traveller saying: 'You can't have the things and the money too!' came strongly to mind.)

On the other hand, of course, I was greatly delighted at the prospect of our new possession – even though I did not realise, at the time, how many doors it would open for me in the Romani life, nor how much pleasure it would afford me. A new lorry, a nice trailer, freedom, and above all, youth and optimism – what more could life offer?

By the time that the collection-date for the lorry had been fixed we had been moved on from the car-park, but had managed to install ourselves on a rough piece of wasteland on the other side of the town, overlooked by blocks of council flats some half a mile away. It was not a safe-seeming place, so we were glad to be joined by a family of our long-time acquaintance, originally from North Wales. It was Manuel Evans, his little wife Anne-Marie and their children – one daughter and eight small sons. Manuel was reputed to have a Spanish grandfather, which would account for his foreign name. By wags he was sometimes referred to as 'the Latin from Prestatyn'! The Evanses were very hard-working and utterly devoted to the cause of their self-advancement in possessions. At the time they owned a fair-sized *gaujo* trailer and a three-ton lorry. (In later years, as their children grew in size, and number, their trailers and motors became quite spectacular in quality and variety – it was nice to see dedication achieving its goal.)

Armed with a wodge of twenty-pound notes, I arrived at the garage and was shown the 30cwt Bedford in all its glory. I was quite dumbfounded by the success of its colouration, and especially impressed by the oak body – the last of the old-fashioned penny-farthing boarded bodies to be built by that particular craftsman before his retirement. All in all, a combination of flashiness and refinement in equal measure. The powerful engine would purr and whine and roar, with marvellous enthusiasm, in an entirely unforgettable combination of sounds.

As I drove from the garage in the first brand-new lorry that I had ever owned, I did imagine myself King of the Road!

Feeling quite elated, I decided to take a detour round the city before going home. As I circumnavigated the town and passed through some prosperous suburbs on its outskirts, I noticed a new-looking truck, somewhat resembling mine, parked outside a row of detached houses. Painted in two shades of pinkish-beige colour, it had similar refinements to my own, and I drew up quite close behind it. It was loaded with feed-bags, standing upright with the tops undone and filled with blackish manure. The driver was visible, calling at the door of a house further down the street. After a few moments he emerged from the garden gate and walked along the pavement towards me, furtively glancing about him as he did so. He was a florid man, in his early thirties perhaps, wearing a brown smock-overall coat, well-polished tall, brown, lace-up boots, a spotted silk tie and blue striped shirt. A curly-brimmed straw hat was perched jauntily on his head, and a diamond-encrusted gold ring shone on his left hand. I knew him slightly, for it was the renowned Henry Lichen. Even at that age, he was famous all over the country as a compost-seller of extreme skill – and, in a few years, was to rejoice in the title of King of the Muck-hawkers! He originated from Devonshire, and still possessed that county's musical accent, despite having left the area in his childhood. I did not know him closely then, though we later became good friends.

'How're you, my booty?' he exclaimed. 'Why, it must be

two years since I seed you last, over agen Chelmsford, I mind. How've you been keeping? Where's you out at?'

I replied to his questions and enquired likewise.

'We'm *atched* behind a *kitchemir* over be Romsey,' he answered. 'With me cousin Andrew an' me brother-in-law, Ben.'

'All mucking?' I asked, not that I needed to ask Henry as he did nothing else.

'Yes,' he said. 'Too many at it, an' some nearly giving it away,' he grumbled.

'There's some *dinilos* who'll always do that – no matter what they're selling,' I replied, with sympathy.

'Nice motor – how long've you had it?' he asked approvingly.

'Half an hour!' I told him, and he smiled.

His forehead was low and broad and his jaw strong; he had a faintly reptilian look, but was likeable nonetheless.

'Pretty colours – it'd be all right for this game, 'cos it *diks* sort've horsey or farmerified, don't it?'

'Well, might give it a try,' I grinned.

After a few more snippets of conversation concerning mutual friends and acquaintances and their whereabouts just then, we made our farewells.

Once back at the trailer, it was not long before Manuel and Anne-Marie returned, having been to the scrapyard to weigh in a load of iron that they had collected. They soon joined Beshlie in admiring my acquisition. Having spent so many years with other people's cast-offs it was a double pleasure to own something brand-new. It is a feeling which can only be appreciated by those whose lives have been spent in the shadow of exacting poverty not of their own choosing, yet of course a condition which has to be borne stoically if one is to maintain the independence of those who survive or starve according to their own immediate efforts.

Manuel and Anne-Marie were very taken by the lorry, and they and all their children, even Horace the baby, gazed wide-eyed with wonderment upon the newness of it. None of us knew the future then, and few could have forecast that, within ten years, Manuel and his family would have prospered to a degree undreamed of in those early days.

Manuel was not over twenty-six years of age, having had Anne-Marie when she was but fourteen and himself sixteen. He was short of stature, but broad and powerfully built. His eyes were black and luminous, with dark circles around them, while his nose was slightly curved, his cheekbones were wide, and deepening lines swept down towards his mouth. His lips were finely formed and the ends turned slightly upwards at the corners, sometimes giving the impression of a smile that was not really there. His hair was thick and dark, and he would regularly treat himself to having it expensively groomed and styled. This caused great disgust in his little wife, who was convinced that he was trying to attract the attention of new ladies into his life – a suspicion which I knew, being his confidant, to be not entirely groundless. In his vanity there was an admiration of himself which seemed quite immoveable. Indeed his fascination and absorption in the quirks of his own personality were both ever-present and almost entirely inconclusive. He domineered his wife, and his children, but by voice alone – he did not ever strike them, rather did he overawe them by threats.

'Strike me dead, that man's the Devil – the wustest day's work as I ever did was to have him!' Anne-Marie would shout when his threats became too severe.

'Take a terrible oath – an' swear you mean that!' Manuel would shout. That she would not do.

When out calling, Anne-Marie came into her own and she was able to persuade and cajole all but the most hard-hearted of house-dwellers to part with scrap-iron, clothes, or any other saleable items in a most generous manner. With braided hair and slanting eyes, faintly oriental, she had been quite beautiful when younger, but at only twenty-four she was already beginning to fade. Stress, strain and the responsibility of so many children were all combining to take their toll on her.

While I had been collecting the new lorry there had been a visit from both the police and the council, who had demanded our removal by nine o'clock the next morning.

We decided to stop together for a while and we began to discuss where we should go, what county, what direction – somewhere had to be decided on.

'How about *hochi* common?' I enquired, to be met with much disgust by Manuel.

'I reckons that must've bin the last place God Almighty made,' he grumbled. 'Talk about a lonely old place!' he continued. 'Why, if you was to see a bicycle-rider go by you'd run out an' stop him, just for the sake of someone to talk to!'

After some argument and counter-argument we eventually agreed to take the coastal road, and head for somewhere within calling-distance of Brighton in Sussex.

'We could try that old common near Ditchling, where we stopped with your father and Ben about four years ago,' I suggested.

'Do you know the way, *mush?*' asked Manuel. ''Cos I'm fucked if I do.'

'Yeah, I'll find it,' I asserted, with a confidence more outward than inward.

'It ain't too soft there, is it?' asked Manuel, suddenly recollecting that it was January, with the promise of rain, or even snow, ahead.

I vaguely remembered that only certain, well-used pitches were negotiable with motor vehicles during wet weather. Even those were mud-filled when we had stopped there previously; however, they were worth trying to recall and harbour in out of the wind, if we arrived there safely. The whole area, and especially the roadside verges, would be swampy and treacherous until at least the middle of April, and to venture on to their inviting surfaces before then would be to court disaster. Few things are more distressing to witness than a heavy trailer-caravan slowly sink in clay or mud up to its axels: such a happening would often cause the ruination of the underworks, usually by virtue of the unnatural strains put upon them when the trailer is hauled out.

'We'll be all right, don't worry!' I reassured the glum little group confronting me.

'Here's a dog's life!' grinned Manuel, resignedly.

'Well, aye!' agreed Anne-Marie, inhaling on a cigarette, and spitting lightly over the head of the infant Horace, who peered up at her through clear blue eyes.

'Who's a little bastard then?' she smiled fondly at the baby. 'Look at his dear little *yoks*,' she murmured.

'Let's you an' me go over an' see Johnnie and the boys, an' we can have a little drink with 'em as we're going away. I'd like to *rokker* to 'em 'fore we *jals*.'

'Just a *little* drink,' I replied, for I wanted to be clear-headed for the next day's journey, especially as it was my responsibility.

'*Dordi*! He don't know what a little drink is,' said Anne-Marie with some malice. Adding, with a faint smile: 'If I kept a *kitchemir* with the likes of him coming in I'd 'dulterate the beer down with water!'

'Hark here!' laughed Manuel. 'Let's go down to that café first – the one with that young *rackli* with long legs with big boots laced-up at the ends of 'em.'

Anne-Marie rose to the bait and swore roundly.

'A bad woman,' grinned Manuel.

Taking his lorry, Manuel and I wasted little time in arriving at the stopping-place of Johnnie and the others. Their belongings were scattered along a wide grass verge, quite close to some large factories, beside a main road. The trailers shone and gleamed under the ghostly fluorescent street lamps; their interiors snug and clean, all illuminated by means of power from one large electric generator which was shared by the families, who were all related by blood or marriage. Several large crossbred semi-lurchers, followed by a procession of yelping terriers, rushed out towards us as we bumped off the road and drew to a halt. Shouts from the trailers, however, stopped them in their tracks and they slunk back under the trailers, or into their kennels, growling softly to themselves.

Some of the men emerged to greet us, and seemed to regard the idea of a farewell drink as being acceptable.

'What shall we do, drive or walk?' asked Johnnie of his brother, Pins, who appeared rather sinister in a black hat and black leather coat.

'What! Walk in this weather?' replied Pins in horror,

despite the fact that it was a fine, if slightly frosty, evening. 'Drive, *mush*, drive! We'll take my little van if we can't all get in the lorry.'

'*Kekker!*' exclaimed Manuel, feeling himself to be the host by invitation. 'Yous can all come in my lorry.'

Eventually the lorry-cab, crammed to capacity, was just about able to contain the figures of me and Manuel, Johnnie, Pins, and his cousin known as Bug. Old Jim and his even older brother Kalup climbed up on to the open back, describing it as old-fashioned, and thus acceptable to them.

All the men in the cab had slicked-down their hair with water before leaving, combing it backwards and upwards at the sides in the fashion of Elvis Presley, and tidied themselves up as best they could without actually donning their best clothes. Manuel took the wheel, with me and Johnnie beside him, while Pins and Bug perched weightily on our laps. The Bedford TK coughed into spluttering life as, with mighty revs, we were swept forward, hurtling on to the main road and taking no heed of ruts or protuberances on the rough ground.

'Good motor, ain't she, Manny?' remarked Johnnie from beside me, his hatchet features so lined and seamed that they seemed almost scarred. He drew in the smoke from a thin hand-rolled cigarette and his cheeks sunk inwards alarmingly under his hazel-brown eyes; he coughed deeply and his chest wheezed brokenly.

'Coughin' well tonight, Johnnie,' laughed Pins.

'God blind me two eyes! These fags is killin' me,' grunted Johnnie, still racked by ill-suppressed coughing.

'It's this bloody weather – it's enough to *mar* anyone,' said Bug from my lap.

'I shall give 'em up, I reckon. On my baby's life, child die, I will!' continued Johnnie, his voice carrying no great conviction despite his terrible oath.

'Where's the sense in that?' demanded his brother irritably, lighting up. 'Didn't me dear old grandfather smoke all his life since he was a *chavi*? An' didn't he live to be eighty-eight? When the dear Lord wants to call you in, well, he'll call you in – it don't make no odds what you does.'

'So long as I can still *ker* some nice young woman I don't care how long I lives to be,' grinned Bug with the brashness of youth, for he was but eighteen years of age.

'Listen to the *dinilo* talking,' gulped Johnnie, between bouts of continuous coughing.

'Hup, there!' cried Pins inconsequentially as we sped along the road towards the city, almost empty of traffic, the harsh ghoulish green lights shining down on us from their ugly concrete standards.

'We ain't going down the town tonight, Manny,' shouted Pins above the roar of the engine. 'There's a nice little public just round the next corner, turn left-handed, an' sometimes a few good sorts gets in there. Generally we only goes down in the town at the weekends. You never seen nothin' like it in some of the places on a Friday and Saturday nights. It'd make you bad if you wasn't careful, ain't that right, Bug?'

'Certainly it is,' confirmed the latter.

'We just come from Cardiff, two weeks ago,' observed Johnnie, who was the eldest of the three brothers, and the strongest character. 'An' there was nothin' like it there, not even down by the docks nor nowhere. The nearest I've seen to it is when we was stoppin' down by Plymouth last summer with Flash Wally and his boys!'

We turned left, through narrow dank-seeming back streets; an air of dimly lit despondency pervaded the rows of small terrace houses bordering each road. Eventually, on Johnnie's instructions, we took another left turn and stopped in front of a mock-Tudor public house. It was tastefully decorated with rows of red and blue electric light bulbs, twinkling in lachrymose splendour across its façade.

'Couple of old *morts* keeps this *tan*,' Johnnie informed us as we climbed out of the lorry-cab, the two older men jumping stiffly down from the back.

'Cold up there,' complained Kalup. 'Me balls is froze like marbles!'

'The two old *morts* used to be on the game, I shouldn't wonder,' laughed Pins, hitting the boy Bug playfully in the ribs and leaping backwards to avoid a left-jab aimed in return.

'Come on, Pins, you'll upset him in a minute,' warned Johnnie, and he pushed open the doors of the bar and we strode in.

'This is a lovely pub. You can go right in and sit down,' said Old Jim to Kalup.

Once inside we chose to sit at a long table, the eyes of the few customers already in the bar focused on us with no great affection in their expressions.

Johnnie and Pins went up to the bar to order the drinks. There were two ageing, peroxided blonde women serving, who proved to be the landladies. They were indeed sisters, and both wore almost identical black dresses of the sort more often associated with afternoon tea-dances. Their white hands were well be-ringed, and their nails lacquered in vivid scarlet. The faces of each were pale and haggard, touched by spots of rouge on the cheeks, while around their eyes were flashes of green and silver shadow. Over both hung an aura of blasé resignation, coupled with expressions of deep self-sacrifice. Their small straight mouths, so red and thin, momentarily curved up into little arcs as they gave us false smiles of welcome, their blue eyes remaining hard and shrewd.

Johnnie pulled a wad of five-pound notes from the front cash-pocket of his traveller-style trousers, and laid one on the counter.

One of the landladies took it wordlessly and handed him the few pence of change. They would be, and had been, free-spending customers, but she remained aloof and unfriendly: a fact which did not escape any of us.

'Them old *rackles* can't a-bear the sight of travellers,' observed Kalup, through a haze of tobacco smoke, to Old Jim.

'That's a nice little pub up the road, ain't it, Uncle Jim?' ventured Bug shyly.

'Certainly it is, my boy – better'n this poxy place,' agreed Old Jim.

'Beautiful microphone an' the best piano-player you ever heard in all your life, an' a lovely *yog*. The only trouble is you got to put your motor out on the main road – an' it's likely to get *poggered* to bits,' said Johnnie.

'Yeah, *or* the big pub next door,' enthused Pins. 'That pub's got two microphones an' a room for a hundred *folki*—'

'There ain't no microphones there, my boy,' interrupted Old Jim, inhaling hard on a roll-up cigarette of sweet-smelling black 'baccy'.

'No harm, Uncle Jim, but there *is*,' protested Johnnie. ''Course there is, Uncle Jim,' he continued indignantly. 'Why, we were all in there over Christmas last year, full of travellers it was – an' all the women was singin' on the microphone, an' me cousin Toby as well.'

'They ain't got no microphones there,' insisted the old

man doggedly. 'Strike me dead, like me dead father, there's no fuckin' microphones!'

'Langwidge, thank you!' said one of the landladies fiercely.

'He should know – it's his country, boys,' said Kalup rather plaintively, loyal to his old friend.

Owing to his age, and out of respect, the matter was allowed to drop, though Johnnie was still aggrieved.

'He's like his grandmother's old cunt at times,' he said quietly to me, his face darker still through wrath. 'I could've *delled* him the other night, with his arguments. If you sez something's white then he'll swear it's black. How I didn't come to hit him I'll never know. Only thing is he's an old man, ain't he? If you did happen to draw one on him, an' hit him a bit *too* hard, it might finish him. You can't be too careful, can you?'

''Course you can't,' I agreed, glad to see that the age of chivalry had not entirely passed. Changing the subject, I asked, 'Is that right that you've got a newish tip-cab Ford two-ton lorry for sale? Only I know someone who'd give you a nice bit of money for one.'

'No, I still got me same motors I had when I seen you last – I can't afford no nearly new ones!'

I wished I had not mentioned it, for both Manuel and I knew that he was jealous of our vehicles, despite his jocularity on the subject.

'That's what I thought,' said Manuel. 'Yet that feller

Nigger swore his life away that you did have one.'

'Well, seein' is believin', my Mannie,' he grinned, managing to swig down a large amount of black beer through a disjointed fit of coughing.

An unhealthy-looking, somewhat mangy blue-grey cat was wandering about the room, rubbing itself against the table-legs, or any other legs, which came in its path.

'I can't abide cats, unluckiest things in the world,' groaned Kalup, adding: 'If it comes near me it'll make me bad for a week.'

At that moment the cat approached Old Jim who, upon perceiving it to be within his reach, swung the unfortunate animal up by its tail and tossed it across the room, where it landed on a table, hissing and spitting in surprise and fury, its uneven fur standing patchily on end.

The landladies gazed at the cat in astonishment, while Old Jim, his face filled with indignation, cried out, 'Did you see that? The Devil's in that cat, madam! He sprang straight at me leg – I never seen a cat do such a thing in all me life! An' me a hanimal-lover too!'

The rest of us, stifling our laughter, stared towards the bar with serious countenances.

'He *what*?' enquired one of the landladies, in increasing surprise.

'The Devil's in that cat – he went straight for me leg!' repeated Old Jim.

'Just playing, I expect, dear,' suggested one of the sisters, placatingly. 'I'm ever so sorry.'

'Well, madam,' replied Old Jim, smiling to reveal several gold teeth. 'You been a nice straightforward lady over the cat, so I tell you what I'm going to do. I'm gonna come over an' give you a nice big kiss!'

'*Dordi*, you'll have us barred,' said Kalup quietly to his brother.

'Charmin',' said one landlady, rolling her eyes heavenwards.

'Here's a way to carry on, you'll definitely have us barred in a minute, Uncle Jim,' groaned Johnnie.

'You might have killed the poor blessed thing, Uncle Jim,' admonished Pins. 'Worstest thing in the world to *mar* a cat, so me dear father used to say.'

'Well, what can you do?' moaned Old Jim in high dudgeon. 'This public's too quiet for me.'

'Put a record on, Bug,' demanded Johnnie, thrusting sixpence at the boy and gesturing towards a huge jukebox which stood in a corner.

Bug duly inserted the coin and, with several clicks and flashes, the great machine broke into deafening sound: the room was flooded by the strident, but by no means unpleasant, voices of the Supremes.

'Lovely singers,' remarked Bug, looking at us for approval of his choice.

'Lovely singers!' repeated Johnnie in disgust. 'Hank Williams or Jim Reeves is what you should've put on – not this!'

'I'll give you a song!' offered Old Jim, the beer getting to him.

'There's a singer!' grunted Kalup. 'He could sing before tunes come out.'

'I likes old-fashioned songs,' declared Old Jim, rather put-out. 'But it ain't no good iffen you'm in the wrong company,' he concluded, staring coldly at Johnnie.

'Anyway, the two old girls wouldn't stand no singing!' said Manuel.

'They looks too monotonous for me,' remarked Pins, rather mystifyingly, flashing white teeth in a smile.

Gradually the time passed away; each of us present had bought a round. Like all mildly dedicated drinkers, we made it a rule never to leave a public house before turning-out time.

As the clock reached the official hour of exodus the remainder of the rather unprepossessing customers had almost all departed, and the sisters were pursing their lips ever more tightly, emitting squeaks of 'Time! Drink up! Time!' After ten minutes or so, without any visible impression having been made, they became more forthright in their determination to clear the house. This was, ultimately, accepted as a direct invitation to leave and we found ourselves outside in the cold night air. Here and there along the dimly lit streets figures hurried along alone, or strolled in pairs, huddled and anonymous together.

Our little party climbed back into the lorry cab, with this time Bug, as the youngest and fittest, being encouraged to climb on to the back.

I sat on the lap of Old Jim, which I found a curious experience, while Pins settled on Kalup. We were soon back at the trailers and, the dogs recognising their owners, all was peaceful.

It had been a restrained evening, and nobody among us was more than just a little merry. The lights were still shining from the uncurtained windows of most of the trailers, as the women waited on the men's return.

We said our farewells, and all expressed the hope that we would travel together later that year.

'They're nice people to stop with,' I remarked to Manuel. 'Good-hearted and not a ringtail among them.'

'Quite right,' agreed Manuel, adding: 'I can't suffer ringtails!'

When we reached our own trailers I went in and enjoyed a dish of broth, some bread and cheese and a cup of tea. All was presented to me by a rather morose Beshlie, who was not over-enthusiastic at being left alone for the whole evening with only Anne-Marie and the tiny children in such insalubrious surroundings. (Ah me, life seemed so much safer then!)

The next morning was harsh and the air was raw and con-taminated with fumes from the surrounding factory chimneys; there was a threat of snow in the air.

But go we must, and before nine o'clock if we wished to miss the council officials and police who would forcibly remove us.

And so it was that by nine o'clock we were ready, all packed, and the trailers hitched-on. All the little children of Manuel were swarming into their lorry-cab, several sitting on a shelf behind the seating, peering out with expectation and excitement at the prospect of new surroundings once more. Barney whined from the recesses of his kennel on the lorry-back, while Manuel's two terriers leaped about, loose and energetic, barking impatiently. All, of course, were essentially outdoor dogs, never having been allowed inside the trailers in their lives, as is the custom of travelling people.

I led the way, the first journey made in my new lorry. Its new six-cylinder petrol engine purred and whined musically; sweet as a nut, as mechanics used to say.

Taking the main road along the coast, and despite a gusty inshore wind, we made good progress, passing two separate little collections of travellers, on grass roadside verges some twenty miles apart. The mixture in age and quality of both the vehicles and the trailers in each gathering suggested that they were almost certainly Irish travellers – the latter tending to be slightly less into the 'birds of a feather' syndrome than English or Welsh travellers.

We had almost reached Brighton before, recollecting some slightly devious cross-country routes, I turned inland towards London, turning off after a while at a right fork marked Ditchling. It was near to this rather smart and prosperous little town, if one could call it that, that the common I was seeking lay. It was large and haphazard, of considerable acreage, consisting of both open and bushy areas, with a variety of well-maintained and exceedingly expensive houses and farms dotted about its environs. The inhabitants of the latter had fought a running battle in their efforts to get all travellers evicted from the common over many years, and it was to be at least a decade more until their self-motivated goals were finally achieved.

For years many travellers had used it for a temporary stopping-place, before moving on of their own accord, as we ourselves had done.

However, for some years local travellers, mostly of a rough and ready kind both in lifestyle and person, had sprinkled themselves about the common on little islands of hard ground. They mainly belonged to two families of rather mixed breeding: Barkers and Whitelows, the first being the most numerous and mainly, in those years, living in bender-tents, which they transported about the common by means of bicycles and hand-carts, or even old perambulators – in a way that I have only myself ever seen among the berry-pickers of Perthshire in the late 1940s. Although both families possessed no excess of Romani blood it was, as usual, enough for them to class themselves proudly as travellers. The Barkers, however, had overtaken the others in worldly possessions, and many of them possessed small trailer-caravans which were drawn about on limited journeys by old family saloons or 'cut-down jobs' – that is to say cars which had been sliced in half and made into little lorries, in the days before pick-up trucks were available.

Only one of their number, known as Banjo Bob, a very aged man of almost complete deafness and exceedingly limited conversation, still lived in the remains of a very roughly built, horse-drawn 'open lot' wagon. His wife had died some years before so he continued to live, alone, in his wagon. He was surrounded by his multitudinous children and grandchildren – upon all of whom he would smile with a toothless grin of great amiability. By being without hearing he had long found any form of communication virtually impossible. One of his sons had once given him a battery-operated hearing-aid which he had begged from an elderly gentleman while out calling for scrap-iron. After applying it to his ear the ancient Bob was, by all accounts, so shocked by the unaccustomed volume of noise emanating from all those around him that he instantly ground the offending apparatus under the heel of his boot, declaring himself unable to stand it! From then onwards he had remained in a state of ben-evolent aural solitude.

Passing through Ditchling that winter's afternoon, we found ourselves to be the object of many malevolent-seeming stares from the denizens, who appeared to sense our destination. (Meetings were regularly held in the village halls of the surrounding neighbourhoods, where it was, with-out fail, decided that 'the Gypsies must go'. But where? This was, naturally, never mentioned during those years.)

Five minutes out of Ditchling, and we approached the common. At the first turning on the right there were three or four separate encampments of travellers, with tents, old trailers and motors of all kinds – united only by age and condition. A few men and youths were stumping about on the muddy ground, or mournfully inspecting the engines of their vehicles. I was sure that they were Barkers. I tooted brightly as we passed them, and they all raised their hands in salute. We took a right turn and then a left, and came upon the piece of ground I was seeking. It was a patch of uninviting land, some fifty feet square, stamped hard and black, oil-slicked and depressed-looking from over-inhabi-tation. A few old travellers' fireplace circles were easily discernible along one side. Lumps of old light-iron (for which there was little market just then), old bicycle frames and wheels, tins and bottles were all too visible in the sparse gorse which surrounded three sides of the patch. It was obvious that little time had elapsed since travellers, of one sort or another, had vacated this barren fastness.

Uninviting though it was, I felt that it would be unwise not to avail ourselves of it, so I pulled on, closely followed by Manuel. We all climbed down and surveyed the area with considerable gloom: it was very depressing and made one feel that life was at a low ebb.

'What shall we do?' I enquired, looking at them in turn.

'How long do you think we'd get here?' asked Manuel dubiously.

'Monty and Jug said they had three months here – and left of their own accord,' I replied, speaking of cousins of Anne-Marie.

'Is that right?' answered Manuel, looking happier.

'Yep, they said you can stop almost anywhere on this old common, 'specially in the summer when it dries out, till you're greyheaded,' I truthfully told them.

'You won't get long here then, *mush*,' laughed Manuel, unkindly gesturing at my badger-coloured hair.

'If the dear sun would shine it'd be a nice place,' announced Anne-Marie, watching her small sons burrowing into the gorse-bushes with great interest, their sister standing primly by with the baby Horace in her arms, a little mother already.

'Come out of them bushes, you boys, you'll be killed by

the snakes and varmints!' cried Anne-Marie, in a change of mood.

After a few minutes doubt, therefore, we finally all decided it would be best to remain there. For where else might we find a good, hard place?

'A Nice Green Field'
and a Winter of Discomfort

There was a piece of flat, low-lying but hard ground of perhaps an acre and a half in size which was situated right next to the little Hampshire market town, behind the shops and away from the bustle, in fact quite hidden from the busy streets. The land was not exceptional in itself apart from the fact that, for several years, small groups of motorised travellers were not turned off it by the farmer who rented it from the local council. Thus, despite occasional complaints by mildly indignant residents, it gradually became a regular stopping-place for travellers from all over the country as word spread of its existence. Generally rather respectable in appearance, with immaculate trailers and motor vehicles, the travellers who chose to spend time there were far from the 'raggle-taggle Gypsy' image of popular conception, and generally proved to be less cowed by authority than their humbler brethren would have been. It was summer in the early 1960s when we pulled on. We were then the proud owners of an eighteen-foot Siddal trailer (now long extinct, but in those days a great favourite among travellers; they were coachbuilt, with a distinctive Art Deco-like shape and two-toned colouration of the owner's choice) and a little A-type Bedford 30cwt lorry. The latter model only existed on the production line from 1953 until 1959 when it was superceded by the more elegant and Americanised J-type model, which reigned as the travellers' favourite for the next ten years. The A-type, roundly bulbous and squat in shape, was nicknamed the 'frog-fronted' Bedford by travellers, and was greatly praised for its stamina and pulling-power. It was truly the 'wagon-horse' of the motor world in its day, appearing indestructible in the face of the ill-treatment it all too often received. When I bought mine it was an uninspiring dark green in colour, so we hastily hand-painted it in the more refined tones of mush-room and cream, which two shades provided it with a superficial smartness which, we hoped, would avert the unwelcome attentions of the ever-feared 'nuts and bolts men', from the Ministry of Transport. For should his eye be offended by the sight of a neglected-looking commercial vehicle, any one of these intractable individuals was empowered to order it off the road, without warning or delay.

Traversing a narrow passageway from the end of the High Street, we soon emerged at our destination. Two separate groups of trailers were already established, with a distance of fifty yards or more separating them.

The first comprised two large Berkeley Ambassador trailers, roomy and stately with spacious accommodation and usually chosen by large families; while nearby was a smaller, more streamlined trailer, which I recognised as a Scottish manufacture – a Balmforth it was indeed. More refined than exotic, it exuded an air of quiet opulence; beside it stood a new Humber Estate, the sort of vehicle more generally to be found outside the premises of stockbroker-belt golf clubs. As ever, incongruity added the spice of life. Beside the Berkeley trailers stood two shining frog-fronted vans, one grey and the other beige – the kind of vehicles almost universally favoured by carpet-hawkers at that time. Three matching custom-made dog-kennels were lined up nearby and five or six lurchers lay in or around them, mostly on chains, leaping to their feet in some indignation on seeing our lorry and trailer passing close by them.

The second group comprised only two trailers: one was yet another large Berkeley, a little older than those of the first group; while the other was a new Jubilee Hornet. The last-named was to increase greatly in popularity during the next few years, indeed until well into the next decade. It was especially liked by middle-of-the-road travellers. It was very reasonably priced and could be ordered in a variety of lengths and interior layouts as required. Some years later we ourselves ordered a new twenty-two-foot model, which was one of the best and most showy that the firm ever produced! With a multitude of shining stainless-steel embellishments applied to the exterior and the interior filled with a proliferation of cut-glass mirrors with intricate designs etched into them, as well as decorative dressing-table 'castle' blinds on each window and exotic chandelier lights, it afforded great pleasure to those of us innocent enough to be so impressed. We journeyed from Cornwall to Scotland in its splendour before, after two years, *chopping* it in for one of the increasingly desired and even more rococo Vickers trailers from Morecambe.

Around the two trailers of the second group were scattered the implements of their trade, and from those objects it was no great feat of detection to realise that they were tarmacadam-layers. Two saloon cars, both clean and new-looking, and a small red Japanese pick-up truck were parked alongside the trailers: an aged alsatian was tied to the tow-bar of the pick-up but, strange in that breed, evinced no interest in us whatsoever. However, from the absence of both people and lorries it would seem that its owners had left for their work. Only the figure of a youngish fair-haired woman could be seen in the Jubilee, duster in hand, engaged in the never-ending task of cleaning up, necessary to preserve the interiors of the trailers of the flash travellers in the state of pristine, almost clinical splendour which is expected of them by their occupants, relatives and other visitors! It is a long way from the cosier, trinketty, colourful and casual living conditions preferred by the New Age travellers.

After a moment's thought we decided to pull on about halfway between the other trailers, as near to the edge of the grass as we could safety manoeuvre without our wheels sinking into the softer ground beside a shallow stream that flowed along the perimeter, at which a few New Forest ponies were drinking without taking any heed of us.

Our journey had been short and unstressful, and it was barely half past nine as we unhitched the lorry and began to arrange ourselves. We were halfway through this operation when our peace was rudely shattered by the sudden appearance of a youth of about thirteen, accompanied by five lurchers and a rangy, ferocious-looking black and tan cross-bred alsatian who was leaping at the back of our lorry in an effort to reach our own dogs, who were growling furiously from the interiors of their kennels.

'Coome down, yer *radj*y bastard,' shouted the youth in a thick Yorkshire accent, adding: 'He'd kill owt, would that *juke*!'

So saying, he raised a threatening gesture at the malevolent animal with a switch that he was carrying, which was enough to cause it to withdraw, grumbling to itself.

The boy, I could see, had his eye on one of our dogs.

'How much would you ask to *chop* for t'alsatian – pure bred, he is!'

'I wouldn't take five hundred pounds for that dog,' I replied sharply: I couldn't be bothered with such a boy.

Disgusted by this rejoinder, he pondered for a minute or so, his brow heavily furrowed under a black fringe, and he turned back towards his family's trailers with one final observation: 'I'm like me dad – I'd *chop* for owt I would. You've got to try, a'nt you – even if you gets *chingered* at!'

I continued unpacking, noticing that the two Bedford vans and the Humber Estate had by then all departed for their day's calling. It transpired that the Humber Estate's owner was the uncle of the youth with the dogs, whose father was working with one of his unmarried brothers – yet another uncle! I later learned that the women went 'out' as well, with lace, the two single sisters together and the two married ones – sisters-in-law – forming a second party. They were rather secretive about their pursuits, apart from their lace – but the word *dukkering* sprang easily to mind.

By quite early in the afternoon the two vans had returned to the ground, to be followed soon afterwards by the Humber Estate. As is the way of travellers, however, we had soon made contact and stood in a group chatting.

They were short, thickset, north-country Lees and

Smiths. Each of the men wore smart business suits and collars-and-ties, their shoes shone: their disguise was complete. There were two unmarried brothers, Henry and Tom, both in their fifties and of remarkably Eastern appearance. The two unmarried sisters kept their distance, both clothed entirely in black and probably older than the brothers. They appeared to be of an unreasonably quarrelsome disposition apiece. Their shrieks of fury could be heard at all hours during the next few days.

'Come out, cat's cunt – and I'll kill you stone-dead!' screamed one to the other after yet another dispute. The abuse was so loud that it reverberated over the roofs of the suburban bungalows which were situated on the townside of the green, causing many a tremor to afflict the curtains thereof!

Accustomed to the more rarefied atmosphere of official *gaujo* caravan-parks upon which they would stay whenever admitted by the precious owners, the north-country travellers affected slight shock at the lack of amenities offered on the green.

'Well, aye, man,' observed the eldest brother to me. 'It's a lovely green field, a man couldn't ask for a prettier place to *atch* – but why couldn't they put up a dear little *ingering kair* somewhere?'

His gleaming black eyes twinkled brightly under the brim of his panama hat and his silk-shot blue suit glistened in the sunlight. Despite his assertion of being 'only a poor old Romani man', he nonetheless spared no expense on his apparel, even his tan-coloured lace-up boots were hand-made and polished almost to excess. His features were sunburned to a rich brown, his hair was greying at the temples, so that he did indeed present a distinguished appearance to the world. Few would have guessed, unless Romanies themselves, that he had passed his childhood and youth living in horse-drawn wagons, on the move throughout northern England and Scotland.

The third brother, Abraham, had more than made up for the celibacy of his brothers and two of his sisters by producing, so far, ten children, six boys and four girls, ranging in age from twenty years down to fourteen months. As is often the case with travellers, his offspring differed remarkably from each other in colour, build and character, though all were pleasantly disposed towards both Beshlie and myself. The one possible exception was the fourth from the eldest, the boy with the dogs, who was called Golly but was generally referred to as Shitty Breeches. This nickname was given to him by the family, his father explained – one's imagination faltered at the implications! Being so great in number, they were, as is frequently the case under such circumstances, almost complete and self-contained within their own ranks – they really needed no outside company for stimulus. Being presently in country that was strange to them and feeling somewhat out of place, their reliance on their own family was even further intensified. The passing of time, through generations, had in no way lessened their old-fashioned Romani family values.

In the evenings, sitting in their trailers, they talked to me wistfully of their own northern stopping-places, the people whom they knew, some of whom were familiar to me; and of the horse-fairs that they still often attended in the spring and autumn.

Superficially, however, their only links with the past were their numerous, semi-wild dogs, all too often running loose in a pack – to the perpetual horror and indignation of those of the neighbouring house-dwellers who refused to be deterred. They continued to exercise their pets, most of which were small and utterly domesticated, despite the constant danger of them being mauled or worse by the lurchers.

To us, however, apart from occasional dog-fights beside or under our trailer, in which our dog Barney invariably came off best, which eventually disinclined the pack to venture within his chain-length, the sturdy little northerners were the most amiable and interesting of temporary neighbours.

The other group on the green proved to be members of the Cooper family: a name spread very widely, especially over southern and central England.

They were Nelson and his wife Leander, who had been

Buckland before marriage, and many of whose relatives were well known to me. They had seven sons, a number which was regarded as being very lucky. All the boys were still 'at home' apart from the eldest, Young Nelson, who was then aged about twenty-seven. He was the owner of the Jubilee trailer, in which he lived with his wife Phoebe and their two small sons.

The Berkeley trailer belonging to Nelson was, despite its size, becoming too small to accommodate the ever-growing six sons and their parents: it was like an overcrowded bird's nest just before the chicks took flight.

In fact, that very day Nelson returned in the late afternoon in his lorry, towing a sixteen-foot *gaujo*-style touring trailer with which he aimed to ease the discomfiture of his family.

Although hitherto unacquainted with Nelson himself, I was quite a close friend of several of his brothers, including one who was reputed to be a millionaire. He drove a new Rolls Royce and lived in a sprawling, ranch-style residence. I will for ever remember him with the deepest respect when I recall a visit to his home and all its splendour. Ushering me inside, he offered me a drink. To my astonishment, he pressed a switch on the wall beside a floor-to-ceiling bookcase whereupon the whole bookcase revolved to reveal a hidden billiard room with its own bar. My astonishment was further increased when I was offered a choice of either red, white or blue vodka! Who indeed could have a better memory to treasure?

'He's got so much money he has to keep it in two banks!' one of his brothers had told me with great pride. Perhaps he hoped for success by association.

Old Nelson himself was one of that curious breed who, though by no means physically attractive, being bald, fat, short in stature with alarmingly crossed eyes, nevertheless compensated for those disadvantages by means of his personality and almost constant good humour. I think that his marriage was a happy one, and his seven sons, most of whom were fortunate enough to inherit their mother's handsome features, were a source of great pride to him, especially later, in view of their achievements in the traveller lifestyle.

He would boast: 'I ain't give none of 'em nothing! What they got is what they got for themselves, strike me dead! If you gives 'em everything they appreciate nothing! That's what my dear old father said an' I'll take my dying oath as it's true!'

I had no reason to argue with him on that score.

In repose, the features of Nelson were mask-like and imponderable, set hard. Little of his thoughts was revealed and when calling at the doors in suburbia in search of tarmacadam jobs, his manner would soon convince all but the most doubting householder that his skills and efficiency were almost unparalleled. Unable to read or write, never having attended any schools, he was by nature a man of inestimable astuteness in business matters.

'You'd have to get up early in the morning to catch our Nelson,' his older brother Joe remarked to me one day in great admiration.

Once Nelson became aware of the fact that I knew so many of his brothers and older relatives he thawed immediately in his manner towards me; we were no longer strangers to each other. As always among travellers, it is all-important for social progress to know who is related to whom, as too is a knowledge of certain respected key figures within the way of life, be they settled-down or still on the road. Without such knowledge, one would be a lesser person.

The same could be said of his eldest son, Young Nelson, with whom I was soon to become friend and business partner: once again matters were assisted greatly when it was discovered that I knew all four of his wife's brothers, and her brother-in-law too, and had indeed stopped with them in Wiltshire before her aged father had died.

Unlike his brothers and his father, Young Nelson was tall and well-built, over six feet, with coal-black hair and eyes; indeed he bore a very Romani look, with sharply moulded features and slightly hooked nose. His kind of good looks was much favoured by the most popular celluloid heroes of the time. Despite his obvious attraction for women, however, he never exhibited the slightest sign of straying from Phoebe.

The latter, with her long blonde hair and white skin, was still unmistakeably a traveller. She was a girl of strong character, with an extremely melodious singing voice – the last attribute causing her to be frequently called upon at travellers' parties where she was much appreciated. 'My Phoebe could sing Teresa Brewer off the stage,' Young Nelson would boast on such occasions.

Old Nelson and his sons (the youngest of whom rejoiced in the name Cuckoo!) were all engaged in the laying of either tarmac or 'tar and chippings'. Of the two options I came to prefer the latter as not only was it cheaper to execute but considerably less stressful. For example, if one slightly underestimated the amount of material that would be required to cover an area it was only too easy to drive to the gravel-pits and buy a little more, sufficient to complete the task. Whereas, should the same set of circumstances arise with a tarmacadam surface, it would always be difficult to 'match up' the small section needing to be 'joined'. Indeed, during our partnership, Young Nelson and I were to experience such a situation on several occasions, and at least twice suffered the greatest difficulty in persuading the householders (who turned, as Young Nelson put it, 'from lambs to devils') not to withhold a considerable percentage of the amounts due to us in retaliation – even though we always blamed the tarmac-plant owners for short-changing us!

I remember, only a few years ago, hearing of a traveller – a living legend in the north of England – who was engaged in the re-surfacing of a large car-park belonging to a five-star hotel near a city centre. He was an extremely wealthy man who only undertook large contracts, generally executed by two or three 'dossers' and himself. On this particular occasion he was, apparently, inflamed with rage that the 'dossers' had not managed to 'stretch' the tarmac over a small patch in one corner – necessitating a journey to the tarmac-plant to fetch about two hundredweight in order to finish the job. Not dreaming that such a miscalculation would occur the man had only brought his new Rolls Royce limousine to the hotel, there being no need for his lorry, he had optimistically presumed. In any event, being so infuriated, he threw good sense to the wind, and sped off in his Rolls Royce to the plant. On arrival, he ordered the astonished staff to pour two hundredweight of the evil black substance on to an old piece of sheeting in the boot of his immaculate car!

Some time later, he approached a leading Rolls Royce dealership with a view to exchanging his year-old vehicle for a new one. Gleaming and immaculate in appearance, it looked faultless. However, after casting an appreciative eye over the limousine, the salesman casually opened the boot: his shock and amazement could well be imagined as he observed the condition therein. As the owner amusedly recalled, the salesman sent for the manager and both stood riveted with disgust and disbelief, staring into the black-stained boot.

The manager, we were told, had been so appalled that he exclaimed: 'I can hardly believe it, sir, but there seems to have been *tarmac* in the boot!'

Having had the situation explained to him, he is said to have continued, 'It is an absolute disgrace! People like you shouldn't own one of our cars!'

Knowing the man involved, I had no reason to doubt the veracity of this story, and it has, in fact, since become something of a folktale related by travellers throughout the country. The Rolls Royce owner would quite often tell the story himself to other travellers, with considerable pride.

The day after our arrival, before I had become partners with Young Nelson, I went out calling in the nearest suitable locality: smart newish bungalows, mostly inhabited by seemingly well-off retired couples, or lone ancients seeing out the remainder of their lives in single isolation. The latter were, generally speaking, of rather uncertain temperaments.

One such, an aged, sparse-haired, bad-tempered old woman barked: 'No, thank you!' and went to close the door.

I repeated the reason for my call, about her front drive.

'I said NO, THANK YOU!' she repeated crossly.

'I'm afraid if I accepted "no, thank you" I might as well stay at home,' I replied jokily.

Her eyes brightened with fury.

'Well, STAY AT HOME THEN!' she spat, slamming the door.

Slightly depressed by this poor start, I nonetheless persevered, and eventually managed to take two small jobs. The first was simple, a short driveway which merely necessitated being re-covered with chippings, after the removal of a few straggly weeds from the inside edge. I estimated that it could easily be completed in an hour. The second was more complicated, comprising a driveway and several narrow garden paths between rosebeds – the whole to be executed in tar and chippings. In those days the black bituminous tar could only be obtained in huge and unmanageable drums which were almost impossible to lift when full and difficult to dispose of when empty.

Ah, the follies of youth! I remember once, when Young Nelson and I were working together, we had completed a small job and, on the way homewards with an unwanted empty drum on the back of the lorry, we sighted an apparent piece of wasteland. We drove in off the road and came upon a kind of cliff-edged valley ahead of us. Casting the drum over the cliff at a venture, we were astonished to hear human cries wafting upwards from below. Creeping to the edge, we perceived the outraged figure of a middle-aged tramp jumping about beside what appeared to be the remains of a small tent. Within the midst of its destruction lay our oil-drum! Fortunately for us that the 'road-pad' had not been reclining within the little structure at that moment. Unseen by him, and slightly alarmed by the near tragedy, we hastened away like two small boys!

The tar and chipping specialist of the successful sort would usually either hire or buy a machine, which not only looked professional but was quite efficient. The tar barrel was lain on its side aboard the 'machine', its bung removed and a tube inserted. It was operated by pump-action, with a spray nozzle: its simplicity was its strength.

However, for those of us who had not then aspired to the richer heights of such technology, an old-fashioned watering-can *could* achieve the same eventual results. Users of the latter simpler method would embroider it with the praise of being 'hand-finished'!

A mile or so outside the town, some old-fashioned local travellers were stopping semi-permanently in a little dead-end piece of abandoned highway in two old broken-down 'open lot' wagons. There were several teenaged sons of the wagon owner who, not then mechanised, were always willing to take a few day's employment for the 'flash' travellers when they were asked to do so. Old Nelson recommended them to me.

'Good old boys,' he reassured me. Adding with some contempt: 'They don't know what it's like to do a bit of *booty* for a hundred pounds a day – a bit of bread's all they looks for.'

So much for sympathy. Those with *equal opportunity* lack pity for those who fail, there being no social or educational barrier on which to blame it.

I drove to where I had been directed and arranged to pick up one of the young men at nine o'clock the next morning. One of his small brothers expressed a desire to accompany us but I refused this firmly.

The next morning dawned bleak and wet and I momentarily wondered whether I should cancel my arrangements. However, true to my lifelong refusal to surrender to anything but ill-health or injury, I decided to go ahead.

I called for my assistant at the wagons promptly at nine o'clock, from one of which he eventually emerged, sleepy-looking and tousled. There was no sign of life from the other wagon.

Nicknamed Creamy (short for Crimea, his mother later informed me), he gazed about him in some trepidation.

'Here's *pani, mush,*' he observed. 'We'll be drownded, wi' mud an' water up to our necks! It's like its granny!'

A gloomy start indeed, but this was no time for politeness on my part.

'Do you want to come or not?'

'Yeah, all right then, *mush,*' he agreed without much enthusiasm. It was his lack of spirit or urgency which did so much to differentiate him from the lively, energetic boys of Old Nelson and their like.

Within ten minutes we had arrived at the gravel-pits and, after weighing my empty lorry on the weighbridge, returned a few minutes later with a load of cleanly washed small-gauge shingle. After re-weighing the lorry I paid the twelve shillings and sixpence at the office, and we were off ... towards Arcadia!

We had a journey of six or seven miles to reach our destination in bungalow-land and the first of the two jobs. This first was the easy one and, despite the weather, was no challenge at all. We parked outside and, armed with a shovel apiece, began hacking off the weeds, taking one side of the drive each, and thrusting them into an old sack. I then reversed the lorry carefully into the narrow drive, almost up to the front door. Creamy, from the back of the lorry, muffled in a ragged, too-large overcoat against the rain, which was still pouring heavily, spread the chippings, to the best of his ability, on top of the sparse remnants which were still present from years before. The effect was quite pleasing as the gravel, being of a golden hue, provided the reserved appearance which I had predicted. The occupants peered out from behind a lightly opened front door, one head above the other. A man and woman in their late seventies, they looked strangely alike, tight-lipped, suspicious and shut-in upon themselves. I marvelled to myself that I had ever taken the job from them. However, they paid me without demur, grumbling about the weather from the comfortable interior of their home: they made no comment about our saturated appearances, but merely held out the cash for me, and we left.

It has long amused me to note that those for whom the climactic conditions are of little moment, cloistered for most of their time in well-heated houses, are the very people whose protests are most vociferous.

I suppose one could learn a lesson from an encounter that I had a year or so ago in Wales on a wet autumn day near Builth Wells.

I called at a small house in a little cul-de-sac, and the door was opened by an elderly lady of fairly amiable aspect. I explained my business to her, and she politely declined my offer, which was bags of compost that I was hawking. As I turned to go, I remarked, 'What a terrible day, I am soaked to the skin.'

Expecting an agreement, I was somewhat astonished when the lady replied, with some tetchiness:

'Any weather the Good Lord sends us is welcome. It is not for us to criticise it!'

'Excuse me,' I asked, 'but are you a Born Again Christian?'

'I am,' she replied, drawing herself up with pride.

'And so am I,' I answered.

'Praise the Lord! He moves in mysterious ways – now what was it you called here about?'

'Well, I have a few bags of compost left . . . ' I began.

'How much are they?' she enquired.

My astonishment may well be imagined when she agreed to take the lot!

There must be something to be learned from the fact that once it was established that it was Christian-delivered compost it was acceptable – how very strange.

As I left she thrust several eccentric pamphlets into my hand, and two of the worst kind of American Evangelical tapes that it has ever been my misfortune to hear.

Just as I had drawn out on to the road a traveller's-style van slowed and then pulled up behind us. Out jumped five travellers, all in their twenties: it was the Windfall brothers, who at that time lived in a council house, still with their parents, in the town. We were really trespassing on their home-ground, but luckily they were good friends of mine and thus bore me no resentment for being in their locality. I thought, however, it was best to make a joke of it.

'Nah!' cried Mosey, the eldest. 'Our name ain't on no gate – neither is yourn: it's every man for himself, brother.'

'Oh *dordi*! You've earned your bit of *moro* today kid, I bet!' said Badger, the youngest, lighting a cigarette.

'A nice little cock an' hen, eh, kid?' laughed another brother.

'That and a bit,' I laughed. 'Here's a struggle for a shilling!'

They were all smartly dressed in suits, no cast-off clothing for them – at first glance they could have been Jehovah's Witnesses!

Likeable and full of fun, they laughed and joked, despite the rain, and we parted happily; it was good to see them and my spirits were lifted considerably.

'Let's go and have a cup of tea and something to eat,' I suggested.

'Yeah! *Kushti*. Me guts is killin' me – I ain't a-had nothin' since yesterday,' agreed Creamy promptly, his pale rather Slavic features lightening slightly, his perpetual frown lessening too.

I knew of a small transport café which lay less than a mile along the main road. Enticingly named Dinah's Diner, it was owned and run by a large middle-aged woman of robust physique. Her complexion was well-painted as protection from the heat of her cooking appliances behind the counter, while her blonde hair was arranged in coils on top of her head and fastened with clasps and ribbons. It was rumoured that she had deserted a career in entertainment before entering the catering industry. In any event, she appealed to her rough and ready clientele who greatly appreciated her jolly humour, riddled as it was with ribald repartee and double entendre, all of which she employed indiscriminately to her customers with total disregard for their social standing.

We found space in the car-park between two juggernauts and entered, pushing between the tables, which were close-set and mainly occupied by lorry-drivers and their mates.

'Hello, darling,' called Dinah on seeing me, continuing, on sight of Creamy, with whose family she was slightly acquainted: 'How's my little Gypsy-boy, then? Sorry we haven't got no hedgehogs on today, lovey!'

Creamy, always shy and 'ashamed' in public, looked slightly hunted at the unwanted attention but realised it was intended as good humour so he weathered it well.

'*Dordi! Dik* the *mort's burkes!*' ('Oh Lord! Look at the woman's bosom!') he remarked to me as a rather private form of reply.

Reference to the size of her bosom was nothing unusual in the café – imposing as they were, they seemed to have a life of their own.

After a little more badinage we found a vacant table and sat down to enjoy a well-cooked full English breakfast, with a mug of strong tea. We sat munching away, placidly sipping our tea, gradually beginning to dry out in the overheated atmosphere. Creamy carefully rolled a thin cigarette and, lighting it from the cigarette of a man at the next table, inhaled deeply, as he had done for as long as he could remember.

'I'd sooner go wi'out bread an' meat than a fag,' he informed me, in a sentence I remembered being uttered twenty years previously by an old traveller round a wood-fire in Dorset. The people die but the words do not.

And so were we engaged when, to our surprise, a piece of

human wreckage suddenly appeared beside our table. It was little Harry Skellington of Norwich. Living with his elderly mother and an older brother until well into middle-age, he was slightly slow of wits in some ways, though not in others. He had, upon the death of both his mother and brother in quick succession, suddenly found himself virtually alone in the world after a lifetime of being cosseted from the hardships of life. Incapable of driving, he had been forced to sell their old lorry and, unable to pay the rent, to leave the trailer-park where they had been for many years. His troubles were not diminished by the fact of his being a chronic alcoholic, to such an extent that his whole day was spent in trying to obtain sufficient funds to enable him to drink himself into oblivion every night. Whenever he was able to afford such a luxury, he would find accommodation in the lowliest of lodging-houses, moving from one town to another, mostly in central England and Wales, as the fit took him. By the law of chance I seemed to encounter him, always unexpectedly, every year or two. On this occasion I had not seen him since meeting him in Brighton two years previously. That experience had been distinctly depressing: it was in the lounge bar of a smart public house just off the seafront where he was offering a rather unwilling audience the benefit of some of his impressions of well-known cinema and television personalities. It was with some amusement that

I perceived that he had managed to button-hole a very middle-class couple who were too polite to drive him away from their presence – he was too drunk to realise that they would have preferred his absence to his company.

Alas, his repertoire was unending – W. C. Fields, John Wayne, James Cagney, a surprising Deputy Dawg, even Max Bygraves – on and on they poured out, some quite accurate, others wildly improbable and ill-judged. Being obviously of surburban temperament, the couple eventually called for the assistance of the landlord in order to be rid of him; the latter promptly gave him an invitation to leave which none but the bravest would have ignored!

He was a small man, no more than five and a half feet tall, with a narrow face which descended from a protruding forehead to a receding chin and skimpy neck; he wore a cloth cap, stained waistcoat and black trousers and boots. Everything about him looked used-up and tired apart, perhaps, from his eyes, black and luminous, which still managed to hint at his Romani ancestry.

'Well, my old cousins, I'm pleased to see you,' he said, gazing rather blearily at us.

'Hello, Harry,' I replied. 'Where are you stopping – down in the town? Here, get a cup of tea.'

I handed him some loose change which he grabbed hastily. Within seconds he was at the counter, regaling a for-once astonished Dinah with a selection of his voices.

'She won't get rid of him now,' I grinned at Creamy. 'He'll *mong* a breakfast off her – you watch.'

In those days I myself smoked, and I rolled a cigarette and soon we were both enveloped in the sickly-sweet odour of the Black Beauty tobacco which, in those days, was the universal favourite of travellers: it lingers in my memory still.

'Me granny's niney-two an' it ain't killed her yet,' announced Creamy, lighting yet another roll-up as we were about to leave. 'The smoke kills all they old germs that's about,' he assured me.

We did not say farewell to Harry as he was by then deep in conversation with a hypnotised-looking Dinah.

We glanced at each other.

'*Dordi*, he can *rokker*,' said Creamy.

Once outside, we discovered that the rain was showing no sign of abating from its unending deluge: if anything it was worse.

'We'd better go and fetch the tar and the chippings – I expect it'll stop very soon, it looks lighter over there,' I concluded, pointing optimistically to a black horizon.

Creamy looked unconvinced.

On the journey back to the trailers, where I had equipped myself with a barrel of tar which I had bought from Old Nelson and a large old watering-can which I had borrowed from Young Nelson, Creamy and I experienced a momentary excitement when we noticed that the lorry's milometer was registering an uninterrupted line of noughts. The little Bedford van had been round the clock, 100,000 miles! Though to be sure, whether this was for the first, second or even third time, I had no means of knowing. The engine was petrol-driven, for in those days diesels were uncommon and backward in development apart from those used on the heaviest of commercial vehicles. The old six-cylinder engines proved to be almost everlasting, despite the almost total neglect received by large numbers.

I was once discussing such matters with a Romani man, long since dead, who always owned brand-new motors in his prosperous later years. 'When you've got an *old* motor you don't never have him serviced, 'cepting for new plugs, do you?' he remarked. 'Yet he goes all right, just the same. Well, if you've got a bran' fine *new* motor it stands to sense as *he'll* go all right wi'out messin' about wi' services, don't it?'

There was, I felt, an incontrovertible logic in his statement which defied contradiction!

Within half an hour, after collecting another load of shingle, we arrived at the second bungalow, which was slightly superior to the first, having neat little dormer windows in its roof, thus elevating itself socially into the category of 'semi'-bungalow: a form of housing which was guaranteed to bring a lifting of spirit in the hearts of all but the most jaded of estate agents!

The rain, sure enough, showed no sign of ceasing – if anything it was falling more heavily. However, we would soon both be so soaked that we would be past the point of complaining.

There appeared to be nobody at home – there being no reply to our sharp knocks, and prolonged rings of the bell, at the front door. We decided it wisest to proceed, and so, removing the bung from the drum of bitumen, we managed to pour enough from it to fill the watering-can without mishap. We commenced to pour it along one of the narrow paths which ran through rose-beds and along the edge of the garden. Alas, however, already almost filled with rain water, there was little accommodation left for the tar and so little more than an oil-slick appeared on the path, with most of the actual bitumen overflowing on to the rose-beds! Not allowing ourselves the luxury of being disheartened by this unfortunate turn of events, we hastily applied a layer of chippings, though the latter had little or no chance of 'gluing' in what was left of the diluted tar. This strangely unsatisfying process we repeated on all the narrow paths, at last assaulting the main driveway in similar fashion. Although no one had acknowledged our arrival, our attention was periodically attracted by surreptitious twitchings of a curtain at a small window set in the front door.

'The old *mush* is *dikkin*' us,' said Creamy, puffing on yet another roll-up of minute diameter.

'He'll be like his grandmother when it comes to paying –
I know it,' I replied, depression beginning to settle on me.

At length, spattered with mud and rain-diluted bitumen,
our clothes clinging soggily to our persons, saturated hair flat-
tened on our skulls, we knocked on the front door – awaiting
developments in some trepidation.

'*Haugh!* Finished, have you?' observed the denizen, a
tubby man of perhaps sixty years of age. He had artificially
black hair slicked down on the top of his head, the sides and
back being almost shaven. He wore slightly tinted horn-
rimmed spectacles; his features were white and puffy, while
his accent bore a trace of the West Midlands and was not
pleasing to the ear.

'Well, how about all that stuff that's washed out on to the
flower-beds?' he asked, pointing to the black rivulets trick-
ling through the roses.

I could see that matters could slide downhill from here on
and that reassurances were called for, even if of an unlikely
nature.

'No, no, don't worry about that,' I coaxed. 'All that is only
the surplus liquid of various additives which are in the tar
these days: in fact it is *good* because it has now been removed
so only the pure bitumen is left. A few days and it will solid-
ify nicely.'

In order to sugar the pill a little more I decided that the
ultimate gesture, the price reduction, might sweeten the

process. I had taken the job for forty-five pounds (which in those days was quite a nice day's work!) so I offered to reduce it to forty pounds 'for cash'. As almost alway,s the ploy worked: human greed will usually triumph, and he paid me like the proverbial lamb.

I had agreed to pay Creamy fifty bob, which was about the usual rate for such assistants at the time. However, in a moment of wild generosity, and in view of the fact that we had actually completed two contracts, I gave him five pounds – with which he was more than delighted.

By three o'clock I had dropped him off at the wagons, the rain had begun to abate slightly, and I was soon back at our trailer, changed into dry clothes, and examining with much appreciation the money I had earned that day.

I gradually became closer friends with Young Nelson, both of us being the same age and with much in common, and we decided to go into partnership for an unspecified period of time. Seeking greater rewards than were generally offered by the humbler 'tar and chippings', Young Nelson preferred to restrict himself almost entirely to the laying of tarmacadam in which the greater profits lay. This seemed to be to my advantage as I was sure that there was much to be learned – which did indeed prove to be the case. Young Nelson, I soon began to realise, was the kind of traveller (not unduly rare!) for whom money was his God: a form of religion to which his wife and most of his family were faithful adherents! This, of course, made life straightforward and uncomplicated in the main: the ambition being to have a Good Day – Every Day.

At times, as experience proved, this could become almost unbearably stressful. Frequently we would 'call' all day, both in uniform suburbia and in pleasant country villages, at new houses and at old, without finding even the hint of a possible contract, returning to the trailers exhausted and ill-tempered, yet forcing ourselves to venture out again in the light summer evenings in hopes of success. Desperation was our master. But eventually, after a complete refusal to submit to circumstance, it was by no means unheard of for a break in our ill-luck to come just as twilight was setting in. Each time it happened, the weariness and depression would slip from our shoulders and we would head homewards well pleased.

Young Nelson, who was lithe, energetic and muscular, could do the work of three men without apparent effort when so called upon, as I discovered – hard-driven as he was in his pursuit of gold.

For his business he was well-equipped, owning a brand-new Bedford J-type lorry – the model having just come on the market – and a vibrating roller, mechanically operated. His great ambition was to acquire a Barber-Greene tarmacadam-layer as used on council highways and the like. He was, I am pleased to say, able to achieve that ambition within but a few years. Even when young it was obvious that, within his own sphere of life, success would be his.

All that summer we worked together, the good times vastly outweighing the bad, in those golden days before inflation and spiralling prices made a mockery of old-time monetary values. Indeed, from the early sixties until at least the mid-eighties the lives of travellers (and perhaps *gaujes* too?) was the easiest it had ever been: brand-new, ever-more flashy trailers, new lorries and vans, even *holidays* were commonplace rather than exceptions. The 'raggle-taggle' had virtually disappeared. Those indeed were the days!

Eventually, however, I began to realise that the eternal strain of trying to obtain quite large sums of money from unwilling householders, combined with the semi-hyperactivity of Young Nelson, became removed from much in the way of pleasure. Matters finally decided me to break our partnership when a retired colonel, whose half-mile driveway we had completed in a specialised tarmac, at great expense to ourselves, 'whipped' (that is to say, refused to pay) when confronted with the cost. His, to us rather lame, excuse was that we had 'failed to follow the course of nature in regards to drainage'. This mystified us both; but in the last resort, after mutual threats of litigation, he eventually paid us a cheque which barely covered our expenses. To say that we were sick as pigs over this was to state it mildly.

The partnership was dissolved without any ill-will, as such partnerships usually are, and I left it with no small horde of savings – indeed more money than I had ever had in my life up until then. There was indeed enough for us to ponder whether to buy a new trailer or a new lorry: for the first time in our lives.

It was autumn as we slipped away, down the flat Sussex coast roads, heading for a piece of wasteland near Brighton, where we had learned that a traveller-friend of mine, known as Northwegion Bob, was stopping.

Having abandoned the lucrative but tension-filled world of Young Nelson's lifestyle, I had decided to engage in the pre-packed compost trade, it being the right time of year: an occupation in which the 'little apples taste sweet' principles of business would apply.

Travelling along the coast in the Brighton direction we spotted a long, deep lay-by on the right-hand side of the highway, just outside Lancing, whereon there were ten or twelve trailers scattered along its length in several groups. At one end were two Eccles Traveller trailers and a new Vickers Morecambe. Beside each stood a new, chromed-up Bedford 30cwt lorry, both painted in contrasting colours in travellers' style; while large step-towbars projected from the rears, upon which to hitch the heavy trailers.

'Prices or Lees,' I said to Beshlie, for their turnouts were always recognisable.

There was a space beside the Vickers trailer so I decided to pull in there to see if I knew that particular branch of either of the families. As we drew along the edge of the lay-by, past the trailers from whose windows children's faces peered, and from underneath which a variety of tethered dogs barked their disapproval, we gradually came alongside the first of the Eccles. Three men emerged, black-haired and lined-faced, and I realised that the women would still be out calling with lace, or *dukkering*, as in those days they were the sole breadwinners – the men preferred to remain at home all day 'guarding the place'.

A stream of dogs rushed out from beneath the second Eccles, mostly Jack Russell terriers and lurchers, barking and growling. Shouts from the men, however, sent them slinking back out of sight.

'Hi, *pal* – how is you? God kill us, I ain't seen you since two Doncasters ago.' The first man greeted me warmly and the other two smiled. They were all dark, almost black of complexion, and each wore a suit tailored in Romani style.

They were, to my relief, members of the Lee family with whom I was on the best of terms, having stopped with them in various parts of the country some years previously.

The old Romani saying 'Hills and valleys never meet – but old friends always do' came to mind.

Like the Prices, to whom some were related, the Lees had

originated to a large degree in Wales, though they are now to be found all over the country. These particular Welsh Lees were, although extraordinarily old-fashioned in themselves, owing to the skill of the womenfolk at the doors able to equip themselves with the best and newest of motors and trailers, with scarce any of their number lagging behind in such possessions. Truly a case of keeping up with the Lees, rather than the Joneses! They cooked on outside fires and travelled with vast numbers of dogs, and often ponies, goats and chickens, which they penned in on the backs of their lorries while on the move.

On the lay-by were Nightingale Lee, two of his grown-up sons, Prince and Blackie, and his son-in-law, also a Lee, called Fearless.

After a few pleasantries, and the assurance by Fearless that Northwegion Bob had moved, having been evicted, and gone to Suffolk, we allowed ourselves to be encouraged to stay beside them.

After comparing the two Eccles with the Vickers we could see that the latter was superior. The owners of the two Eccles had themselves *chopped* theirs with a 'good man, kid' further along the coast and were awaiting collection of their new Vickerses within days.

The Vickers, or Morecambe as it was sometimes called by travellers, was to sweep the board in popularity during the sixties and seventies among travellers of all classes.

Manufactured to order, they could range from plain to those whose rococo and flashy design, both inside and out, could satisfy the most ostentatious among us: wonderful coachbuilt monsters, like luxury land-liners. They were unrivalled by any firm other than the Westmorland Star, made in Penrith, which somehow managed to combine the flashiness of the most ornate Vickers with a curiously refined tastefulness. Rising inflation in the early 1980s eventually caused both firms to cease production: indeed the last Westmorland Stars to be made had been offered at something in the region of £25,000! They are now the stuff of legend, like many of the no longer existing motor-car manufacturers.

We spent several days with the Lees, during which I laboured away like a thing possessed: compost supplies were plentiful from a local mushroom farm and sales in the opulent suburbs of Brighton and Hove were rewarding.

The women of the Lees, all strikingly Romani-looking and still addicted to long skirts and colourful Gypsy-style apparel, would all go off together in the morning like a little flock of gaudily plumaged birds, often (after a good day one surmised) returning by taxi-cab in the early afternoon, laden with *monged* clothes and foodstuffs; the little children seemed to have new clothes every day, as brightly coloured as they could find.

We also managed to drive to the 'good man' along the

coast and discovered that he had ordered an extra Vickers at the time of obtaining the two for the Lees. It proved to be a nineteen-foot model, rather plain on the outside – this was before the travellers demanded an emblazonment of stainless-steel ornamentations eventually to become so extreme that very little of the entire surface was not so encrusted, sometimes on the front and back ends of the roof as well! This Vickers, nonetheless, was of the usual graceful shape, and internally, in the fashion for decades to come, was entirely surfaced in off-white marble-grained formica with wide stainless-steel strips at intervals down the walls and across the ceiling – from which two chandelier-style lights were affixed. It possessed cut-glass display cabinets for china and ornaments and full-length cut-glass mirrors on each wardrobe door, glass-fronted lockers all round the roof. All the furniture fronts were bowed and little fiddle-rails bordered all the flat surfaces in the manner of custom-built yachts. A large Parkway solid-fuel stove stood on one side, and the dealer offered a fully fitted thick cinema-foyer-style carpet of a bold and swirling design, which he knew would be appreciated by travellers.

Beshlie and I were so tempted that we had a deal there and then. Eleven hundred pounds to *chop*. It seemed such a great sum then.

Just before collecting the Vickers, I managed to find a temporary private stopping-place near to the Sussex town of

Haywards Heath, in a small field where we remained for two weeks, Beshlie spending the time in making the Vickers less impersonal, more homely.

It was almost the end of the year when we returned to Hampshire and, following the main road across the New Forest near Stoney Cross, we sighted a little group of motors and trailers which we both recognised.

'Old Nelson and his boys,' I cried to Beshlie, swinging off the main road without hesitation towards them.

It was about three o'clock, a grey wintry afternoon, the light already fading. The lorries and cars were all parked around the trailers so we knew that they were at home. Indeed as we neared the Berkeley, Old Nelson appeared at one door, his wife at the other, the Berkeleys having the unusual benefit of two doors.

Munching a piece of white bread held in one hand and a slab of bacon in the other, Old Nelson regarded us quizzically; his small eyes, well crossed, twinkled engagingly.

'Dordi! I can see who's been having it off! Nice brand fine new trailer – there ain't no flies on you, my old cousin!' He laughed, his voice rapid and highly pitched, as though he was shouting in the face of ferocious elements.

'See who this is, my gal?' he enquired of Leander, who smiled as though to herself, her features seemingly cut in leather, dark and lined beyond her years.

'He's a Nelson!' she remarked of her husband, rolling her eyes heavenwards. One felt she regarded him as eccentric, but still faintly lovable.

She looked back at us, slightly mournfully, and then peered at the sky.

'Comes in dimsie-dark at this time o' year, don't it? I can't bear it.'

'How's Nelson treating you?' I grinned at her, for despite their constant superficial battles they were very fond of each other in their way.

'I hit him over the head wi'a tin of plums yesterday,' she told me. 'That quietened him down for a half-hour.'

'A half-hour,' I replied.

'A half-hour, that's all!' she answered. 'Since he've had his new *mumblers* he chats all the time, on my life he do – just like a *dinilo*!'

'Well, this won't buy the baby a new frock,' I said to Old Nelson.

'No, you wants to get your bits of things set up afore it gets dark, if you're stopping along of us – which I hopes you are,' he replied, by then gnawing on what appeared to be a piece of smoked salmon.

And so, pulling to one side of them while the boys waved from the interior of their tourer, we started to install ourselves for the night. In those days, very few travellers owned portable generators so they had to rely on Calor Gas, paraffin lanterns, or candles for lighting. Most trailers were fitted with solid-fuel stoves for heating.

Young Nelson was the first member of his family to furnish himself with a generator, which though remarkably noisy, lacked much power and could only provide enough current for one trailer. It did allow him to run electric lights and a little black and white television set which was the envy of his brothers. (Being a little behind the times ourselves, it was to be 1963 before we became the proud owners of a twelve-inch screen black and white portable television, which ran successfully from the twelve-volt battery of our lorry, and from which we derived untold pleasure.)

After Beshlie and I had eaten a fairly substantial stew of pheasant and vegetables, it had become quite dark. I walked round to Old Nelson's trailer, and was beckoned in when they heard me outside. Not to have visited them would have been thought stand-offish.

It was Friday evening, and it transpired that Old Nelson was intending to spend Saturday in trying to find a privately owned stopping-place somewhere in the Romsey or Southampton area, with the possibility of remaining there until after Christmas. It was very necessary to find such a place as during the festive period Nelson and the boys always occupied themselves with Christmas trees, holly and wreath-making on quite a large scale – difficult to achieve from a piece of wasteland with the ever-present threat of eviction looming over them. Especially so for Leander and the younger boys and their wreath-making operation, which was performed with inherited skill and amazing rapidity. It is, of course, all part of the daunting challenges with which travellers are unendingly faced, and it is a great credit to their resilience and stamina that they survive.

Young Nelson, however, had taken it into his head to do 'no Christmassing' that year and was intent on finding a place to stop on his own – a course of action which rather aggrieved his parents who took it as a direct slur against themselves. They chose, however, on the surface, to blame their daughter-in-law for such unorthodox behaviour.

'She ain't got no proper traveller's ways,' grumbled Leander. 'She's half a *gauji* so what can you expect?'

As it was a private family matter I did not pursue the subject with them. Privately, however, I disagreed with them. Young Nelson's wife, despite her breeding, had always seemed intensely proud of being a Romani, with little or no *gauji* ways that I could detect.

I, too, though invited by Old Nelson to accompany them, was not anxious to end up over Christmas in some closed-in yard on the outskirts of Romsey or Southampton, neither of which town I had found to be very lucky for me. So I decided that, like Young Nelson, I would do my best to find someone in the Ringwood area whom I could persuade to allow us to stop just over the next two or three weeks.

The next morning I set off early, bypassing Ringwood in the direction of Fordingbridge, keeping to the back roads across the Forest. I was looking out for anywhere with a reasonably wide gateway through which I could negotiate the trailer without the risk of taking a side out against a gatepost. Eventually, after but a few possibilities presenting themselves, I found myself on a little byroad, though not too narrow, some three miles from Fordingbridge. I espied a bungalow of the smallholding variety, with a good-sized empty paddock to one side of it, bordered by a thick strip of woodland. There was an enticing double gate on the far side, away from the bungalow, against the wood.

Without too much optimism, I knocked on the door of the homestead, and it was opened by a rough and ready man, red-faced, attired in a worn cap, torn navy blue waistcoat, matching trousers, and a striped collar-less shirt of flannel. His wellington boots were turned down.

He did not look very promising and emitted only a low grunt when he saw me. Accepting this as being his own private form of vocal economy, perhaps, I told him my plight – and offered him rent for two weeks in advance. In retrospect this offer almost certainly swung his decision, even though it was only ten shillings a week. He nodded favourably and, upon receiving the small rental, his hitherto inexpressive countenance came about as close to a smile as could be hoped for.

Unbeknown to me, and in an example of the strange coincidences which not infrequently occur within the traveller's life, Young Nelson had himself, but minutes before, been fortunate enough to secure a pull-in for his family no more than a hundred yards up the same road as ourselves, behind the battery-houses of a nearby chicken farmer. Out of sight of the road, if a little smelly due to the constant aroma from the broiler-house's occupants, it was *somewhere*.

Returning to our respective trailers, we were both pleased and surprised at the quirk of chance which had caused us to be such close future neighbours. Although not actually stopping together, we would still be 'company' and of mutual aid in the event of need.

It was soon after noon on Saturday and it was decided that we would all go out to the nearest town and obtain provisions, to be ready for an early departure on Sunday morning.

It was no great journey for Young Nelson and myself, nor Old Nelson either. He had, as we had thought probable, found a stopping-place in an old disused yard near Southampton, which was owned by one of his many relatives in the area, who had used it for storing tyres. It was convenient for him, and I knew the place by sight, but not for us; to be confined within its tall-fenced enclosure, with no view of any sort, was too penned-up; it would have offered us little benefit and caused too much claustrophobia.

(In later years, of course, with the advent of sites either council or even privately owned it became necessary to adapt one's psyche to accept both fences and walls surrounding the trailers on such places: little framed plots and attempts by officialdom at controlled and soulless orderliness – unnatural though such conditions were, to myself and many others, a far cry from 'the Wind on the Heath'.)

Just before setting off for the shopping, two of Nelson's sons remaining as lookouts, we were standing about in idle conversation, when our attention was attracted by warning barks from Barney and their ageing alsatian. To our astonishment, upon looking towards the main road we beheld two travellers' trailers heading in our direction.

'Is that me Uncle Caleb?' suggested one of the younger boys. *'Kekker, dinilo!* He ain't got no trailer like either of them two,' replied Old Nelson in disgust.

The trailers, each pulled by a motor van, were both of a design which was unfamiliar to us; they were new and very pleasing to the eye. Their vans were older, though tidy. The first was a Morris one-ton LD – interestingly enough, this was the last mass-produced commercial vehicle to be made with the body panels affixed to an ash-wood frame. I owned one myself for a few months and, though lacking comfort or grace, with a noisy engine roaring away within the cab, it was of great roominess and mechanical reliability. The Morris LD was attached to a magnificently ornate trailer, of swirling shape and considerable length. Upon the side the legend *Lonsdale Eagle* was inscribed: a make that was unknown to us then. The cab of the van appeared to be packed with the heads of small and middle-sized boys, some carroty-haired, others black as ravens. Amid them sat a small thin woman, a hint of Romani in her face, which was taut with strain and agitation – a not uncommon condition when one is on the road with no specific stopping-place in mind.

The second turnout, slightly smaller overall than the first, consisted of a 15cwt Austin 'sausage van' (as was their travellers' nickname), red-painted and tinged with rust. The trailer was a Vickers Lunedale, a name so close to Lonsdale that confusion often arose. I was very taken with it, in many ways preferring it to our own. I was especially attracted by its patterned leaded-windows with coloured glass inserts – which died out with that particular model, being largely regarded as too old-fashioned. I myself, however, would have liked them on our own new Vickers, had they still been available.

Each had a stainless-steel chimney projecting from the off-side of the roof. Like ourselves, the majority of travellers of that era would not countenance a trailer without a coal-and-wood-burning stove. 'A *yog* gives a nice dry heat – not like that old gas,' travellers would rightly assert. Alas, one can only sadly report that by the end of the 1980s just one firm remained who had resisted the lure of bottled gas, which was affected to be preferred on the grounds of 'cleanness'.

The trailers swung round beside us on the hard surface of what had once been a wartime airfield – upon which nobody was allowed to encamp between dusk and dawn, such was the peculiar-seeming New Forest rule. We had been remarkably fortunate ourselves to 'catch' a night or two there unmolested by authority in one form or another.

The two men jumped down from their driving-seats. The owner of the first turnout was heavily built, swarthy and surprisingly bespectacled; his features were pitted and heavy, as was his nose. He looked about fifty years of age. His companion, who proved to be his brother-in-law, was younger, fair-haired with a bright red complexion and cornflower blue eyes of an unusual brightness.

'We seen the trailers from the road, we kenned it was travellers,' announced the older man. 'We've no been down in this country before so we dinna have any idea where to *atch*. Can anyone stop here?'

His accent was strongly Scottish and pleasantly soft in tone.

'You won't get much time here, brother – no harm but that's how it is,' replied Old Nelson, adding quickly, 'We're all goin' away ourselves tomorrow – we just bin out an' found a bit of an old *tan* to pull in. It's worse than goin' out to get a livin' to try an' find a place to stop!'

'Would you mind if we get a night here along with you?' asked the fair man, his accent even more agreeable than that of his brother-in-law.

''Course not, my old cousin – we'm all the same breed, ain't we?' beamed Old Nelson amiably, his eyes in a state of chaos.

The new arrivals parked a reasonable distance away from us and finally all emerged from their respective vans, which they left hitched on to their trailers, merely lowering the rear legs in order to steady them.

The younger man seemed to only have one child, a small ringletted girl of about three years old. His wife was pale and in no way Romani-looking. (Indeed it is not at all uncommon in Scotland to find travellers who seem to have little or no Romani blood at all yet are still, in some almost indefinable way, quite separate from the rest of the population.)

'Here, my gal!' Old Nelson exclaimed to Leander, having kept his attention on the older arrival's van. 'I've *dikked* seven boys come outa that motor, like me dead father! They must've got seven sons, like us!'

His delight knew no bounds when, having hurried over to determine whether or not he was correct, he returned in a few minutes looking self-satisfied and overjoyed to find that he was right.

'My blessed Lord!' he shouted. 'The luckiest thing in the

world it is, for two sets of seven sons to stop on the same ground!'

It proved to be an exceptionally agreeable meeting, all of us seeming to become the best of friends in so short a time: it was a great feeling of kinship which, for me, was to last several decades ahead, even up in Scotland, as I will later relate.

I took to them so much that I offered to escort them to the owner of a small caravan-park near Bournemouth who would often allow a few travellers into his park during the off-season winter months, providing that they were respectable and well-recommended. Thus, quite early on the Sunday morning, the two Scotsmen and I drove over to see the place and, the owner taking my word as to their character, for we had ourselves stopped there a year before, it was agreed that they would pull in later that day.

They were exceedingly fulsome in their thanks and, I later learned, proved admirable tenants for a couple of months.

I never encountered the younger man, whose name was Fraser, again, though I heard that he settled down near Falkirk.

However, my astonishment may well be imagined when, some ten or twelve years later, we were stopping near Edinburgh for the week of Musselburgh Fair which, alas, is now closed down, finished by authoritarianism, but was then the largest travellers' fair north of the border. It was held annually in August and was attended by travellers from all over Scotland and a handful from England too. That year it was during a heat wave and tempers were on edge in the crowded atmosphere, not helped by the presence of a stifling red dust which settled on humans, animals, trailers and vehicles alike. It was therefore no great surprise when, one afternoon, a fight broke out, with seemingly a dozen or more young men involved.

Five or six were actively assaulting each other with their fists, dust flying even more thickly around them, when suddenly one of them, catching sight of me, flung his arms in the air and, ignoring his surprised opponent, emitted a cry of greeting! The fighting ceased altogether and I was surrounded by the youths and young men, all stripped to the waist, some bleeding profusely from facial wounds.

'Aye, look, Nathan! See who's here!' shouted one to another.

'Aye! Bobby! Jimmy! Do you ken this man?'

They all scrutinised me carefully, their faces glowing with pleasure.

Suddenly my brain began to function and I realised that most of the young men were the very same seven brothers, at the time so small or half-grown at most, whom we had met long before in the New Forest.

Once again: 'Hills and valleys never meet – old friends always do.'

The eldest son told me that, sadly, his father had been dead for three years; but his wife, Nathan's mother, was alive and well, and was in fact present in her trailer at the fair.

'Aye, me faither thought the worlds of you taking the time to be away with us down to Bournemouth to get us fixed up with a wee place to stop,' he reminisced. 'He was always asking for you ... I can tell you this, brother, you're always welcome in Scotland – just mention our name if you meet a barm-stick!'

We continued talking for some minutes when, without warning, they all resumed fighting, the brothers eventually routing their opponents triumphantly – one of whom was so terrified that he dived through an open trailer window, scattering the indignant occupants inside, and emerged from another window on the opposite side before streaking away like a greyhound dog.

I was soon to discover that the seven brothers were feared and respected throughout Scotland: few, if any, bested them in their feuds.

That welcome at Musselburgh was a rare reward, and perhaps a just one, for a kindly action.

By half past nine that Saturday evening we were all abed, looking forward to going away on Sunday morning.

The next day dawned bitterly cold, with a biting wind

sweeping across the desolate area of scrub which made up that part of the Forest. By half past ten we had all, the Scotsmen included, packed down (or packed up, as some might say!) and were ready to go. We were making three roads of it: Young Nelson and ourselves taking the short-cut on narrow roads across country; Old Nelson was taking the Southampton road; while the Scotsmen were heading in the opposite direction towards Bournemouth. We had found the company of the Scots people so agreeable that we felt quite sorrowful on saying our farewells.

Little did any of us dream we were speeding towards the worst winter in living memory. Rather were we all filled with self-satisfaction at our achievement in finding various places to stay for Christmas. Upon reaching our goal Beshlie and I negotiated the double gateway into the pasture without hazard, apart from a little wheel-slip in the mud on the incline from the road to the gate itself. (Experience taught me in later years that it is folly to attempt the pulling of a large trailer-caravan by a lorry through a gateway of less than ten feet wide; the neuroses and anxieties caused by attempting a narrower access are too distressing to try more than once!)

Once we found ourselves actually in the field we drew in against the fir-tree forest which bordered it, and although the outlook was rather restricted, it nonetheless gave us a certain sense of security, combined with the knowledge that even the council could not demand our withdrawal before the 'twenty-eight days in any one year' had elapsed. So much for freedom – for tenant or landowner alike!

The next morning I decided, despite both the climatic gloom and the proximity of Christmas as well, to venture out with a load of chippings, intending to strike at an area of reasonably opulent suburbia which lay between Bournemouth and the little town of Poole in Dorset.

In truth it was a lucky day. I called at only two houses before, at the third, taking a small but very rewarding task of re-surfacing two footpaths of a stucco seaside-looking dwelling which appeared to be a good example of some of the architectural follies of the 1930s. The owner, a graceful lady of fading beauty, chain-smoking and fashionably dressed and coiffed, was rendered almost speechless with delight by the result of my labours and paid me happily in cash.

It was by then only ten o'clock so I thought it would please me to seek out some company, and possibly enjoy an hour or so's conversation.

At that time, which was before the commencement of the building of council sites for Gypsies, travellers were to be found in visible numbers on roadsides, pieces of wasteland, future house-building sites and old commons throughout the country, their presence periodically causing a complete breakdown in tolerance in the minds of the local *gaujes* whose 'Ratepayers Unite' cry would regularly seep into the pages of their newspapers, demanding the removal of such 'undesirables'. Their most frequent complaint was that 'these are not *real* Gypsies', rather were they described as 'unhoused slum-dwellers', human rubbish. All of which was completely untrue and heavily tinged with both racism and snobbery. It was a bad state of mind, even affecting some of the county councillors, whose outpourings would not, I am sure, be allowed today.

As an example of the above, there was a large area of so-called commonland, much of which was in fact part of a vast estate, lying on barren and unenticing land near to Poole which was a favourite haunt of old-fashioned travellers, many still with horses and wagons, others just beginning to change over to motors and trailers – often giving up good horses and colourful wagons for ancient trailers, many small and damp, with a variety of knocked-about trucks or vans to pull them. I was well-acquainted with most of the people thereon, some of whom rarely left its insalubrious confines, and I usually visited them when I passed through the locality. There was always somebody stopping there, either beside the road or in little gatherings scattered almost as far as the eye could see across the heathland. That year it seemed that more than ever before had congregated there, from all over the south and west. It was even rumoured that some 'foreign travellers' were there.

It was rather early in the day for visiting, and most of the people were out calling. So after a short time talking outside his bender tent to an old man called Righteous, who, nearing eighty-two, was in a poor state, I bade him farewell.

Wearing a black hat, old black suit, and black and white spotted scarf knotted crosswise, his eyes running due to the smoke from a small stick-fire smouldering on the ground, he was one of the almost extinct breed of Romanies. One of twenty-one brothers and sisters, his relatives were spread widely throughout Dorset, Wiltshire, Gloucestershire and Somerset.

His memories were fascinating indeed. He remembered the McEvoy brothers, Patrick and Christopher, whose charming book *The Gorse and the Briar*, published in the late 1930s, gave such an accurate and personal account of the travellers' life during that period in Wiltshire.

I left him sadly, seeing his days were numbered. In fact he perished within weeks of my seeing him.

I drove Beshlie and myself over to Poole on Christmas Eve, where we spent an extraordinarily lively evening at a small public house, situated in a gloomy back street, which was much frequented by the travellers from the common, to the exclusion of everyone else. The landlord was a vast curly-haired Irishman, in his fifties, of at least six feet six inches in height and with the build of an ox; he combined his own authority with that of his bejewelled little wife, known charitably as Diamond Lil. There was the minimum chance of any fracas becoming out of hand – any potentially troublesome customer was physically carried outside and ejected on to the pavement.

Little Eli was there in the crowd, and gave a show of step-dancing for our entertainment, his small but heavy boots clattering out the most intricate of tap-dances on a little square of wood which was kept especially for the use of such performers.

Order was called repeatedly and a young girl with a sweet and clear Romani voice gave a fine rendering of 'The Black-bird', while several older women sang long and varied ballads that they had learned in childhood.

A young man, with curly black hair and an almost Indian look, gave us a version of Cliff Richard's 'Travelling Light' that was so close to the original as to ensure his popularity with any young unattached girls present, of whom there seemed to be plenty.

When we all left at what is sensibly referred to as 'turning-out time', somewhat the worse for wear, it was generally agreed that we would all meet there again on Boxing Day evening.

That, in fact, was not to be. By midday on Boxing Day heavy snow had commenced to fall unceasingly, quickly pitching, and gaining rapidly in depth as the day wore on.

Little did we know it then, but the snow was to continue falling for the next few days – to remain, deep and unyielding, right through until the middle of March. Nobody, no matter what their age, could recollect seeing its like.

In the field where we were stopping, huge drifts accumulated, up against the side of the trailer and almost submerging the lorry, while the temperature remained well below freezing. The air and atmosphere was zingy and unreal.

Man and beast suffered equally. Taking a walk to the edge of the Forest with Beshlie, we noticed a lone Forest pony, some twelve hands high, standing ominously still by a clump of holly bush. Closer inspection revealed, to our dismay, that it was frozen solid where it stood – stiff and dead on its feet!

In the afternoon, I walked down the road to the trailer of Young Nelson and found both he and Phoebe as worried as I was at the bleak prospect of earning sufficient money even for our living expenses under such conditions. Privately we both knew we had some savings – but to dip into them would have been an admission of failure in the face of the elements.

Unlike George Borrow, safe in Mumper's Dingle, we neither of us had the benefit of scholarship with which we could philosophically while away the hours!

'I rang up me cousin Dorfy this morning,' said Young

Nelson, 'and he's told me that all the travellers is going out with logs – an' there's a man over Firwood who's selling 'em for the right money. I'm going over meself in half an hour – follow me if you like. 'Viding we can get the old motors started!'

As his lorry was almost new I felt sure that he would have no fears there. Mine, on the other hand, was eight years old and had had a hard life; time would tell.

I told Beshlie of my plans, and we proceeded to virtually unbury the lorry which was necessary before I was even able to insert the starting-handle and give it a few turns. I then climbed into the cab and, with careless optimism, pulled on the self-starter. Little or nothing was the result, but on the second try, with only the briefest of hesitation, the engine fired and, after some mighty revs, it gradually simmered down to a steady chug-chug. A few minutes later Nelson stopped outside the gate grinning – and, I knew, surprised – to find my old lorry's engine running.

'Good old motor,' he grudgingly admitted.

So we were off, through a strange white world, snow drifts on all sides, hedgerows all but obliterated. Had it not been for us being able to follow in the tracks of an early-morning tractor as far as the main road, it is doubtful whether we would have been able to make out the actual road itself, and would almost certainly have landed up in one or other of the ditches on either side of it. Youth and need drove us into actions which the more mature might have wisely baulked at.

Arriving at and joining the Salisbury–Ringwood road, we found the conditions to be a little less harrowing, though the road-surface was of a slipperiness which would not have disgraced an ice-skating rink, the snow having been compacted by the wheels of heavy goods vehicles still doggedly pursuing their routes. After three miles we turned off on to a minor road to end up, a mile or so on, within the precincts of an enormous asbestos-sided barn. Catching a glimpse of the interior, we could see it was a hive of activity. Despite the fact that it was afternoon and the temperature well below zero, there stood outside the building, waiting for admission, seven or eight unmistakeably traveller commercial vehicles, ranging from 10cwt trucks and vans up to the always-favoured 30cwt lorries, mainly Bedfords. Most were hand-painted, rather shabby, and of some age. Their owners were standing about talking and smoking, several raising their hands to Nelson and myself as they recognised us. In front of them, inside the barn, were two other lorries and a van, each situated beside one of the three antiquated band-saws which were all operating at full speed, and were attended by a collection of roughly clad, undernourished-looking men, all of whom, without exception, had small cigarettes in their mouths.

The screaming sound emanating from the elderly band-saws was truly excruciating, but it was staunchly ignored by the gallant operators with bovine stoicism.

The logs supplied were almost all round when loaded on each vehicle – to be taken home and split up with an axe, thus converting them into three or even four logs before being presented, bagged-up, at the doors.

Experience over the next months was to prove to me, new as I was to its rigours, that this was back-breaking toil of the worst kind. As a small comfort, however, it did at least offer me some return, even if hard-earned. Some would assert, of course, that hard-earned money is the most satisfying: but the reverse has always been my experience!

Perhaps two vehicles in front of us, awaiting its turn to enter the barn, I noticed an old bull-nosed Bedford 30cwt lorry of almost vintage age – I judged it to be a 1938 model. It was in an especially frightening state of decay and bodily disrepair. Without the benefit of any remaining paintwork, with mismatched doors and mudguards, dented and eaten out with rust, its rotting wooden body tied up with baler twine – one could but marvel at its ability to move at all, let alone carry a load of logs. It transpired that it belonged to an ancient local man called Old Scamp, a half-traveller, who resided with his son Scamp Boy in a collapsing showman's living-wagon on a little piece of land which they owned.

'Motor still going all right, Uncle Scamp?' I enquired as he greeted me.

'*Dordi!*' said Nelson, under his breath.

'Like a bird, my son – she got a few years in her yet, like me, I hopes!'

He was of the breed of no longer to be found dealers who, though financially more than secure, chose to conduct their lives as though they possessed no worldly wealth of any kind, yet had the private satisfaction that they could probably buy out almost any of their prosperous-looking neighbours.

He grinned sheepishly at me from under the brim of his old felt hat: once again the glittering black eyes gave away the secret. In truth, like many another *posh rat* – half-Romani – he looked more like a Gypsy than most who boast of their pure Romani ancestry. The fact that he knew himself to be regarded as a man of means, despite his appearance, gave him a faint complacency. But despite that, he was one of the nicest men I have ever met.

Declining his son's request for some more baccy, he declared, 'You smokes too much, boy. It'll make you bad!'

'Huh! It ain't made you bad,' grumbled Scamp Boy, who sported a yellow knotted silk handkerchief worn crosswise. But he did not wish to upset his father, whom he secretly greatly revered, though he would never have the latter's charm.

'Here's a poverty old game to be on – I'm surprised at you,

with all your money,' observed Old Scamp, coughing bronchially and smiling lopsidedly at me, his black eyes twinkling.

'My God above!' I exclaimed. 'Talk about the pot calling the kettle black – you've got more money than I'd ever see in two lifetimes!'

'Take a oath!' laughed Scamp, evidently pleased.

'How's Old Nelson?' asked several bystanders of Young Nelson, whose new lorry impressed them greatly. Some were friends and some were enemies. Like all 'characters', Old Nelson had both – but to me he was always a friend.

It was growing dark before Nelson and I were able to get our lorries loaded, for two pounds each; and we both grumbled at that!

Although illuminated by the reflected whiteness of the snow-covered landscape, it was virtually dark when we reached home.

I reversed into the field gateway as far as possible, ending up on the patch whereon the lorry had spent the previous night and I offloaded the logs as near to the hedge as I could. I noticed with not too much surprise that Beshlie, always one to utilise resources, had built up a wall of snow in my absence, to a height of at least five feet, to act as a windbreak for me during my arduous task of splitting and bagging up the logs, prior to reloading them on the back of the lorry. It was virtually an igloo.

Thankful for the coal-fire in the trailer, we were soon devouring yet another of our winter stews before, armed with a long-handled axe and a small paraffin lantern, I went out to attack the logs. I had, by chance, found the stump of an old tree alongside the hedge and this proved to be admirable for use as a chopping-block. After working incessantly in the manner of a lumberjack born and somewhat exhausted, I found that I had filled thirty-five plastic ex-cattle-feed bags that I had *monged* from a farmer. The average bag contained about seven logs. (After a few days, however, I abandoned the use of bags and, like Nelson and most of the travellers, secured an old 'bushel-basket' which I filled out and carried into the houses, emptying the contents where directed.)

I will not bore the reader with a prolonged description of such an unrewarding occupation. Suffice to say that it kept us, and many other families too, from the brink of starvation during that arctic period of almost three months. Disconnected, as ever, from the Social Services, the ease of living even if humbly afforded by receipt of the dole was not to be ours.

Sorrowfully one has to admit that, within only a few years, many of the poorer classes of travellers, unwilling or unable to adjust to the switch-over from horses to mechanisation, allowed themselves to be manipulated by councils, do-gooders, sociologists and educationalists (all misguided to a man!)

to the extent that they found themselves being allocated council houses, being drawn into the system. Many continued to exist indefinitely on the small weekly income provided by the state. It did little to encourage their self-respect, completely unsettled them in their minds, and so they all too often fell into a half-world – not fully that of the traveller or the *gaujo*. It is interesting to note that quite large numbers have been known to leave their council-housing and return to the roads – a harder but more independent and proud way of life.

The weeks dragged by into months, the snow still set and unmelting, with long icicles hanging from every branch and even from the water-spouts at each corner of the trailer. Everything seemed brittle, and the walls of the trailer would crackle alarmingly in the stillness of the night. The two dogs scarce stirred from their kennels, which we stuffed with straw for their comfort.

Each day, thankful that my little lorry would start, I would trudge round my chosen pieces of suburbia. The hard work was only lightened faintly by the fact that, after a couple of weeks, I actually had something of a round!

But suddenly, after a seemingly interminable length of time, by then well into March, the weather broke and a rapid thaw set in. Within two days scarcely a vestige of snow remained: our relief was great.

Young Nelson, not a great wanderer by choice, despite being as true a Romani as could be found, showed no inclination to leave his hideaway stopping-place.

For me, however, it was time to go.

The Purley Way

I t was a beautiful heat-hazy May morning and I wished that we were not on a lay-by on the main Dorking road in Surrey. But there we were, three long trailer-caravans, two big tip-cab Ford lorries, and our twin-wheeled Transit van. It was the kind of morning when one would have preferred to be in a green field or on an old common, somewhere far from the roar of rush-hour traffic. I crawled from my bed, opened the top half of the trailer door and inhaled some health-giving fumes!

There was a slight stirring in the other trailers and soon Concorde emerged, looking bemusedly about him to see if any of the rest of us were about. In fact it would have been rather futile if his brother Alfie, the owner of the other trailer and lorry, had been outside too as they were not on speaking terms, and had been in such a condition for three months or more. Despite travelling together they had maintained a stony silence toward each other, and each had vowed not to break it. Hence their sole means of communication was through their respective wives, children, or me. They were true Surrey travellers and rarely left the county's boundaries other than to make rare forays into Sussex.

Concorde was a fine figure of a man, tall and broad, and dark-skinned: his only visual defect was the possession of a nose of extraordinary size. It swooped down over his mouth in a long curve, beak-like and predatory. Once the large aircraft had been manufactured, and spotted in profile, it was only a matter of time before his nickname was pronounced and adopted.

His brother Alfie, a year or so his junior, was not burdened by the unfortunate nasal organ and was thus more pleasurable to look upon. Alas, however, he was the victim of a stammer of almost apoplectic proportions: any conversation was pre-empted by a vicious gulping and gargling, words eventually pouring forth cataclysmically at a speed often impregnable to the listener's ear.

Old Alfie, their father, described their shortcomings thus:

'When they was babies,' he would say, with a leer, 'I used to push 'em out in a pram together, one each end. An' when my Concorde wanted to sit up I'd catch hold of him by his nose an' pull him up! Then when my Alfie wanted to git up I'd catch hold of him by his little *cori*! That's why the one's got the big nose, an' the other stutters so bad!'

Suddenly a small pick-up truck, hand-painted and battered, plunged into the lay-by from the flow of traffic without signalling, causing several of the following car drivers to toot with indignation and glare in annoyance in our direction.

'Go and fuck your mothers!' shouted the occupant at the passing motorists, more in amusement than malice.

We were pleased to see that it was Bronco Brown; he was a small rotund fair-headed man, with incredibly pale blue eyes that seldom registered any expression, more was it as though they were forever consulting the infinite in cold indifference. A ferocious little fighting-man if the occasion demanded, he was also kind-hearted and generous to a fault to those who could claim his affection, of whom I was thankfully one.

'Where you stopping, Bronco?' asked Concorde.

'Right down in the town, on an' old building-ground, bruv,' replied Bronco, his eyes peering up and down the row of trailers appraisingly.

Our three trailers were almost identical, being Astral Lavengroes. At that time they were the favourite trailer in the category of the less expensive caravans which were specifically made for travellers and showmen. In order of merit it would probably be correct to say that, during the decade of the 1970s, they could be placed: Westmorland Stars, Vickers, Lonsdales, Jubilees and Astrals. Other makers tried to cater for the traveller market but few were really successful in that period. Later, of course, there came the Aaros, Portmasters, Buccaneers, Romas, Nuvardas and the German trailers – the latter being greatly in vogue today.

Concorde's Astral was but two months old, Alfie's under a year, and our own was fifteen months in age. Lined with formica and wood, with large coal-burning stoves, they provided a warm and comfortable home for many a travelling family.

'Which way are you going?' enquired Bronco, his cold stare everywhere and nowhere.

'Somewhere down towards Brighton way, Bronco,' I answered.

'I'll tell you a pretty place, bruv,' said Bronco, with much enthusiasm. 'Go on down to Purley an' turn left-handed towards Mitcham. There's a great big green common on the left an' it's packed with trailers – there's gotta be fifity, on my mother's life, an' plenty of room for more.'

'What sorta people's there, Bronco?' asked Concorde, looking worried. 'Only I've got my dear little gals, an' I don't want 'em round no dossers an' that.'

'Nah!' cried Bronco, looking suitably scandalised by

having his judgement questioned. 'There's all sensible people there, anyway certainly all down the left-hand side. Over on the right there's a few Irishmens, well, maybe twenty or thirty trailers, but they're all by theirselves – they ain't mixed-up with the others.'

'Iiiiirrrrrrissssshhhhmennnsss!' gulped Alfie in strangulated tones of alarm. He, like many of us, had experienced both good and bad at the hands of Irish travellers. The latter appear, on occasion, to have become possessed by the Devil when leaving their own shores; sometimes even stooping to steal from English travellers – or at least encouraging their children to do so. Happily this is not always the case, and indeed some Irish travellers greatly enhance the roads by the charm and poetry of their discourse. Bronco began to lose patience slightly and his eyes became colder still.

'Hark, bruvver,' he continued. 'I'm just telling you about the place – you don't have to go there. Anyhow, there's a heap of English travellers there, on their own, so you can stop with them – I 'spects we'll pull there tomorrow ourselves.'

'Who's there, Bronco?' enquired Concorde pacifyingly.

'Old Sam's there with his boys, an Do Shit an' Don't Shit, an' Chrome-Legs, an' Digger – I tell you there's dozens there, bruv. Anyways, this won't buy the baby a new frock! I shall have to get on ...'

'What're you doing, Bronc, a bit of painting?' asked

Concorde, his face split sideways in a long lopsided grimace under the shadow of his nose.

'There's a nose, bruvver!' remarked Bronco, eyeing the ponderous organ with feigned awe. He continued: 'Still doin' a bit of painting round the *kairs*, anything, this an' that! I'll drive over an' see you later ...'

And so saying, he let in the clutch of his old truck and sped out into the passing traffic with much tooting and gesticulating.

'He don't care, do he – he's a Bronco!' said Concorde. 'But he's the nicest fella you could ever meet if he takes to you. He'd cut the heart out of his body if he thought you needed it.'

Stunned by this picture of filial generosity, we each retired to our trailers for breakfast, having agreed to try the 'pretty place'.

We had not unhitched the trailers during our one night stop on the lay-by, nor unpacked any but the bare essentials, so it was not long before we were on our way, gliding like great land-liners, along the suburban route to Purley. Indeed, with no other mishap than one of Concorde's greyhounds leaping suicidally from the back of his lorry as we halted at traffic-lights, the journey was smooth and uneventful. Concorde's young son and daughter were able to catch the offending dog and fling him back aboard the lorry before the traffic-lights had changed to green for the second time!

And so it was that we eventually found ourselves proceeding along the large main highway towards Mitcham, and it was not long before we sighted the travellers' trailers scattered about on wasteland on our left. There were indeed many trailers there, of different age and quality, each group seeming to comprise trailers of a similar standard: gravitating together as if by some secret signal, it was the 'birds of a feather' syndrome in its finest hour.

Across to the right-hand side of the common, some five hundred yards or so away, were the Irish travellers. These, it transpired, were part of a large and admirable family-band who were then dealers in second-hand and antique furniture. They always moved about together, often forty or fifty trailers strong, wandering the length and breadth of England, Wales and Scotland. Their astuteness in business and their ability to acquire the latest traveller-style trailers, combined with new Volvo Estates and Transit vans, caused both wonderment and envy among the rest of us, many of whom were driving equipages of considerable age and dilapidation.

Concorde was in the lead, then Beshlie and myself, closely followed by Alfie and his wife Phoebe, with their three little children. Concorde, never a man to hesitate or explore dangers, swung directly in from the main road and headed towards a group of trailers of similar appearance to our own. Despite slight agitation on the part of Beshlie, who always preferred to scout ahead, it proved to be a reasonably sensible path to follow and we soon found ourselves within an acceptable stopping-distance of those alarmingly named twin brothers Do Shit and Don't Shit.

Their mother, Seni – to whom I had attached the prefix Ob! – never a woman to mince words, had once described to me in some detail the miraculously opposing workings of the brothers' alimentary canals during their infancy, which had resulted in their evocative nicknames, which were to remain with them for the rest of their lives.

The wives of Do Shit and Don't Shit stared out from their respective trailer doors on seeing our arrival, while various tow-headed little children stopped what they were doing to gaze at us. Three or four greyhounds and lurchers, all chained to dog-boxes, set up spasmodic barking.

'Hullo, Phoebe!' called Do Shit's wife to Alfie's wife, who was her first cousin. 'Here's a lovely day. We heard you was comin' this way – pretty place, innit?'

'It's all right,' agreed Phoebe, adding: 'I could do with a nice place to stop for a week or two. I'm sick of the movin' – they been drivin' us about like dogs, Anna Maria, an' me nerves is all in shreds.'

'Oh *dordi*!' exclaimed Alfie in a rare moment of perfect speech, his eyes rolling heavenwards behind Phoebe's back.

'Come, on, let's git the trailers off an' have a cup of tea,' urged Concorde.

'Let's do that,' I concurred.

We pulled round to form a three-sided square, with the trailer doors opening into it, and thus providing ourselves with our own private space from which all but close friends would feel excluded. Within a quarter of an hour or so, we were well towards feeling settled and were enjoying the freedom of being off the road, away from passing traffic, and surrounded by apparently congenial company.

'I shall have to try an' git me motor done today,' stated Concorde, glancing at his lorry. 'She's got no guts – she wouldn't pull a greasy man outa bed! She ain't bin no good since I lent her to me father.'

'Ccccoorrrrrr!' gurgled Alfie, winking at me.

Concorde ignored this and went on: 'When I went over to fetch her back I could tell she weren't no good the moment I drove her ... In fact, I said to him, "No disrespect, Dad, but you've fucked the motor right up!"'

'What did he say?' I asked.

'You know me dad,' replied Concorde. 'He just laughed – you wouldn't git no change out of him!'

'Well, I must go out and see if I can earn myself a shilling,' I declared.

'Hark here!' cried Concorde. 'You got more money than I've had hot dinners! Still you're right to go out an' try – it's better than sittin' at home all day, scratchin' your head!'

I was at that time, and indeed still am to this day, engaged in the hawking of compost and manure which, back then, I used to bag up myself. Riding schools have usually proved to be the best source of supplies, and as they have proliferated about the country in recent years material is not generally too difficult to obtain. In truth, I can boast proudly of having bagged up manure at such establishments from Land's End to Aberdeen. (Not a boast to which many would aspire, I instinctively feel!)

So, within an hour of arriving on the common, I was off it again and out in a search for supplies. I had plenty of empty bags with me, having been fortunate enough to obtain a large quantity which had been intended for pre-packed coal but which private enterprise had diverted to me. I headed towards Epsom and had only covered four or five miles when I saw a rather grand-looking equestrian school. And, eagle-eyed as ever, I detected an enormous mound of wood-chip bedding and manure beside some loose boxes in the yard. As it was a Saturday morning there were large numbers of well-washed children, mostly girls, milling about around the stables, some mounted and others grooming their ponies. My presence encouraged some little curiosity, but I was soon able to approach the person most likely to be the school's owner: this was a gentlewoman of uncertain age, whose garb suggested straitened circumstances but whose manner did not. However, after a few moments of questioning me about the motives for my visit, all was settled. In fact, she was anxious for the heap of manure to be reduced, if not entirely removed, and she asked no payment for it. This was, of course, an encouragement in itself for, apart from petrol, I could look forward to a day of complete profit.

After waiting for a few minutes for the diminutive equestrians to move into an adjoining paddock for schooling, I pulled up beside the midden and, snatching my fork from the van, I proceeded to bag up like a thing possessed! In those days it was my achievement to be able to bag up sixty in an hour, so driven was I by the spirit of financial advancement.

I recollect once, when we were stopping near Edinburgh, in the autumn, and I was, as ever, bagging up most vigorously in company with two Scottish travellers at a riding school hitherto unknown to us. I had filled perhaps a dozen bags when, plunging my fork at a venture into the steaming innards of the midden, I pierced a wasps' nest full amidships. Its demented inhabitants, outraged by this sudden intrusion of their privacy and fearing, doubtless, for the safety of their monarch, poured forth by the dozen. Their aggressive little bodies pitched with abandon upon the surprised persons of me and the two Scotsmen, stinging us unmercifully about our hands, arms, faces and necks. Worse still for one of the Scotsmen, Dodie McPhee, was that he had an unwarranted aperture near the seat of his trousers, into which two or three of the insects explored. He was therefore even further distressed than the rest of us, beating with abandon at his crotch. As one, we rushed to our motors, leaping into their cabs, and shouting in pain to one another, we hastened from the yard, leaving even the filled bags, such was our condition. We negotiated the narrow lane from the riding school with record speed and drew up on the first lay-by that we reached in order to compare our suffering. We were all severely stung and sadly out of temper.

'You daft barm-stick,' complained Dodie, 'could you not have seen the wopsies?'

'Now, now,' said his friend placatingly. 'It wasna his fault – och, indeed the poor man's stung as bad as any of us.'

'I wouldna say that,' retorted Dodie, 'he wasna stung in the privates like me.'

'Aye, well, if you hadna had the arse of your trousers hanging out neither would you have been, so I should say you're more the barm-stick, Dodie,' observed his friend.

I began to sense a sharp antagonism welling up between the two, and as one in a strange land – a foreign land to me then – I felt that my withdrawal could only be of benefit to me. I had no wish to become the lynch-pin of a quarrel. Later I discovered that the two were brothers and were but a quarter of a family of quarrelsome brothers who were, in their own way, a power among the travelling people of Scotland.

I managed to return to the trailer, where we were stopping in a field with two other English families. There I collapsed, ever-swelling and in increasing pain, to which I was forced to yield for two days. The company with whom we were stopping did not increase my optimism of an early recovery, constantly regaling me with stories of fatalities that they had witnessed or heard about which were caused by merely *one* sting, let alone dozens. It was with some relief, therefore, that, having been apparently snatched from the jaws of death, I found both swellings and irritation greatly diminished at the dawn of the third day and on the fourth I was back out calling.

In any event, that day near Epsom, I managed to beat my own record and had completed sixty-five bags within the hour, though I was somewhat dehydrated in the midday sun. It was a lucky day: my memory served me well and I recollected an avenue of secluded homes near Esher at which I had called a few years previously when we had been stopping on the Epsom Downs for Derby week. I had obtained considerable reward there, I remembered, so I decided to try the same area again. Having, fortunately, a memory of almost photographic quality concerning neighbourhoods, roads and individual houses at which I had been successful on previous missions, I was soon able to distinguish the correct route to my avenue. The mock-Georgian and Tudor miniature mansions, each standing in their own grounds, welcomed me as to the Promised Land. A short halt to get my bearings and my brain was fully engaged; it was one of those days about which even a hardened knocker will reminisce with fellow-spirits in tones of deepest nostalgia. At the very first house upon which I called, after the briefest persuasion, to an old gentleman of military appearance, I sold thirty bags. The remaining thirty-five I disposed of in two lots, both to houses upon which I had called before. '*Audocious!*' as an old Irish traveller of my acquaintance was wont to say upon any stroke of luck coming his way.

Much elated by this agreeable turn of events, I was soon headed for home, and felt myself impatient for the sight of the trailers and for the comradeship that I would find there. Happy the man who could say that, say I!

Beshlie was surprised to see me back so soon, and even more astonished and pleased to find that I had had what an elderly Devonshire traveller used to describe as 'a nice little day'.

It was still only early afternoon and few of the men had returned from their daily struggle for the proverbial crust of bread. The hours which travellers actually work are perhaps not extravagant; but the tension and stress which uncertainty and desperation cause are severe. *Trying* to gain a living by knocking on doors, with few things in one's favour and many against, is enough to make the average securely paid worker fall by the wayside, or at least into the arms of his union!

The sun shone down upon me and I sat on the trailer steps enjoying a cheese sandwich, while around me the children played their own games, not straying from their homes, their mothers ever watchful of them. Far across the common faint cries and shouts were dimly audible from the Irish travellers; and as I looked in their direction I saw that one of their Volvo Estates, its full-length chromed roof-rack shining in the sun's rays, was slowly driving towards me. As it grew nearer, I was able to discern that it contained two blond men, a red-headed woman in some disarray, and five or six freckled children of the sort generally associated with the advertisement of cornflakes.

'How are you then, kid?' asked the driver, his accent as strong as though he had only left Ireland the previous day. 'I see you just pulled on. Did yous come tru Bristol or Bath? Only we've lost me wife's brother an' his wife an' childer, an' he doesn't know dis country at all—'

'What motor and trailer has he got?' I interrupted.

'Ah sure, he has an old Eccles trailer—'

'Ah no, it's an old Morecambe trailer,' interrupted the second man.

'Oh Jesus! Sure enough,' agreed the first man. 'He has an

old Morecambe trailer an' an all-coloured lorry wit' a burnt-out front!'

'If you sees him, young man,' pleaded the woman, sticking her head out of the window, 'would you tell him to meet us next week where the baby had the stitches in?'

Assuring them that I would do so should I happen to encounter the lost family, I returned to my sandwich.

'Whatsever they want?' demanded Anna Maria from the trailer as the metallic-silver Volvo glided back across the common.

'They've lost some of the relatives, or something,' I replied.

'I can't a-bear them people – they've ruined the country for the likes of us,' she grumbled, her strong Surrey accent grating after the musical brogue of the Irish. 'Some of 'em's all right, but some of 'em would *chor* the boots off yer feet – an' then swear their lives away as they never done it!'

There was some truth in what she said, though it was rather ironical and sad to hear one kind of traveller so berating another – not a rarity, I fear.

I felt the inclination to doze in the sunshine but this was not to be, for I heard an oncoming vehicle and saw a large Bedford TK lorry speeding over the common from the main road. It was brown and cream, with the cab and body lined out, traveller-style, in a dying-out fashion. Buckle-belts encircling scrolled initials were painted in the centre of each door. I could soon detect the driver and his passenger, both small-faced, dark of complexion, with thick raven-black hair: it was Do Shit and Don't Shit, back from their day's excursion.

'Hello, my old *mushy*,' cried Do Shit, his eyes glittering.

'All right, bruv?' enquired Don't Shit, leaping down from the cab and drawing himself up to his full five feet six inches.

'Good day?' I asked politely.

'Oh, mate, don't ask!' moaned Do Shit, flinging himself down on the grass and propping himself up on one elbow. 'I never knowed a wusser day in all me life! Believe me, on my baby's life! *Please* believe me! Ask him ...'

Don't Shit rallied to the occasion well. 'I hope my child's lying stiff an' dead in the trailer, it's the truth he's telling you, bruv! Oh, mate! We took three different jobs to do trees – an' every one of 'em whipped afore we could start. *Every one!* All we done is spend money – I've had me hand in an' out of me pocket like a fiddler's elbow!'

And so saying, he drew bars of chocolate and sweets from his coat pocket and cast them in the direction of the children, who had all been waiting expectantly for them.

'It has definitely gone very tight round here for our sort've work,' declared Do Shit solemnly. Adding for my comfort: 'Not that I want to put you in bad heart, my old bruvver. 'Cos often a new face can have new luck. It's just that we bin round about here too long an' the old place has got a bit tight, don't you know, bruv?'

I agreed, for I appreciated exactly what he meant and knew its truth. However, I was a bit disconcerted when Don't Shit remarked:

'Anyhow, we've all got to git off here on Monday, ain't we?'

'We didn't know,' I said, a bit put out by the news and wondering if Bronco had known when he sent us here.

'They'll all be down by nine o'clock on Monday, with tractors an' *gavvers* an' all,' Don't Shit replied. 'An' if you don't git off then they'll pull you off – an' they don't care if they breaks your bits of things neither. Proper fuckin' bastards they are, you knows that.'

I did, and it has long been beyond my understanding how it is that seemingly pleasant council workers can allow themselves to be turned into inhuman monsters, wreaking havoc on men, women, children and their homes purely at the whim of dark-suited bureaucrats, who always supervise such operations under the protection of the police or sometimes even of private security firms.

Some minutes later, Concorde returned with Alfie seated silently beside him in the cab, possibly for moral – if not vocal – support during his quest to remedy his lorry's deficiencies. The engine sounded healthier and, with exaggerated revs, Concorde and Alfie alighted.

'Got the motor done?' I asked, somewhat superfluously.

'Yeah,' replied Concorde. 'Found a lovely man, a proper rampant *dinilo*, an he'll blow the old motor over [spray-paint it] one day next week if I takes her in.'

'Pay for it all in one go, I suppose,' I grinned.

Concorde winked.

Do Shit and Don't Shit stared as though hypnotised at Concorde's nose, faint grins playing about their features.

'There's a nose, my bruvver,' breathed one to the other, though just loud enough for Concorde to hear. Without warning, he launched himself upon the hapless pair and, seemingly in fun, spun them both to the ground, laughingly delivering sharp blows about their persons; they suddenly became three Gypsy boys again, fighting like children on the ground. Luckily, however, it was all taken in good part and did not develop into any form of malicious combat. And so we were soon all drinking cups of sweet tea and exchanging news of mutual acquaintances and friends, and discussing all matters peculiar to our insular way of life. Not least, of course, where we might make for after the promised eviction on Monday.

Our discourse was interrupted by screams of fury from Concorde's wife Prissy, apparently directed towards her ten-year-old son who had been demanding money from her.

'My blessed Lord!' she shrieked. 'It's five years since I've seen a monkey, 'cept him over there. Go away, man-child! You poxy *divvy!*'

The boy, face contorted with rage, rushed over to one of his small bicycles and started to demolish it with a sledge hammer.

'Look at that! Look at pig's-ears!' Prissy called to us. 'He might have got angel-white skin – but the Devil's inside it! Look at his dear arms, wavin' 'em about like that old *rai* on the telly, Magullus Pipe!'

Roused at last, his father shouted, 'If you *poggers* that *treader* you won't get nothin' but bread to eat for a week, an' that's the God Almighty's truth!'

The boy, who was not of a tractable nature, continued to hammer the bicycle with abandon, knowing himself to be safe from all but verbal abuse.

'There's a brazen boy,' observed his father with a mixture of annoyance and admiration.

'We seen old Amos today,' said Do Shit, changing the subject. 'His pony've kicked him an' broke his leg: it's in plaster of palaces, and he's on two crutches.'

'All he seems to git is bad luck these days,' joined in Don't Shit. 'Dear, civil old man he is too, not a liberty-taker.'

We nodded in sympathy and agreement.

'An' now he've got to git off that bit of land he bought, by Dinilos Corner, so he sez,' continued Don't Shit. 'Once he got hisself a chalet on it, the bastard council went an' put a 'pulsory compurchase order on it, an' they're gonna git him off it.'

'Where's he going?' I asked.

'God in heaven knows,' replied Do Shit, sadly. 'But them *gaujes* don't care what happens to travellers, even dear old people, do they? All they wants is us out of their sight – they don't care if it's on a lonely old mountain, or down agen a sewerage-works, they thinks that's good enough for travellers. Believe me, bruvver, travellers is classed as worse than dogs by most of 'em. Yet some of them council people is very classical *folki* what should know better.'

I felt momentarily very depressed by these sentiments, not because they were not true but rather because they *were*. How distressing and unjust it is that in these little islands there is a section of society that is so badly and unthinkingly treated. Indeed, if such treatments were meted out to any of the immigrant groups then great would be the protest from almost all shades of political persuasion. But travellers seem to be excluded from the net of sympathy, perhaps because they are too independent and too averse to being boxed in by so many of society's rules. Can it be, perhaps, that jealousy or envy of those qualities are at the root of the matter?

Within the next hour or so, most of the other men had returned, some a little richer, others less fortunate. It is an

unwritten rule that one does not disclose one's actual earnings to anyone but the closest of family members, unless,
perhaps, one stumbles upon a piece of good fortune beyond
one's wildest dreams. 'No good' would normally signify a reasonable return for the day's efforts, while 'ticking over'
might assure the listeners that success had been achieved.
However, as the only muck-hawker pulled in on the ground,
my own occupational rewards were of some curiosity to the
other men, most of whom were either scrap-collecting, tree-
topping or roof-repairing.

It was getting towards dusk and the majority of the men
and some youths were gathered, sitting on the ground
together, smoking, coughing and talking. Gaunt, grey Old
Sam, his age allowing him to be direct in his question without causing insult, enquired suddenly of me: 'I'm gonna ask
you a question, *mushy*. How much can you make of a load of
them old bags you takes out every day?'

'Well, Uncle Sam,' I answered, looking at him blandly.
'Sometimes I go out calling, and I call and call, *all day long*,
from nine in the morning till six at night.'

I paused for dramatic effect, my audience hanging
expectantly on my words, and then continued: 'And do you
know, on my mother's life, sometimes I don't take more than
twelve hundred pounds!'

For an instant a stunned silence reigned, before they realised
that I had not been serious and they all rocked with laughter

that they had been deceived, not least Old Sam, whose respect for me would have dwindled considerably had I been cretinous enough to disclose my business in such a public manner. I have known only a very few travellers who would come home each day and boast of their earnings, and those unwise persons were widely viewed with both distaste and disbelief. There is an old saying: 'What's in *his* pocket doesn't help me!'

Sunday morning dawned bright as the previous days, the magic of May, even in sight of a trunk road, undimmed. Bronco, who liked to engage in part-time horse-dealing, had heard that there was to be a trotting-race near to Staines that morning, solely a travellers' event, to take place on a length of straight main road which would hopefully be little used by traffic early on a Sabbath morning.

Several of us decided to go, and Do Shit, Don't Shit, Old Sam, Digger and Concorde all managed to squeeze into a small Ford Escort van which was owned and driven by Young Sam. We comprised a pleasantly Gypsy-looking little crew: the older men wore coloured silk handkerchiefs about their necks, and all of us wore suits and yellow or tan elastic-sided boots for the occasion.

We made good speed along various back roads, keeping to the latter in the hopes of not been stopped by police patrol cars, for the van, although insured, was bereft of road-tax.

'She runs as well without it!' laughed Young Sam, with the happy-go-luckiness of youth.

'I can't a-bear a motor with no tax,' grumbled Digger mournfully, adding: 'One thing leads to another and before you knows it you're locked up.'

'We old uns can remember when a pound *was* a pound,' observed Old Sam inconsequentially.

'I suppose you can, Uncle Sam,' said Do Shit. 'You must be knockin' on a bit now, Uncle Sam?'

'Over fifty now, I dare say,' replied Old Sam, giving every appearance of being an octogenarian in poor condition. 'If I never had no water-troubles I'd be so good as new!'

These musings were interrupted by the sight of a huge aircraft taking off from nearby Heathrow airport.

'There goes yer airyplane, Concorde!' laughed Don't Shit and Young Sam as one.

'Fuckin' bastards!' said Concorde, but he said it with a smile.

The next moment we approached a junction and emerged on to a wide road, a straight highway along the verge of which were numerous motor vehicles of the sort favoured by travellers, also several new German limousines belonging to wealthy settled-down travellers from London. These last were at once visible, standing together in a knot, in expensively tailored suits and with occasional camel or vicuna coats about their persons.

Young Sam drove slowly down the road until he came upon a space, and was able to edge his van carefully in between a huge horse-box and an elegant Mercedes saloon, finished in metallic cherry-colour and shining in the sun.

'Nice motor,' remarked Do Shit admiringly of the Mercedes, and we viewed it with some envy.

'That's Boxer Tom's,' Concorde informed us. 'He had it out new on Epsom for the races last year: it ain't twelve-month-old yet.'

'He've a-done well,' said Old Sam. 'Yet his poor old father couldn't never do no good at all – he couldn't take salt for a tater!'

'Often happens that way,' agreed Don't Shit philosophically.

A very dark, chubby-featured, almost Indian-looking youth drove by in a new 4x4 pick-up truck and tooted a greeting at us.

'He's a nice fellow,' said Young Sam. 'He's off that new trailer-park by Woking, the one they got passed for travellers.'

'Who's he one of?' demanded Old Sam.

'He's one of them down-country travellers, he could be a Pinfold but I ain't sure. But he's a nice young fellow, he ain't braggy, don't you know?'

Young Sam, and especially his father, were of a very

oldfashioned kind of traveller, proud of their Gypsy heritage and clinging to many of its old traditions with great ferocity and ardour. Old Sam would boast that he had not spent one night of his life under a house roof. Born in a bender-tent, he had travelled with horses and wagons until after he was married; and then, after becoming mechanised, he had gradually pulled himself up from battered little trailers and motors to his present state, in easy stages. At the time he owned a new trailer and an almost new Bedford TK lorry. His trailer-caravan, a vast and imposing Westmorland Star, was one of the best on the road: coach-built with graceful lines and ornate applications of stainless-steel designs, the exterior was a pleasure to look upon. The makers knew exactly what Gypsy people wanted in a living-wagon and catered accordingly. The interior was of marble-grained formica and elaborately bowed furniture, with fancy lamp fittings and numerous full-length etched-glass mirrors. The floor was covered in luxuriant carpets and rugs, and the china display-cabinets were lockers stuffed with Crown Derby and Royal Worcester china. Even the windows were decorated with cut-glass images of fruit and flowers. In truth, Old Sam's trailer was more rococo, with more extras, than almost any other that had been produced by the firm, and to my mind was all the better for it. As far as I was concerned its only drawback being its exceedingly heavy weight, which necessitated the possession of a three-ton lorry to draw it about the country.

Some five or six hundred yards along the road the people had begun to huddle around four sulkies drawn by trotting-ponies, and before we reached them they had set off in our direction at a furious pace, hurtling towards us in a line and causing us to leap on to the grass verge in alarm.

As they drew closer I recognised two of the competitors as semi-local travellers, one settled-down and the other still moving about; but the two others were strangers to me. One was driving a very rough-coated grey pony whose action and speed belied its appearance, while the other unknown was behind a very lanky bay of extraordinarily long reach. Davey and Bobby, brothers, were each driving a black pony of similar aspect.

It was soon evident that both they and the lanky pony were outclassed by the rough grey pony, which soon took the lead and gave every indication of maintaining it. Indeed, as they sped to the turning-point a half a mile or so away and commenced the return, the rough pony began to increase its lead, despite frantic efforts and cries from its three followers.

'My *mush*, *dik* at him goin'!' shouted a lined-featured London-man, smoking a cigar and wearing a camel coat. A few diamonds glittered from a heavy gold ring on his left hand. 'I'd a-thought Davey's would've beat that any day . . .'

On closer inspection I saw the winning pony to be driven by a man called Levi, a London-traveller long settled-down with his own prospering car-front. His thin face was taut with achievement and excitement as he reined the pony to a halt and skipped down and ran round to its head.

'He can go on all day like that,' he laughed. 'A good sort!'

'Leave off, Levi!' shouted one of the London-men, his Cockney accent heavy and hoarse, his black eyes shining.

'I tell you what, boys,' challenged Levi: 'I bet five hundred pounds I can win the next one too – how about it?'

Much murmuring talk ensued before the challenge was taken up. And off they went again, this time the rough grey being severely tested by a blue roan horse belonging to a cousin of Billy the Kid Kidd, but nonetheless Levi triumphed again. His flush of pride, however, was interrupted by the arrival of two police cars, the occupants of which emerged with severe expressions and proceeded sternly towards us.

'Have you been racing those horses on the public highway?' asked a sergeant, to our astonishment. Was he out for a full confession? Did he presume that he had an open and shut case? Much intrigued, I listened with amazement.

'Racing, policeman? Nah!' exclaimed several onlookers, their expressions those of misunderstood innocents.

'Here, you!' continued the sergeant, fixing his eyes on

Levi and his heavily sweating animal. 'Have you been *racing* that horse?'

'Me, sir?' said Levi, looking hurt. 'Nah! Why, this old pony couldn't do no *racing* – he pulls an old greengrocer's cart, that's what he does. Race! Cor! He couldn't race a blind man through a wood! Nah!'

The sergeant and the constables seemed rather put out of countenance by these denials, all backed up by dozens of witnesses, and at a loss as to what course of action to take. After much consultation with their superiors by means of their radios, they suggested that we should all withdraw from the locality, and issued many ominous cautions as to what proceedings would ensue if actual racing was discovered thereabouts in the future.

'Well, that's it, boys,' shouted Levi. 'No more today – let's go down the *kitchemir* and have some beer.'

And so we did.

On Monday morning we were all up and about by eight o'clock, knowing that the council officials would arrive by nine o'clock or thereabouts. We stood in groups, men and women separately, awaiting the inevitable. And sure enough, just after nine, two or three cars turned in off the road, followed by three police vehicles.

'*Gavvers* an' all,' observed Digger in disgust. 'You'd think we was murderers an' hooligans!'

The council officials descended from their cars and gathered together, inspecting various documents and glancing around the common. After a brief conversation they split into two bands, one proceeding towards the Irish travellers and the other lot coming in our direction. As they reached the first trailer, belonging to a man called Pincher, one of the officials broke away and made towards it with the seeming intent of knocking on the door. Four or five greyhounds rushed out, barking and growling menacingly.

'Watch them *jukels* – they'll have him,' smiled their owner, who was standing near to me, in some satisfaction. The rest of us watched in pleasurable anticipation. At that point the dogs became even more fierce and one, a large black animal, snaked in and bit a lump of cloth from the trouser-leg of the man's dark suit. He frenziedly beat at the dog with his sheaf of papers before making a strategic retreat: his was the indignation of the self-righteous, and no less comical because of that!

Our amusement, alas, was short-lived. One of the sharper-eyed among us detected the ominous shapes of no less than four large tractors, bright yellow, moving in unison along the road towards us: council vehicles, no doubt of that.

As they entered the common, three of the tractors broke away and headed for the Irish travellers, the largest collection of trailers in one place, while just one approached us.

From the Irish people's encampment there suddenly appeared a vast army of children, who had seen the tractors and were aware of the reason for their arrival. The children ranged in age from about four years to possibly eleven or twelve, both boys and girls. There were probably fifty or sixty of them, their straw-coloured and ginger heads showing up in the morning sunshine.

Unbeknown to us but seemingly known to the Irish, the council tractors had been equipped with ball-hitches with which to tow the trailers from the common, should any refuse to budge. These fixtures, being rarely required in routine council work, were affixed to each tractor by means of a pin-fitting which could easily be removed when other forms of apparatus were needed.

Our delight and approval knew no bounds when we realised that the Irish children, swarming like locusts about the yellow tractors, had removed the ball-hitches and their fixing-pins and were triumphantly wafting them across the commonland and finally hurling the appendages far out into the centre of a stagnant and evil-smelling pond which lay there, and from which discarded flotsam of all kinds projected, covered in green and yellow slime.

Our hysterical applause for the action of these wise and knowing children had diverted our attention from the lone tractor that had entered our own precinct. It was only the loud screams of abuse from Pincher's wife, Evie, that made us realise that his own trailer was, despite protests from the woman and dogs, about to be attached to the huge tractor.

We sped forwards, Pincher just ahead of us.

'If you hitch on that tractor to me trailer I'll break your jaw!' he shouted at the driver who, despite the presence of both police and council officials, did not look proud of his task.

'Listen, my mate,' continued Pincher somewhat more calmly, sensing a crack in the man's armour. 'We're shifting tomorrow anyway, so where's the sense of you breaking up me bits of things, an' frightening me wife and babies?'

The driver looked hesitatingly at the policeman. 'I can't do it,' he said, ashamedly.

'Carry on!' ordered the policeman, cold-faced.

But the driver made no move to comply.

'You are in breach of a Health and Planning regulation,' said the council official, in a curiously minced-up voice. His face was a pale yellowish colour, not healthy-looking; it was rather suggestive of one who had been reared almost exclusively on under-cooked meats, complemented by over enthusiastic devouring of custard tarts.

'You'll all have to go, today,' he decided, a false smile momentarily fastening itself to his mouth.

'Well, where *can* we go if we leave here?' enquired Do Shit sarcastically.

'That's not our concern, it's up to you. But you can't stay here – you choose to live like this, so you'll just have to find somewhere else.'

So much for the tolerance of authorities for varying lifestyles!

The council man's features betrayed no emotion other than stolid disapproval, reinforced by the attitude of the police.

'See him – he's like his grandmother!' said Young Sam, showing both disgust and resignation at the situation, one all too familiar to us.

'They'll have all the travellers off the roads in time,' pronounced Old Sam, adding prophetically: 'An' they'll try to git us all penned up in them old sites as they're building – there won't be no free roamin' life no more.'

'You're right, my Sam,' agreed his old friend Digger. 'They wants to do away with travellers altogether if they can.'

'They'll never do that, Uncle Digger,' asserted Young Sam with the optimism and authority of youth.

Eventually a complete impasse was reached, culminating in a visit from a high-ranking police officer who decided that we would be allowed to remain for that day; but our removal was demanded on the next morning, and we were assured in no uncertain terms that our failure on that score would undoubtedly result in many arrests and the consequent issuing of summonses.

'Here's a life,' grumbled Concorde. 'I'm fucked if I know where we can go.'

'Well, I'm goin' away, my old boys,' said Digger. 'There's no sense in me hangin' on here, jist for today.'

'Where you goin', Uncle Digger?' asked Young Sam.

'Somewhere down in Kent, my son. I knows a few old places where you can stop an' catch your breath down in that country. We been runnin' here an' there ever since Christmas, an' I could do with a week or two in one place. Come down with us if you like – it'd be a bit of company, wouldn't it?'

After some discussion, we all eventually decided on our movements and choice of companions and even, vaguely, our destinations.

Having become a little tired of the brothers Concorde and Alfie, and not wishing to stay with Do Shit and Don't Shit, who were remaining within the London boroughs, I decided to journey to Kent with Digger and the rest, and to go with them that day.

'Right then,' said Digger brusquely. 'Let's have a nice cup of tea an' a bit of bread an' meat, an' then we'll *jal*.'

Restless by nature, some might think slightly unhinged, I was quite happy to leave, even though our stay had been so short. To swing through the countryside, drawing one's complete home and all one's worldly possessions behind one, is to me the ultimate happiness – which I believe only illness or death will destroy.

By noon we were all packed down – five long, elegant, chrome-encrusted trailers and our lorries and vans. The open lorries plainly showed, even to the uninitiated what we were, their backs crammed with the accoutrements of the travellers' life; each contained several lurchers or greyhounds, loose or tied depending on their age or temperament. Digger led the way and I chose to be last as I am not addicted to being sandwiched in a convoy. With much tooting, shouting and yipping, we were out, off the common and, once more, on the road.

Trouble and Strife

It was not long after Christmas, in the mid-1970s, and Beshlie and I had packed up all our possessions on an icy winter's morning and decided to make for the outskirts of London, where there would certainly be acquaintances or friends with whom to stop during that cheerless time of the year. The skies were leaden and the qualities of the land-scape, both good and bad, were curiously accentuated. The threat of snow was in the air, though none had as yet fallen. At that time we owned a twin-wheeled Transit truck and a heavy Sambrookes trailer which was almost too much for the lorry to pull. I avoided the motorway, preferring to take the older, more devious roads with which I was familiar. Eventually, on the outskirts of Swindon, I drove cautiously on to the forecourt of a filling-station for fuel, noticing another obviously travellery lorry at an adjoining pump.

When the driver came back from the payment office, I recognised him with some pleasure as my old friend Bonny. Small of stature, dark-skinned and luminous-eyed, he was, although perhaps thirty-five-years-old, the eternal Gypsy boy. He sported a coloured handkerchief about his neck, a Romani-style yoke-backed jacket, narrow trousers and yellow elastic-sided boots. His little Transit lorry was laden to overflowing with tree-toppings. He smiled and we greeted each other cordially.

Finding that we had no planned destination he immediately suggested, with the friendliness of a true traveller, that we should pull in with him and his family.

'Who's there, Bonny?' I asked, with slight caution.

'Just me farver, an' me two brothers-in-law, Tom an' Frank,' he replied. 'It ain't a bad old place, nice and hard and plenty of room.'

As an afterthought he added: 'That Nelson an' Blackie an' them is over the back, but they ain't too close.'

I was rather relieved to hear that, as the last-named were of quarrelsome natures, prone to fall into conflict with all around them.

He explained in some detail as to how I could find the place, although, as is often the way of some travellers, he did not know the name of the area, nor of the nearest village. Indeed, he could only say it was about three miles from Slough and was a piece of wasteland. The whole locality was faintly known to me from the past, so I had no great difficulty in puzzling out his directions.

Within a little time, we had left the trunk highway and were heading through quieter, narrower roads towards the village he had tried to describe. Keeping a sharp observation, we suddenly perceived several travellers huddling in separate groups some distance across a rough and charmless, litter-strewn landscape. From the road there was a gap in some spiky bushes and broken fence-posts through which all traffic to the stopping-place was forced to pass; it was muddy and rut-filled by the numbers of motors having to use it. Upon sighting us in the characteristically sharp-eyed way of Romani children, there was some agitation within the clusters of young ones around, who interrupted their play around the trailers; at their instigation, several doors opened and adult figures were silhouetted, poised within the door-frames, surveying our approach with curiosity. New arrivals on such a stopping-place would always cause those already ensconced to be pulled in two ways emotionally. Being naturally gregarious, they would generally welcome the excitement of new company, combined with the greater sense of power which a large gathering always feels it possesses in the face of eviction threats from the local council. However, at the same time, they would be forced to acknowledge that the greater the numbers so would the speed with which the authorities would feel impelled to act be greater.

'Let's take it a bit steady as we go through the entrance,' suggested Beshlie cautiously. 'We don't want to get stuck halfway through.'

'Nah! We'll be all right,' I replied, in customary sympathy!

I recognised Bonny's and his parents' trailers, with two others beside them, lying some two hundred yards or so to our left across the common, and bore in that direction, the trailer creaking in protest at the unlevel, rutted ground. It was an insalubrious place, having obviously become an unofficial rubbish-dump to which local inhabitants from the neighbouring village and housing estates had generously contributed. Heaps of old cardboard boxes, builders' rubble, mattresses, carpeting, broken items of furniture, old tins and bottles, evergreen hedge-clippings lay in profusion. The remaining pressed-down earth was embedded with fragments of glass. In those days it was a common habit of householders to tip rubbish near to any temporary stopping-place of travellers, safe in the knowledge that the latter would receive the blame.

We pulled slowly across the debris-strewn ground until we reached the trailers of Bonny and his family. His father and mother, Joe and Mary-Anne, were at home with some of their grandchildren, who gazed fixedly at us from dark eyes. Their trailers were each clean, shining and bright despite the glowering skies. Smoke poured upward from the old couple's chimney, and the cut-glass mirrors and fine china glistened within the interior.

We exchanged greetings and, pulling forward a few yards, managed to find a level spot for the trailer. We joined them for a welcome cup of tea, which was served to us in Crown Derby mugs.

The other travellers, in two separate encampments across the common, were not so prosperous-looking. Their turnouts were shabby and unpolished, mostly of poor quality and in utterly neglected condition. Beside one of the trailers stood a large and aged lorry on to which two rust and grease-covered figures were loading scrap-iron from a heap on the ground; they, strangely, paid no heed to our arrival.

'Just as well you never *jalled* in by them old *dinilos* over there,' said Joe contemptuously. 'Proper cranks – they calls theirselves travellers but they ain't worth a light! *Gaujo*-bred bastards, I call 'em!'

Beshlie managed to clear a patch of ground behind our trailer for Barney's kennel, throwing quantities of old tins and bottles into some bushes nearby.

'Look at the mess,' grumbled Joe, gazing about us. 'If it was travellers who'd made it, instead of them *gaujes* fetching it out of their *kairs*, there'd be murders. Yet on the papers we're gettin' the blame for it – always the same, ain't it?'

We had just finished unpacking when a very smart little Bedford CF lorry turned in from the road, speeding with great abandon over the deepest of ruts and bumping up and down over the protusions. It was pale blue, lined out in both red and straw-colour, old-fashioned traveller-style. When the vehicle drew abruptly to a halt, it revealed two men and a youth in the cab: it was Frank and Tom, the sons-in-law of Joe and Mary-Anne, and their nephew, who was the son of their eldest sister. The boy was about fifteen, named Jobi, and was staying on 'holiday' with his uncles while his parents were travelling in Wales – a country which he affected to dislike.

'How's your luck, brother?' cried Frank, a handsome young man of very Romani features, with sleek black hair and eyes like those of Bonny. His brother Tom grinned, and the boy looked on expressionlessly.

'How long've you been here?' I enquired.

'We've *atched akai* since well before Christmas,' replied Frank. 'I do believe you can stop here as long as you like. Me uncle Siddy an' me cousin Lias had five months here once, an' they moved of their own accord. But there've been some dirty people here since, brother, an' them old *gaujes* has been makin' it fuckin' bad for us. Here's a state of a place to be in!' He looked around him and shrugged.

He tapped his fingers up and down relentlessly on the bonnet of the lorry, his heavy gold buckle ring clicking as he did so.

'Me feet's froze,' remarked the youth, and the men stared at him in wonder.

'Hark at dog's-face!' exclaimed Tom. 'He bought hisself a bran' fine new pair of them Hush Upperties, or whatever you calls 'em, an' since then he's done nothin' 'cepting go on about how his fuckin' feet's froze – I never knowed a boy like it. He don't know what it is to have to get about wet-footed. Like me dead farver he's had it too easy! Much more of it an' I shall give him his walking-papers!'

His tone, however, was of no great severity, and the youth grinned, pleased to be the centre of interest.

'That boy's like a little old *mush*, strike me dead!' observed Joe. 'Ain't that right, Frank?'

'Sure it is, Uncle Joe – fuckin' sure it is!' agreed Frank.

'Women's his trouble – I never seed a boy like it in me life!'

'Fuck anythin' he would,' smiled Tom.

'Would you fuck a goose, boy?' enquired Frank.

'Sure I would,' announced the boy indignantly, and we all laughed. He reddened slightly at being made fun of, kicking rather absently in the direction of a passing whippet, with no malicious intent. The dog, sensing this, continued on its way without any reaction.

The sky, which had grown more overcast and ominous since our arrival, had turned truly leaden, and flecks of snow began to fall, settling at once.

'Look at this,' I observed to Joe, somewhat downcast. 'I've just got here and the bloody snow starts. How about if it keeps on for a month?'

'You was lucky not to have been *kotched* on the road,' rejoined Joe, adding: 'It won't last long, not at this time of the year.'

'I don't know, Uncle Joe,' mused Frank, who had wandered over. 'How about that bad winter, ten years ago, when it lay for four months, or was it six? I had to go out log-sellin' with me Uncle Bon an' me Aunt Jane. I never did so much *booty* in me life, an' all for a few poverty shillin's a day, it very nigh *marred* me!'

He recalled the experience with some exaggeration, for he was capable of the kind of labour which few but the hardiest could rival.

When dusk fell, the snow had pitched and was by then several inches deep and worsening by the minute. The lights in the trailers shone out, the generator-powered ones bright and dazzling, those more humbly lit by candles more restrained; the little homes, both of the wealthier and the not-so-well-off, were tiny islands of comfort on the detritus-strewn wasteland. As to us, our generators chugged happily in the cold night air. In order to prevent condensation forming on the windows of their trailers, this being before the advent of double-glazing, most travellers preferred not to draw their curtains or let down their blinds until late in the evening; rather we built up our fire-stoves in order for the heat to absorb the moisture in the atmosphere.

The temperature was low and the snow lay deep upon the ground.

From about five o'clock onward the road past the stopping-place would become busy with homeward-bound workers from the nearest town and the surrounding factories, weary after their long day's toil, yet safe in the assurance of their security. Those who bothered to glance at the trailers might do so with indifference, or perhaps, very occasionally, with slight envy. Yet none, I imagine, had more than a fleeting desire to emulate our way of life, and those who did would quickly use some form of ready-made excuse, such as the needs of wives and children, to prevent them from following their inclinations.

Feeling somewhat exhausted, we went to bed early and slept well, with pleasant friends nearby.

Next morning, to my disgust, showed that the snow had melted only a very little, some of the ground being covered by a thick, brackish slush. Fortunately we had enough food and water in stock for at least a day ahead so were not obliged to fetch either. Rather regretfully, I decided to remain at home and take a day off work for, as Joe put it, 'the Queen'.

Bonny, who was at that time enjoying one of his periodic separations from his wife and children, was living alone in his trailer. Deciding not to go out himself either that morning, he spent most of it sitting in our trailer reminiscing about old times we had shared during past years. Towards midday a faint sun shone and the slush melted further so that the whole ground became water-logged. Suddenly the dogs began to bark in an urgent, definite manner and, to our surprise, we saw that a little trailer and motor van was leaving the road, seemingly in our direction. As it neared we could see that it was an obsolete little egg-shaped tourer of but ten feet in length, of almost vintage manufacture, towed by a very battered van of a half-ton capacity of the sort more generally used for postal deliveries in rural areas. It was probably twenty years old, rusting, dented and hand-painted roughly. The dreary little turnout came closer and closer until it seemed that it was going to set itself within a few feet of Bonny.

'Put yer *yoks* on this!' exclaimed Bonny in consternation. 'These ain't travellers, not with *poggerdi* old *covels* like this kid. We don't want no fuckin' *dinilos* up agen us, eh, brother?'

So saying, he grabbed his coat, as did I, and we hastened outside.

The van was driven by a sandy-haired man of about forty years of age, unkempt and wearing a stained knee-length anorak, while at his side was a small wizened-faced woman probably fifteen years his junior. She was fully muffled within an oversized man's duffle-coat, torn and stained; her features were thin yet puffy, and devoid of any generosity in the way of either natural or artificial aids to beauty: she had a glossless simplicity of expression and a faint hint of dementia in her blind-looking pale-grey eyes.

'Could you pull up a bit, mate?' requested Bonny placatingly. 'Only me cousin an' his family is comin' in sometimes tomorrow with his two trailers, an' he wants to stop agen us, you know?'

The driver stared uncomprehendingly at him for a moment before answering, in a strong Glasgow accent:

'Och aye, friend – I'll be away a wee bit.'

And, so saying, he jerkily moved forward, wheels spinning in the slush and mud. After about fifty feet or so, with the trailer lurching from side to side, like a ship in a storm, there was a mighty cracking sound as the towbar of the trailer snapped in two – causing the caravan to rear upwards from the front, crashing back on to its rear end in an alarming sit-up-and-beg position.

The couple wordlessly climbed out from their van and stood as though petrified at the spectacle of their minute home tipped up at such an angle. However, their wits gradually returned to them and they grasped what remained of the towbar and succeeded in lowering the trailer to a more dignified position, and while so doing managed to swing it round, just off the hard trackway. We observed that the trailer did not possess even rudimentary let-down supports (or legs as we call them) at any of its four corners. Hence the man was forced to search among the debris around them until he was able to find several old bricks and two tin drums, which he used to steady the trailer at each end.

'Well, I tell you what, my *mush*,' said Bonny, 'I never seen such a turnout in all me life. My baby's life, I ain't! I'd be 'shamed to take it on the roads. A fuckin' eyesight! Why I'd soon have me a bender-tent an' a bicycle than stuff like that.'

I listened, and in some ways agreed, though without knowing a little more about the two strangers I was less ready than Bonny to condemn them completely. My interest has always been in reasons, principles and prejudices. In fact, I must admit that, like Dr Johnson, I sometimes believe that one prejudice is worth a dozen principles!

As fate would have it, the newcomers were more than fortunate in their time of arrival, for within minutes of them levelling up their tiny trailer more snow began to fall heavily, almost a blizzard.

'Here's weather!' grumbled Frank. 'It's enough to make you *jal* to *voodrus* an' have a good *suti*, innit?'

I agreed, and Bonny and I went back up into my trailer. I sat and peeled a peach, which Beshlie had bought for me in an uncharacteristically spendthrift moment.

'That's foreign – it'll make you bad,' warned Bonny, darkly eyeing the peach, adding for good measure: 'I wouldn't eat one of them, not if you was to give me a five-pound note – on my children's lives I wouldn't.'

I laughed, and swore softly as juice spurted on to my silk tie.

'Well, I don't know what to do – I can't a-bear sittin' about at home all day, you'd soon go *radji!*' said Bonny, restless as a terrier.

Tom knocked on the door and walked in.

'This weather's like its grandmother,' he remarked, drawing a strange comparison.

'I ain't going out, is you?' he asked me, and on receiving a negative answer he continued: 'Where's the sense in takin' the motors out on the roads, an' most likely gettin' them heat up? I mean, I ain't short of a few bob, an' I know you ain't, brother. If I was then I *would* go out, mind – 'cos I ain't the kind of man as sells his breakfast to get his dinner, you knows that, Bonny.'

Bonny agreed placidly, having digested these comments. He was, however, knowing Tom so well, ready for him to change his mind completely and suddenly decide on an opposite course of action. In a way it was part of his charm, a many-mindedness, not necessarily a weakness.

Seated drinking cups of tea and, as ever, smoking ceaselessly, our attention was gradually distracted by the sound of hammering coming from the direction of the little trailer and van. Our amazement knew no bounds when we were able to perceive that the sound of heavy blows was due to the fact that the Scotsman had engaged himself in the task of demolishing the little caravan with a long-handled axe.

'He's gone *radji*!' declared Bonny.

'He has, an' me *a-suti* an' all,' grumbled Frank.

The very considerable noise made by the Scotsman during his course of destruction had even caused a few of the travellers from the other side of the common to peer forth from their trailers in some faint puzzlement.

Owing to the great age of the little tourer, and the consequent fragility of its wooden framework, it needed no Herculean effort to raze it to the chassis within a surprisingly short time. Parts of its construction consisted of hardboard and plywood, while some of the external panels were of thin-gauge aluminium. The man lit a small fire and started to burn up the wood and board, consigning the few thin sheets of metal to a little pile on one side. As the flames leaped upwards, the rotted plywood and hardboard burned speedily and vividly against the backdrop of snow, the smoke swirled skywards, acrid with the smell of paint, and occasional splatters of red ash blew across the snow, to land, black and dead, some feet away.

Old Joe, Bonny and the others, still greatly surprised by the destructive activity, speculated with curiosity as to how the desolate pair planned to exist, especially under such arctic conditions.

Towards London, in full view, there rose great tower-blocks of newly constructed flats, the inhabitants of which could, should the fancy take them, stare down upon our trailers from afar.

While, there again, possibly even worse off than the Scotsman and his companion, a mile or less distant, on a small piece of grass-covered scrubland where it was too rough to drive a motor or trailer, there lurked a number of aged tramps and a few meths-drinkers. The former, often having spent half a lifetime living in the open air, had almost all provided themselves with *some* sort of cover, be it only old boxes or a canvas or plastic sheet in the lee of an old perambulator; but the meths-drinkers seemed both immune and indifferent to the weather and lay huddled or slumped in postures of complete resignation, their tell-tale bottles clasped lethargically in their hands or lying empty beside them.

Although everyone thereabouts could perhaps be described as outcasts from the general goings-on of society it was, nonetheless, only the travellers who were *proud* of their circumstances and way of life. And rightly so, for they had proved that it was possible to lead a decent and in many ways generous existence, in pleasant little homes, despite the sometimes embittering experience of having almost every hand turned against them without let-up. Some, throughout their whole lives, knew nothing but persecution and discrimination; and the idea of being allowed to stop in one place for more than a few days at a time was but a wistful ideal, not much more than a dream. To be taunted, from childhood, as 'gyppos', 'diddikais' or 'pikies' often leaves its mark, deeply engrained, but it rarely diminishes the spirit. Only the weakest have ever wished to veer from the true traveller's course. No proper traveller would look upon himself as a variety of 'poor white' or 'trailer trash', but would rightly adjudge his powers of survival to be vastly superior to those of many of his fellow-men under similar conditions.

Meanwhile, the Scotsman and his little woman stood, possibly nostalgically, by the dying red embers of their fire that was all that remained of their erstwhile accommodation, apart from the chassis, wheels and an unimposing pile of bent-up aluminium sheeting. This lay, paint-flaking on the one side and shiny on the reverse, jagged and unimpressive in the snow.

Bonny and I sauntered up to them, for we were curious to find out more about the pair.

'Howdy-do,' greeted the man at our approach, grey-faced and unhealthy-looking, and the woman stared silently, her face wan.

We did no more than glance at her, lest he were a jealous man: neither of us had any desire to be the cause of dissension concerning a young woman of such unprepossessing appearance.

'Nice bit've fire,' observed Bonny.

'Aye,' said the man.

'Come far?' I enquired.

'Aye, a fair ways,' said the man.

A silence descended on us. It was eventually broken.

'I've a wee bit of metal there, going for scrap,' remarked the man casually, pointing to the aluminium. 'Do you ken where there's a scrapyard? Or would you like to buy it – to save me takin' it doon the yard?'

'How much do you want for it, my mate?' asked Bonny, though I knew that he was asking only for his private interest since there was not sufficient to warrant him taking the time and trouble of weighing it in at a yard himself.

'I'd take five pounds for it,' suggested the man hopefully.

'Oh, my mate!' exclaimed Bonny apologetically. 'I couldn't give you that for it. To be honest, I ain't on the iron-cart just now.'

Conversation flagged completely after that, making me realise yet again how far is the rift between the traveller and the *gaujo*. Had the unfortunate pair been Romanies they would have had the best of welcome, sympathy and very probably assistance to help them on their way.

Alas, for this unprepossessing pair, there was no bonding or fellow-feeling of any sort between us. I often wondered, in later years, why they ever pulled in with travellers at all. A very strange occurrence.

Bonny and I wandered back to our trailers, picking our way carefully through the protrusions in the snow.

'Five pounds!' repeated Bonny in shocked disbelief. 'My dear man, there was a quarter of a fuckin' hundredweight there, if that. I *should* like to give five *bars* for that! You know I would!'

'I'd sooner give him five *bars* for the old motor,' I laughed.

'Think he'd take it?' asked Bonny, half serious. 'I reckons I could go up to seven if I was pushed!'

He laughed, rather unkindly, if one considered the dilapidation of his own possessions in the not too distant past. Or indeed, of course, of my own!

'Poor sods! They must have their troubles,' I said. 'If they're going to sleep up in that little old motor tonight in this weather, I'd sooner it was them than me.'

I screwed up my face at the thought.

''Course, bein' Scotch must help 'em,' replied Bonny. 'I mean, you often hears of snow in Scotland near enough in the middle of the summer – so they probably thinks nothin' if it, being so used to it, don't you know?'

During that day, the roads began to turn slushy once more, and patches of snow on the wasteland began to melt, especially that which had lain on various old car-bodies, dotted about here and there in pugnacious colours like giant late-winter flowers.

At intervals, as the day progressed, the lorries of the trav-ellers came and went, slithering and skidding their way through the slush and mud; and several vans and pick-up trucks containing visitors who were stopping within not too wide a radius drove in for short conversations with friends or relatives.

Within the confines of the trailer-caravan existence, as also used to be the case with wagons and horses, there is a great pleasure and a sure sense of freedom. Paradoxically, however, this can entail severe personal restrictions, in some ways an almost entire loss of privacy. Most itinerant trailer-dwellers seem to feel the urge to get away from the claustrophobia of their surroundings, and will rarely volun-tarily miss going out each day unless circumstances force it upon them.

As the day began to fade, the temperature again dropped considerably and the brown slush turned to ice. The trailers creaked as the occupants stirred within; and the drinking water that was left outside in old milk-churns froze solid. The dogs crept further underneath the trailers – those older and more cunning would lie directly beneath the coal-burning stoves for extra warmth, while the less fortunate ones would nuzzle close together.

For the next days the weather showed little sign of improvement: each time a partial thaw set in it was imme-diately counteracted by further hard, white frosts.

Throughout the first two days and nights after the incineration of their little trailer, the Scotsman and his woman appeared to remain within the cramped confines of their motor van, its windows and windscreen covered from the inside with greyish blanketing. They did not venture out except for absolute necessities, and they made no attempt to converse with anyone else on the common.

On the third day, however, after energetic cranking of the starting-handle, and much misfiring, they were eventually successful in getting the engine going. Enveloping us in blue smoke, they jolted slowly on to the track and moved jerkily on to the main road. Within minutes they were swallowed up in the traffic. They had left without a word or gesture of farewell; all that remained to show that they had been there was the rusty chassis, its wheels and the little ring of ashes. They had taken the tiny heap of aluminium.

Old Joe was still abed, but Frank and Tom were out on business when the derelict pair had departed, having become unable to bear the strain of living on their saved resources for more than the first two days of the snowfall. Bonny, too, had left early, his destination unknown to us.

Frank and Tom returned in the afternoon and were interested to note the disappearance of the motor van.

'No chance of a five-pound motor now, eh?' laughed Frank.

'I wonder where they've *jalled?*' queried Tom.

'Back to Scotland I shouldn't wonder – best fuckin' place for 'em!' rejoined Frank.

For those who roam continuously, the departure of any-one, no matter what the circumstances, often stirs up a feeling of restlessness in those who are left behind. Sometimes, indeed, the latter feel impelled to pack up and move of their own accord, such is the feeling of desolation which overcomes them. For though the grass rarely *is* greener on the other side, there is always the possibility that it might be.

Quite suddenly the temperature rose and a thaw set in, followed by a sharp downpour of rain: once again dark pools of water formed at random across the uneven land-scape.

It was Old Joe's fifty-eighth birthday so there was some cause for celebration that evening. We had decided to hold it at a little local public house called the Dog and Drum, the landlord of which seemed to like travellers and be accus-tomed to their ways. Beshlie and I arrived at about half past eight, the low-ceilinged bar-room was by then filled to capacity with travellers. Some were from a nearby council site, others from their own properties, and the remainder were from the old common on which we ourselves were *atched.*

The women, of whom there were perhaps twenty-five or

thirty, some with children at their knee, sat crammed together at one side of the room. The men were apart from them, seated or standing at the bar counter.

It was a pleasant evening, well spent in amiable chatter and exchanging of news, which, towards closing-time, was interspersed with hoarse shouts of 'Order!', as aspiring singers were sometimes not accorded the respect which their relatives felt that they deserved.

'Do you want a song, or do you want to talk?' demanded a large blonde middle-aged travelling-woman, whose spirited rendition of an early Gracie Fields classic had been all but drowned out by the hubbub of shouting and laughter; she sat down in her seat, huffing and puffing with indignation.

Her mood was not improved when reverent silence was accorded to the next performer, a good-looking girl of perhaps eighteen whom I had heard singing before in the West Country. Her voice was unchanged from the days of Borrow, and she sang 'The Blackbird' so musically and so charmingly that she was given a respectful silence, to finish on a round of heartfelt applause and praise. Her closest rival in popularity was Frank: that evening his version of 'Old Shep' was so true to the original by Elvis Presley, so soulfully and sentimentally delivered, that it brought tears to the eyes of several of the women, even his wife Kizzy – upon whom his magic still appeared to be effective.

At closing-time, the night still seemed young, so it was decided to take back several crates of beer and a few bottles of whiskey, to carry on old Joe's birthday celebrations. In order to finance this, we all put five pounds apiece into a tankard, thus raising a goodly sum to spend.

The evening had turned mild, the rain had long ceased, and the moon and stars shone down in a friendly manner upon us as we returned to the trailers.

Bonny, already there, old-fashioned as ever, began hauling wood of all kinds from where some had been dumped by a builder, and soon had a huge crackling fire burning cheerfully. The beer flowed copiously, and maybe fifteen men and a few small boys gathered round the fire, talking and laughing. I noticed Big Bob in the shadows, which was rather daring as he was 'on the run' at the time from an open prison.

The women, girls and the smallest of boys had all retired to the trailers – knowing that the men would go on drinking probably into the early hours, at least until their drink supplies ran out. A small rat-like man called Ebbi found a small platform of wood, two feet square, which he threw down beside the fire and on which he began to step-dance, traveller-style, accompanied by his brother Jack on the melodeon. Irish and Scottish jigs, strathspeys, and reels all flowed effortlessly from the skilled fingers of Jack on the German instrument. After Ebbi tired slightly, his place was eagerly taken by others, anxious to prove their ability. All went well, everyone enjoying the scene, until, during an active step-dance routine effortlessly performed by Bonny, a tall and strongly built Romani-looking man called Black Jim suddenly tried to elbow him from the board impatiently.

'Git off the board, dog's-face,' he demanded. 'I'm gonna give you a song.'

'Don't push me, bruv,' said Bonny quietly, his eyes gleaming, and I knew that his temper would break at any moment.

'I ain't pushin' you, fuck-mother! I just wants to give a song,' announced Black Jim.

'Why don't you go back to the pea-country where you was born?' enquired Joe nastily.

Several of the bystanders, sensing trouble ahead, slid silently away from the fire and disappeared in the darkness.

'I'll *jal* where I wants to *jal* – I don't need you to tell me, Uncle Joe,' replied Black Jim, lunging unsteadily at Joe, who side-stepped and caused the lumpy figure of Black Jim to trip and fall heavily against the fireside, singeing his leg in the process.

Seeing him on the ground, Bonny, who was half the weight of Black Jim and at least a foot shorter, kicked him savagely about the ribs. Drunk though he was, Black Jim was able to catch hold of one of Bonny's legs and overbalance him. For a few moments they fought in rough-and-tumble style in the light of the fire; mud-covered and bleeding, they rolled over and over. We watched with some alarm this ill-matched contest.

'*Dik* here!' shouted Joe. 'Call yourself a man, Jim – fightin' with a little feller half yer fuckin' size. Have that!'

And so saying, he picked up a firebrand and held it against the side of Black Jim who, screaming at the burns, let go his hold on Bonny, who rolled cat-like from his grasp and stood, sparring up Gypsy-style, some feet away.

Black Jim's brother Nelson, who was not a quarrelsome man, gripped him by the arm and half-dragged him away from the fire and back into the darkness towards their trailers.

The huge fire had burned low, and most of the men had disappeared, many unwilling to become embroiled in the fighting or its consequences. Even Joe had gone to bed, leaving me, Frank, Tom and Bonny still discussing the events.

'He's a ringtail, that Jim,' declared Frank.

'A proper bastard – not like his brother Nelson at all,' agreed Tom.

'I could've beat him with one arm tied behind me back, on me mother's life I could!' asserted Bonny, with the confidence of the semi-intoxicated.

I was about to bid them goodnight and go to *voodrus* when

we suddenly became aware of thuds and bangings, roars and screams wafting across the common from the direction of the trailers of Black Jim and his family. Strange, bloodcurdling shrieks, like those of an animal in pain, rent the air, coming ever closer.

'I'm gonna kill that Bonny! I'll kill him stone-dead, like me dead father I will . . .'

There was no doubt. We recognised the voice of Black Jim.

'Keep out've the way,' urged Bonny, seeming quite unafraid of his large and dangerous antagonist's intentions. 'I'll soon *mar* him! I'll kill him stone-dead.'

'He's coming back, Bonny,' warned Frank and, apart from Bonny, we all looked apprehensive.

'Keep out've the way,' repeated Bonny. 'I'll soon *ker* him!'

And so saying, he leaned into his lorry cab, withdrew a curved billhook and stood waiting as the fearsome threats grew closer and closer in the night air. Suddenly, it seemed, the lurching figure of Black Jim, his face ashen and haggard in the moonlight, his trousers burned and shirt ripped all down one side, tottered around the front of Bonny's lorry. But Bonny, crouching in the shadows, waited, then pounced. He hurled himself at the immense body of Black Jim, striking him a sickening blow straight down one side of his face with the curved blade – blood welled from it.

Momentarily taken aback, Jim fell forward on to his face, whereupon Bonny flung himself across his back, slashing with the wicked reaper across his rib-sides.

Frank, with great presence of mind, rushed from the darkness and seized the weapon, wrenching it from Bonny's hands.

'*Kekker!* Leave him, Bonny, leave him – you'll *muller* him,' he cried, and flung the billhook far out into the middle of a deep pond some way behind the trailers.

Tom came over, and me too, and we examined the damage to the semi-conscious Black Jim, who was in no condition to feel pain. Blood continued to well from the gash.

'Let's take you to the hospital,' urged Frank. 'You needs stitchin' up – that's a bad cut on yer face.'

The wound was deep and long, from brow to chin; the blood from it covered his once-white shirt in a jagged pattern.

'Nah! I ain't goin' to no hospitals,' protested Jim feebly.

However, after a few minutes, his brother Nelson and his old widowed mother drew up in their lorry and forced the blood-soaked and unwilling Jim to go with them to seek medical assistance.

The old woman was of evil demeanour and in very ill-humour at what had befallen her son. 'I'll get my Bill and his boys over tomorrow,' she threatened, 'an' they'll be certain to burn you lot out! An' we'll get he what done it transported!' she concluded. One wonders if this was the very last occasion upon which that particular threat was uttered within the environs of Slough?

By then it was nearly three in the morning and, discussing what repercussions we might expect, we all spent the rest of the night wide awake, drinking tea and fearing the worst.

It later transpired that when Black Jim had arrived in the casualty ward of the hospital and shown his injuries to the doctors, they were unwilling to believe his rather noble assertion that he had 'tripped on some broken bottles'. And, at length, his evil-minded old mother, pride hurt at her son coming off worst, had given a full account of what had occurred, even naming Bonny as the culprit.

At first light, therefore, our surprise was not extreme when a line of police vans and two patrol-cars drove at speed across the common and their occupants spilled out. Our own trailer, being nearest to the fire after Bonny's, was the first to be visited by the plain-clothes men, an inspector and a detective sergeant.

After taking our names and ages the sergeant demanded: 'Now just tell me what happened here last night.'

'Well, I don't know,' I replied. 'I've been asleep all night – I didn't know *anything* had happened. What has?'

'Oh, yes!' he said, eyeing me coldly and adding to the inspector: 'Always the same, isn't it?'

'Listen, son,' said the inspector loftily. 'This is an attempted murder enquiry. We know who did it – we just need some witnesses to wrap it up.'

'Who did it?' I asked, innocently.

'You know,' he replied severely. 'We'll subpoena you, and you'll have to come to court and say what you saw.'

'I can't tell of what I didn't witness,' I answered doggedly.

'We'll see,' said the inspector grimly, and they left us.

Meanwhile, the uniformed men and women and two dog-handlers were combing the immediate surroundings in an effort to discover the whereabouts of the weapon of assault.

Bonny himself, of course, had quit the scene before daylight, leaving his trailer with his parents, and gone to stay with some relatives who were fifty miles distant.

Before leaving he had said goodbye and, surprisingly, did not seem to be unduly perturbed by the course of events.

'Don't worry, my old bruvvers,' he joked. 'I've bin in worser stews than this!'

The incident did, however, make the rest of us feel distinctly uneasy and, despite not having had the benefit of any sleep the previous night, we agreed that it might be a wise plan to move, lest some of Black Jim's various brothers and cousins might descend on us in revenge.

Funnily enough, a few days prior to this drama, Frank and I had found ourselves driving past what appeared to be a derelict hotel standing in its own grounds, about fifteen miles distant. Inspection had proved to us that it would be possible to pull in behind the hotel, where there was a large courtyard with stables to one side of it. There would, we had estimated, be room for at least five trailers.

We decided to go there.

Without more ado, we busied ourselves packing our possessions, hitched on the trailers and were off again. Frank's wife's car, which was an extra to our towing needs in normal circumstances, was used to tow Bonny's trailer in order that we would not have to make a return journey to retrieve it – during which time vandalism by Black Jim's relatives might have occurred.

The hotel yard proved spacious enough to accommodate us without undue closeness and also to provide us with complete privacy from the outside world.

'Nice quiet old place, ain' it?' remarked Mary-Anne, looking about her in some curiosity.

'It'd be all right if we could put away a month or two here, till the spring of the year, when the daffodils is out an' you feels like pullin' on to a nice bit of green grass,' observed Joe, waxing quite lyrical as he wound a blue-spotted silk handkerchief around his neck.

'I tell you what, Uncle Joe,' said Frank. 'I'll go down to the box an' phone up me aunt Minna and tell her to let Bonny know where we're stoppin'. Otherwise he might go back over there an' get hisself killed by that big *dinilo*.'

'Quite right, my Frank, very sensible,' agreed Joe.

'Pity they ain't got everything switched on – we could have had a nice bit of electric then!' grinned Tom.

The hotel itself was white stucco, its plaster hanging off in great lumps like a moulting polar-bear, while most of its windows had been put out by passing stone-throwers. Its appearance suggested that it must have been standing empty for well over a year.

Over the following weeks we remained undisturbed and our tensions gradually eased for, though we realised that Black Jim's family would soon have learned our whereabouts through the traveller grapevine, we received no unwelcome visitors.

Feeling rather too enclosed in the courtyard, we decided to move out on to what had once been the hotel's front car-park, where our retirement from the world was not so complete.

We were not displeased when, after we had been there a week, two other trailers joined us. These were nephews of Joe, his brother's two sons and their wives and children. They were affable and lively young men and their presence was a welcome addition to our numbers.

On most evenings Bonny would slip round to see us and

entertain us with nerveracking accounts of his activities, both social and business. Bonny, though of small physique, was lion-hearted in the face of adversity: a person to whom the meaning of fear was unknown. For those of us who do not tip the scales at more than ten stone he was a great inspiration.

Beshlie and I stayed on with the family until the spring – my 'Best on Earth' compost provided us with a living. Those were prosperous times and, that spring, I was able to afford to buy another new vehicle. This time, I chose a long wheelbased Landrover. The time to look legitimate had arrived.

Ends and Means

Over the past few decades, and onwards to the present, a small number of travellers all over the country have been, usually after much opposition, granted licenses for the creation of their own privately operated trailer-parks, as they are called. Most of such sites are inhabited by the kind of travellers who are still itinerant from choice, living a modern version of the old Romani way of life, and do not desire to be anywhere permanently. Such trailer-parks are, almost invariably, spotlessly clean and completely litter-free. The residents are proud of the fact, sensitive and anxious to be seen as far removed from the 'dirty Gypsy' tag. The latter is often indiscriminately attached to all travellers by the misinformed, who refuse to believe that there are differing classes and standards among Gypsy people just as within the *gaujo* society. These trailer-parks are rather widely spaced and exclusive. I am myself in the fortunate position of being welcomed on many of them.

Periodically over the years, travellers have purchased fields and divided them into little plots, with electricity and water on each, and have either rented or sold them to any interested travellers within their own sphere. Optimism prevailing over sound reasoning, they have sometimes not bothered to apply for planning permission before installing themselves upon such pieces of land – hoping to present the council with a *fait accompli*. When eventually accosted by the authorities, they would at once apply for planning permission and, if refused, would merely continue to re-apply. Until relatively recently, such appeals and applications could stretch over years; indeed, one with which I am familiar has been fought over a period of eight years – and the battle still continues. However, owing to changes and amendments to the law, I am led to believe that appeals are now severely limited, both to the planning authorities and the county council and to the Department of the Environment. Should the appeals fail, I am told, then the issuing of enforcement notices follows and the sites have to be cleared, with heavy financial penalties imposed if such orders are ignored.

As such trailer-parks have, in my experience, generally been established in comparatively secluded positions, at no cost whatsoever to the ratepayers of the local councils, it has long been a mystery to me why their presence should engender such animosity in the local authorities – who might eventually be forced by government legislation to bear the substantial costs of providing their own council sites, at their own expense, possibly in the same localities as the ones which they had ordered to be removed!

Still feeling rather depressed after our experiences on a council site and only slightly uplifted by having handed in our rent book (the only such document that I ever possessed in my life, before or since), we arrived at the large, privately owned trailer-park where we had arranged to pull on. The park, which lay alongside the M25 motorway, from which it was screened by high wattle-fencing, was a credit to the industry and imagination of its proprietor, a young Romani man in his late twenties, who had purchased it as a piece of rough land without much apparent value. Besides the fencing, he had freshly gravelled the entire area, and fixed a number of water-taps and electricity points at intervals around the perimeter, leaving an island of lawn in the centre upon which the children could play. Tall lamp standards stood around the edge, their light shining down upon the trailers at night, and no houses were nearby, so nobody would be disturbed by the comings and goings of travellers' motor vehicles. Apart, perhaps, from the ferocious and continual roar of the traffic on the motorway, only partially muffled by the fences, it was an ideal spot for a travellers' trailer-park.

We found a space towards one end of the ground, under some trees, without the poultry-run fencing of the council site and with friendly and quiet neighbours on either side of us. Almost without exception, the trailers were of the latest design, each one sparkling clean, with a square-framed tent beside it. Polished stainless-steel water-carriers stood on low tables outside most of the trailers, and large green cord-carpets were spread on the ground in front of the doors and the tents. An air of quiet prosperity prevailed in the atmosphere: nobody was actually *settled* there, all were itinerant by their own choice, and so there was no trapped feeling in evidence. Everyone was as free as their own circumstances allowed them to be. We remained there for a month, until restlessness set in again.

In such opulent trailer-parks, I have noticed, there is possibly a little less of the camaraderie of the less affluent travellers – but less too of the envy and jealousy which, alas, all too commonly afflicts the less well-off in this world.

Unfortunately, within less than a year the dream of the trailer-park owner had been destroyed. Finally, enforcement notices were issued and all the travellers were forced to leave. A few months passed and the ground began to revert to weeds and dereliction: vandals smashed the lamps and pulled down and stole the majority of the fence panels, while local residents took it upon themselves to create their own version of a municipal rubbish-tip. Bogus principles, one could not help but surmise, were at stake.

Funnily enough, just a very few years previously, several Romani families had clubbed together and acquired another piece of land in the same area, which had formerly been a dairy and market-garden and had lain abandoned for many months. The purchasers cleared the land and divided it up into a dozen or so individual pieces, some of which they kept for their own immediate families and the rest they offered for sale to other travellers. Within weeks, all the plots were sold, and each one was re-surfaced with tarmac or gravel and divided from one another by low fences. At their own expense the travellers had provided themselves with a pleasant little self-contained community. All the families were clean and respectable with a pride in their possessions – no debris soiled their plots. Yet, despite this, every effort was made by the council to dislodge the occupants. Although not an owner myself, we were staying there on the plot of a friend and planned to remain there for the whole winter. At length, not long before Christmas, the council decided to hold a full public meeting to try to decide our fate. Before this took place, however, the travellers banded together and hired a barrister from London who, it was rumoured, was very sympathetic towards travellers in their attempts to provide their own forms of accommodation. I met the barrister and found him to be a person of much character, a little short of breath but not of words: he was, I judged, as good a man as would be found.

At the public meeting, in a large hall nearby, the attendance was solely of travellers and officials, with no members of the general public in sight.

The case of the council rested upon their assertion that the land was green-belt and that it was essential it be returned to agricultural usage. Upon the latter decision they were all united, said their spokesman. The barrister spoke well and volubly, but their insistence on the 'return to agricultural usage' seemed implacable and nothing seemed to have been resolved. Indeed, by early spring the matter was still without resolve – though the threat of enforcement notices was regularly spoken of by the time we pulled out in early March.

My astonishment may well be imagined, therefore, when I learned later that spring that a large firm of building contractors had placed bids with the council, which they had accepted, and it was planned that scores of houses would be erected on the land. And so it was that the firm, having obtained planning permission for its scheme, was able to make the travellers offers of such magnitude for their plots that they felt unable to refuse. In *some* ways the travellers emerged the victors, though only materially. And after their incessant demands that the land should be returned for agricultural usage, how could the council justify the construction of a housing estate thereon?

With the best will in the world, it was difficult not to believe that their main aim had always been the eviction of the travellers at whatever cost to their principles with regard to the preservation of green-belt. It was, for me, a very disenchanting example of the intricacies of local politics.

Every time I drive by the housing estate I am surprised, and when I pass the rotting, once-immaculate trailer-park beside the motorway I am depressed. Always, it seems, man's hand is turned against his fellow for some very inadequate reason – usually either through social or religious motives, or merely through plain intolerance.

With over fifty-five years of experience of the traveller's life, I continue to feel a sense of gratitude for what has been given to me, both through the people with whom I have talked, and those with whom I have shared chunks of my life. When I was very young, a very ancient Romani man once said to me, 'If you'm a proper traveller, and you got your health an' strength, then you'll never starve, my son.'

And that, I have found, with optimism and an athletic mind, has proved to be the truth. To climb up the ladder of the travellers' society is an unrivalled adventure, both in pursuit of self-confidence and in mutual respect for those also within the way of life. Somewhere inside me there has always lurked an unquenchable enthusiasm both for the travelling people and all that they stand for, and I am more than grateful to whatever celestial powers that may exist that they still remain.

I recently attended the funeral of a very old Romani friend of mine who expired from what he believed to be a defective 'Fosters' gland. Upon being operated upon, alas, more ominous complications had been discovered and he died within weeks, at just under eighty years old.

He was known as London Mushy and was a man I truly admired. Born to parents who moved only in and around Middlesex, with an annual journey into Kent for 'hopping', he was brought up in a bender-tent, transported about on the back of a four-wheeled trolley pulled by a pony, without a day's schooling in his life. Mushy, however, was wise and shrewd, driving a motor by the time he was sixteen and skimming up the slopes of prosperity, buying and selling firstly ponies, then motor vehicles, and finally even property. He was married by the age of seventeen to a Romani girl, and quite wealthy before he was twenty. Young and flash, he was wont to drive about in a variety of huge fish-finned American cars, long and low-slung in the fashion of their times. Slightly more adult in outlook by his late twenties, and the father of six children, he gradually adopted a more sober form of transport, favouring the more refined BMWs or Mercedes saloons. His trailers were always of the latest fashion – with many extras and adjustments to his own taste. His lorries, too, were always 'lined out' and unmistakeably travellery. He was proud of being a Romani – and was pleased with his success in a way which made others feel pleased too!

Even when I visited him in hospital, not knowing that he was on his deathbed, he showed me brochures of a new four-wheeled drive vehicle that he had ordered. 'Once I gets out've here an' on me feet we'll be off up to Scotland,' he assured me cheerfully. But I could see death in his face and could only feign encouragement. I left feeling so very sad.

When special, outstanding people leave this world one is left wondering who will replace them, will they stay for ever in one's memory?

My thoughts turned to his funeral: it would undoubtedly be very well attended, both by travellers from London and its surrounding counties, and down-country travellers too. London Mushy was an exceptionally well-known and well-respected man.

Romani funerals are, and always have been in my memory, most elaborate and spectacular events. The numbers of mourners is in itself a tribute, often so many that they overflow from the church during the memorial sermon, while later, at the graveside, floral arrangements dazzle the eye with the amazing intricacies and variations of the wreaths and tributes. The latter are quite commonly fashioned into shapes and objects that conjure up memories of the departed: miniature Romani wagons, greyhound dogs, horses, pints of beer, or even boxing-gloves are fairly popular. Perhaps the most bizarre that I have witnessed was at the funeral of a middle-aged man who had been a road and drive contractor for most of his life. His sons had ordered, out of respect, a floral representation of a tar-spreader, in red and white flowers, to be created in his memory. This had been executed with considerable skill by a florist to whom the request must have been something of both a surprise and a challenge! It seems to me to be an endearing way in which to pay respects to the dead and the living also.

Besides funerals, weddings too have become more and more splendid of late. Beshlie and I were recently invited to a wedding and reception held at a large country club type of hotel in Surrey, and were suitably impressed by its splendour. We were seated in groups of eight or ten at separate tables, each with waitress service, and presented with an elaborate three-course meal and a variety of liquid refreshment. A middle-aged traveller and his wife were seated on my left-hand side. Both were of the darkest complexions, the man's white hair ringing his face in a sharply contrasting aura, long sideburns diving down below his ear-lobes. Heavy lines etched his entire features and his black eyes were pouchily set. He wore a metallic-looking suit of silver colour, a startlingly white shirt and a red-spotted silk tie.

The hand that held his cigarette was made more interesting by the presence of two gold-mounted diamond rings of imposing size. His name was Skylark, though he was always called Larky.

After several glasses of white wine, Larky was in reminiscent mood. 'See me now,' he said in wonder, 'I can't believe I'm sitting here, in a *bori tan* like this – an' being waited on like a fuckin' lord!'

Several of the other diners at our table regarded him with some curiousity, which he ignored. *'Dordi! Kek!'* said his wife quietly to him.

'When I thinks of how me dear old mother used to have to go out with a basket on her arm, with a bit of lace or a few flowers, and how we five boys would be waiting round the *yog* for her to come back, the *gavvers* round us all day, with a bit of bread and meat – I can't believe it. Life is so easy today that the young ones don't even know what hard times is! But it's nice to see, mind.'

Noah and his wife were on our right and some young marrieds were opposite to us, in a world of their own. 'Hey, mushy, where was you born?' enquired Noah, grinning.

'Blackbush Common,' replied my neighbour.

'Poxy little place that is, full of varmints,' said Noah, still grinning, lighting another cigarette.

'Not another fag, Noah!' exclaimed his wife Ellen, a rather attractive woman with a loud voice, her person almost smothered in gold chains and necklaces, bracelets, and rings on every finger. 'He was a-smokin' twenty a day an' I told him to his face – you can't have no more sex unless you cuts down,' she continued, glaring at him and then smiling at us.

'Cor! Fuck me! I smoke fifty a day now!' laughed Noah, winking at me.

'Did you hear that?' asked his wife Ellen, feigning disgust.

As we made our way through the 1980s, with extraordinary speed, I looked forward with slight trepidation – and backwards with no little astonishment. To those who affect a contempt for wordly possessions or scorn any advancement in those terms, I suppose that the traveller's world of today must hold little charm or enticement. Yet for those within it, the ability to acquire new motor vehicles or splendid new trailers is a sign of achievement in the battle for survival. As I have written before, in days gone by the Romanies were admired for their picturesque and ornate wagons and their beautiful horses, so they are merely striving for the equivalent in the world of today. Those who look down on such aspirations are all too frequently those who could never manage to obtain such things for themselves – and therefore seek to present themselves as occupying the moral high-ground.

Yes, things *have* changed from the times of *Smoke in the Lanes* and *The Wind on the Heath*, and the ideas of the romantic Gypsy life that once abounded – even the heath has changed. Thinking back on the old ways of farming and agriculture when horse-power meant just that, it all seems in retrospect that much more colourful and more of a spectacle in itself. The coming of the motor vehicle, despite its incredible convenience, somehow sapped both city and countryside alike of life and vibrancy. The same may be said of the popular idea of the Romani life, the horses and wagons, colourful and raggle-taggle, amid what today would be referred to as 'litter'.

Yet through it all the Gypsies have survived, mostly still a society quite apart, and all the better for that. Differing classes and differing ways of life have evolved as travellers used their natural abilities to adapt. Unfortunately for travellers, the academics at present rather fashionably have what they term *Roma* or *Roms* in their sights. Alas, a large percentage of these learned people, mainly intent on discovering rare traits of language or genealogy, have little or no personal friendship or even acquaintance with actual Romanies other than on the most distant level. Even worse, such people only too often feel compelled to offer 'solutions' regarding travellers that are born of a purely *gaujo* outlook. Some even count the nebulous New Age travellers as being part of the traveller community, which is really rather pathetic – and utterly untrue. Almost every principle of the Romani lifestyle is at odds in every detail with the outlook and philosophy and aspect of the New Age traveller – completely separate.

Through it all – persecution, bureaucracy, hardship and even the attentions of academia, which have conspired against them – the Romanies have survived and even flourished. To have spent so much of my life among Romani travellers, among such open, generous and hospitable people, as their guest, friend and brother has been my great good fortune. For which I will always be grateful.

Old-fashioned

When we stop travelling, the first thing in mind,
It's tent-rods and ridge-poles as we got to find.
We tied the old pony's legs, and away he did go.
Where shall we find him? The Lord only knows.
We got up next morning, and searched all around.
Where did we find him? We found him in the pound.
We *jalled* to the old *rai*, and what did he say?
'Pack up your old trap, and clear right away!'

Modern-style

When we stop travelling, the first thing in mind,
It's a piece of good standing as we got to find.
It can be a lay-by, or even a yard –
No matter what, so long as it's hard.
Unhitch the motors, and trailers as well,
And off we go out, to buy or to sell.
We'll stop for a day, or maybe a week,
And then for a new place we'll have to go-seek.

The Mechanised Years
in Photographs

Our first trailer, bought for £20: an old hardboard Willerby.

The old Austin 1940s two-tonner – our first lorry – which cost £17,10s.

A Traveller's Special – one of the many wagon birdcages made by Beshlie.

Getting larger: our first 23ft Lisset trailer and 1955 A-type Bedford, in the early 1960s.

Our first all-new turnout in 1965: Jubilee Butterfly and Bedford J-type 30cwt lorry. We were Kings of the Road!

Our 16ft Baby Portmaster, in mid-Wales in the early 1980s. (Young and successful!)

Stopping on Chobham Common in the 1970s. Jubilee trailer, Beshlie and Barney.

Short-term ownership in the late 1970s: a 'flashed-up' 23ft Vickers trailer, alas too heavy for our J-type Bedford.

Snowed-up in Lincolnshire in the 1980s: our first German vehicle.

The 18ft Buccanner which we had in about 1990, complete with double-glazing. Still made with a solid-fuel stove.

A homely scene: the exterior of another Buccaneer in the 1990s. The water-carriers have been with us since 1966.

The Roma 'Crazy Band' trailer and its ageing owner.

Our pick-up in 2003: the Silver Bullet!

Glossary of Romani Words

akai	here
atch	stop
atchin-tan	stopping-place
awved-in	pulled-in
bar	pound (coin or note)
baulo	pig
Beng	the Devil
booty	work
bori	big, important
chat	thing
chavi	child
chinger	swear
chitty	tripod cooking frame
chop	deal, trade, barter
chor	steal
chordi	stolen

cor	fight
cori	penis
covel	thing
dell	hit
dik	look
dinilo	fool
dordi	(oh) dear, (oh) Lord
dukkering	fortune-telling
folki	people
gaujo/gauji/gaujes	non-Gypsy man/woman/people
gavvers	police
hochi	hedgehog
ingering kair	toilet
jal/jals	go
juke/jukel	dog
kair	house
kek/kekker	no
ker	do
kinder	manure
kipsy	basket
kitchemir	pub
kushti	good
lovell	money
lubni	prostitute
mar	wound, kill
mong	beg
moro	bread
mort	woman

mui	mouth
muller	kill
mumblers	teeth
mush	man
muskeros	police
owli	yes
pal	brother
pani	water
pogger	break
poggerdi chib	literally, 'broken tongue' – Anglo-Romani
rackli	girl
radji	mad
rai/rye	gentleman
rati	night
rawnie	lady
rokker	speak
Roma/Roms	used here to describe East European Romanies
suti	sleep
swigler	pipe
tan	place
trashed	frightened
treader	bike
vongar	money
voodrus	bed
yog	fire
yogger	gun
yok	eye

SMOKE IN THE LANES

*Happiness and Hardship on the Road with
the Gypsies in the 1950s*

Dominic Reeve

In the 1950s the Romani people lived on the brink of great
change. In their bright wooden wagons, they journeyed
between horse-fairs and traditional stopping-places – stoic,
humorous and wild, often poverty-stricken but protective of
their freedom – on the fringes of a society that was soon
to close around them.

Dominic Reeve describes his life among his proud people:
the feuds and fairs, the sharp deals done and rings run round
country policemen, the love affairs, dancing and open-air
feasting. *Smoke in the Lanes* is the vivid, memorable and
unsparing record of a disappeared world.

'The real deal . . . a fascinating, unflinching portrait of the
rich diversity of characters and traditions of the Romani life
at a time when it was threatened as never before'
Choice

Abacus
978-0-349-00003-9

RABBIT STEW AND A PENNY OR TWO

Maggie Smith-Bendell

The *Sunday Times* bestseller

Born in a Somerset pea-field in 1941, the second of eight children in a Romani family, Maggie Smith-Bendell has lived through the years of greatest change in the travelling community's long history. As a child, Maggie rode and slept in a horse-drawn wagon, picked hops and flowers, and sat beside her father's campfire on ancient verges, poor but free to roam. As the twentieth century progressed, common land was fenced off and the traditional Gypsy ways disappeared. Eventually Maggie married a house-dweller and tried to settle for bricks and mortar, but she never lost the restless spirit, the deep love of the land and the gift for storytelling that were her Romani inheritance.

Abacus
978-0-349-12361-5